How to Write a
KILLER LinkedIn® Profile

...and 18 Mistakes to Avoid

by

Brenda Bernstein | www.TheEssayExpert.com

To say this book is a "Must Have" is like saying you should have a Bible.

– J. R. Hollingsworth, JD, Director of the Job Seekers Network

ISBN: 978-1629672342 (Paperback)

ISBN: 978-1629672359 (Hardcover)

Library of Congress Control Number: 2022906764

For Cataloging in Publication Data Block information visit: https://lccn.loc.gov/2022906764

How to Write a KILLER LinkedIn Profile

is the only book we know of that is updated
to the new 2022 interface!

Here's just some of what's been changed in this e-book edition (16ᵗʰ Edition):

- Add Pronouns, Former Name, and Pronunciation Audio to Your Introduction Card (Mistake #1)
- New Career Gaps options with Stay-at-Home titles (Mistake #1)
- Tips for keyword searches (Mistake #1)
- Why it's a good idea to turn off "People Also Viewed" (Mistake #5)
- Auto-Away Messages & Unread Message Badges (Mistake #7)
- Emojis hover function (Mistake #7)
- Video Cover Story (Mistake #8)
- Future of Skills & Career Paths search tools (Mistake #12)
- New article ranking "dwell time" (Mistake #13)
- New search functionality (Mistake #13 & 16)
- Publish articles as your page (Mistake #13)
- Creator Mode (Mistake #13)
- Turning comments into posts (Mistake #13)
- LinkedIn Polls (Mistake #13)
- New Featured Section (Mistake #14)
- Volunteer Marketplace (Mistake #14)
- New "Open to Work" feature (Mistake #16)
- LinkedIn Learning Hub (Mistake #16)
- New Special Section for Businesses
- Tip for following hashtags on your Company page (Special Section for Businesses)
- New Product Pages (Special Section for Businesses)
- Tips for getting employees engaged in branding (Special Section for Businesses)
- How to set up LinkedIn Ads (Special Section for Businesses)
- "Open for Business" is now "Providing Services" (Special Section for Businesses)
- Services Reviews Feature (Bonus Tip #2)
- New Character Limits (Appendix B)

Please email TEESupport@TheEssayExpert.com if you have a topic, idea, or question you'd like me to address. I'm listening!

APPRECIATIONS

I don't know what I would have done without my Virtual Assistant, Jeanne Goodman,[1] who has spent countless hours revising images and instructions throughout this book. She keeps me sane, able to focus on my business, and available for the speaking opportunities drummed up by my dedicated publicity guy, Scott Becher.[2] Appreciation goes out to all my clients, as well, especially the ones who offered to have their profiles included in this book. Thank you, thank you!

Brian Schwartz[3] of SelfPublish.org continues to do a wonderful job of converting edition . . . upon edition . . . of *How to Write a KILLER LinkedIn Profile* into Kindle format. And Robin Krauss works magic each time I tell him it's time to publish a new hard copy version.

Each person who has written a recommendation for me on Amazon has made my book continue to reach thousands of people who benefit in their businesses and careers.

Thank you to all of you, and to many more I did not mention, for making *How to Write a KILLER LinkedIn Profile* a longstanding success!

And thank you in advance for your generosity in considering reviewing this book on Amazon. Your support makes a difference.

Post a review on Amazon![4]

TABLE OF CONTENTS

REVIEWS

"Within a few weeks of my complete profile overhaul, I was contacted on LinkedIn by a Director from a company completely outside of my industry. I applied for the position, which was a PERFECT fit for my skills and work style. I got the job!"

— **Sara Kay**, Project Coordinator, Los Angeles CA

"I reached [the] top position for my area of expertise and location, [which led to] several offers from headhunters and CEOs. Just this month, I started a new job—and guess what? The CEO of my new company contacted me through LinkedIn!"

— **Charlotte L.**, Editor, Barcelona, Spain

"I saw a sustained 4-5X traffic increase on LinkedIn by the time I was done. [My new profile] led to many new business contacts as well as an invite for an advisory board seat at a top university."

— **Joseph P.**, Board of Advisors at NJIT, New York, NY

"I got an interview within a week of implementing the changes."

— **zmyers**, Amazon Reviewer

"I used this book to improve my boss' profile and got him 20% more views."

— **Danielle**, France

"My LinkedIn rating went from 17% to 95%. I have received calls from recruiters who called after looking at my revised profile. This is a very worthwhile investment—can't recommend it enough!"

— **Simon A.**, Writer, Production Manager, Vancouver, Canada

---

"I got a job interview! I am at the top of the search function list for my industry in a 50-mile radius."

— **Matthew W.**, EMT, Orange County, CA

"I have had a 73% increase in profile views in the last week. Thank You!"

— **Simon Crowther**, Project Manager, Greater Manchester, UK

"As a LinkedIn trainer myself, it's good to know I have a resource like this for my clients to help them after they've left my classroom."

— **Michael Phelps**, LinkedIn Trainer, Little Rock, AR

ABOUT THE AUTHOR

| Certified Master Resume Writer | Certified Advanced Resume Writer | Certified Executive Resume Writer | 2013 Best International Resume 2nd Place Winner | 2013 Best Sales Resume Nominee | 2012 Best New Graduate Resume 3rd Place Winner | 2012 Best Re-Entry Resume Nominee | 2011 Best Creative Resume Nominee |

Brenda Bernstein, Founder and Senior Editor at The Essay Expert LLC, is a #1 best-selling author, an in-demand speaker & consultant, and an award-winning resume writer, holding Certified Executive Resume Master and Certified Master Resume Writer certifications from Career Directors International. Her first book, *How to Write a KILLER LinkedIn® Profile*, has been featured in *Fortune* and *Forbes* Magazines; the book has consistently ranked in the top 30 in Amazon's business writing skills e-book category since July 2012. Her other e-books, *How to Write a WINNING Resume . . . 50 Tips to Reach Your Job Search Target*[5] and *How to Write a STELLAR Executive Resume . . . 50 Tips to Reach Your Job Search Target*,[6] have been met with rave reviews.

A top-notch editor, Brenda has 20+ years of successful written communications, experience from C- level executive resume development to business copy editing to Ivy-League-bound student college essay consulting.

She holds a B.A. in English from Yale University and a J.D. from the New York University School of Law, graduating from both schools with honors. Brenda's clients report that they gain clarity about themselves and their message, in addition to having that message deliver sought-after results.

Email: BrendaB@TheEssayExpert.com

Web: TheEssayExpert.com[7] / TheExecutiveExpert.com[8] / KILLERLinkedInProfile.com[9]

LinkedIn: LinkedIn.com/in/brendabernstein[10]

Facebook: Facebook.com/TheEssayExpert[11]

Phone: 718-390-6696

NOTE TO READER

There are 200+ hyperlinks (URLs) contained within this book. Because links continually change, we've created a web page with a current list of links. You can also go here to report any broken links and sign up to receive updates. Simply point your favorite web browser to this URL:

https://theessayexpert.com/killer-linkedin-resource-links/

Or scan this QR Code:

Thank you for reading *How to Write a KILLER LinkedIn Profile!*

Yours truly,

Brenda

INTRODUCTION

Why You Should Read This Book

LinkedIn, owned by Microsoft, hosts the profiles of nearly 800 million people in over 200 countries and 2.8 million locales—and up to 47% of them are active users. LinkedIn reports 97 million monthly unique visitors worldwide, 57% of whom log on via mobile devices. In the U.S., 27% of adults (180+ million users) have LinkedIn profiles. Over 30 million companies have company pages on LinkedIn. Furthermore, according to LinkedIn,[12] there are executives from every Fortune 500 company using this social network, and 95% of those companies[13] use LinkedIn's licensed recruiting software to search for job candidates.

LinkedIn is reportedly the most trusted social network in the U.S.,[14] with 73% of users agreeing that LinkedIn protects their privacy and data. That's way higher than Facebook at just 53%. This is good news for LinkedIn's job search audience of 40 million people per week.

U.S. News reported in 2017 that about 95 percent of recruiters[15] utilize LinkedIn as a major candidate sourcing tool. Evidence also suggests that most people who make hiring decisions have decided NOT to hire a candidate based on what they've found online. Here's the clincher: A whopping 89% of all recruiters report having hired someone through LinkedIn (as opposed to 26% from Facebook and 15% from Twitter). So if you're going to conduct a job search using social media, LinkedIn is the place to be.

Still not convinced? According to 2018-2019 research conducted by ResumeGo,[16] job applicants who have LinkedIn profiles are 71% more likely to get called in for an interview, and the more comprehensive your profile is, the better. Here are the numbers from that study:

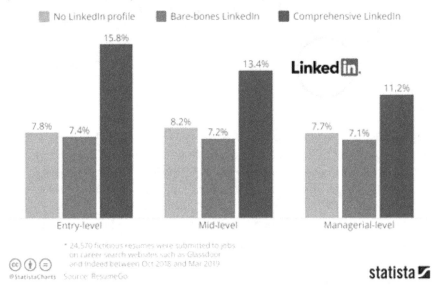

Study: A Comprehensive LinkedIn Profile Boosts Job Chances
Job seeker callback rates by level and state of LinkedIn profile on their resume*

No LinkedIn profile ■ Bare-bones LinkedIn ■ Comprehensive LinkedIn

* 24,570 fictitious resumes were submitted to jobs on career search websites such as Glassdoor and Indeed between Oct 2018 and Mar 2019

@StatistaCharts   Source: ResumeGo

statista

As you can see, no matter what stage of your career you're in, having a comprehensive LinkedIn profile gives you a big leg up on those with either no LinkedIn profile or a bare-bones one. And you're actually slightly better off NOT having a LinkedIn profile than doing a half-baked job on the one you have.

Maybe you're saying, "I'm not far enough along in my career" or "I'm too young." Well, LinkedIn is not just for seasoned professionals. In fact, the minimum age for membership in the U.S. is 16 (see LinkedIn's User Agreement[17]) and LinkedIn Higher Education Pages[18] give students a place to get information about and engage in discussions with universities worldwide. If you are a high school student, now is the time to start building your network and exploring career opportunities! (See High School Students: Embrace your skills, show your professional side, and create a LinkedIn Profile.)[19] Join the over 39 million students and recent college graduates who have already taken the leap (also see Appendix E for more on how students can make the most of LinkedIn).

What's crystal clear is that every single EMPLOYER or CLIENT who considers hiring you will Google you, click on your LinkedIn profile, and assess it. Whether you are a high school or college student, job seeker, company owner or other professional, your profile MUST impress your audience if you want results from this social media treasure chest.

Guy Kawasaki told CNBC Make It,[20] "If you're not on LinkedIn, you might as well not exist in this world. Everybody needs to be on LinkedIn."

If you happen to be unemployed, one of the top 3 most important things you can do is maximize your value on LinkedIn (writing a standout resume and networking are the other two). While there is no one right way to do this, I have provided my best advice on how to make LinkedIn work for your job search, from how to write an optimal Headline to how to use the robust LinkedIn Jobs feature. If you're looking for a job, you simply can't afford to have a mediocre LinkedIn profile.

Are you getting the results that you want from your LinkedIn profile?

If you're not getting the results you hoped for, this book is for you. I provide you with 18 detailed strategies and writing tips, plus seven bonus tips and additional materials, that will teach you how to get found on LinkedIn, how to keep people reading and want to take action after they find you, and how to leverage this platform fully.

Using LinkedIn to its full potential can lead you to results you never imagined. Many of my clients have been amazed to get hired solely on the strength of their LinkedIn profile activity and content. I personally have built my business through the connections I've made on LinkedIn. My clients have shared many success stories, which you'll see in this book and on my website. But don't take it just from me. Read the LinkedIn Official Blog[21] and check out the narratives of people like account manager Sabrina Lee (Finding My Way Home on LinkedIn)[22] and digital marketer Mei Lee (My Secret Career Weapon: LinkedIn).[23] You must optimize your profile to get results like theirs.

Okay, so how will this book help you get the results you want from LinkedIn?

Since 2009, I have worked with social media experts, business people, recruiters and employers and have identified EIGHTEEN common weak points in LinkedIn profile strategy and content. These errors can be fatal if you want people not just to find your profile, but to continue reading once they do. By following the advice below, you will avoid these errors and create a frequently viewed AND highly effective LinkedIn profile. Remember, your LinkedIn profile might never be perfect—but don't let that stop you! It's time to take action.

Use these 18 tips to create a POWERFUL profile—and show your target audience you're serious about your online presence. What's the reward? That depends on what you're looking for:

A new job . . .

An unexpected partnership . . .

A lucrative account . . .

YOU get to choose.

> ▶ **Important Note on Compliance:** Some industries and companies, such as finance, insurance, real estate, law, and others, have strict legal or corporate guidelines about what you can include in your LinkedIn profile. Nothing in this book is meant to contradict or override those guidelines. Please consult with your company and/or an attorney before making changes to your profile that might conflict with company policy or the legalities of your profession.

> ▶ **Important Note on LinkedIn Changes:** LinkedIn changes its platform frequently. In an interview with SocialTimes, Amy Parnell, Director of User Experience at LinkedIn said, "We are in a constant state of evolution with our site and app designs, and strive to push the experience and product value to new heights on an ongoing basis."

> I do my best to keep up with these changes and release new editions regularly. If you discover any outdated information in this book, rest assured that an update is on its way! Check out the Important Opportunities to Give and Receive section of this book to read how you can get free new editions of *How to Write a KILLER LinkedIn Profile* in PDF format!

▶ **Important Note on Tone/Non-US Profiles:** The advice in this book works no matter what country you live in. However, the tone of the samples is geared toward the United States job market. In some countries, a subtler tone might be warranted.

LinkedIn® Profile Nuts and Bolts

This section covers some fairly straightforward "nuts and bolts" for the "Introduction Card" section of your profile, including your Headline, photo, websites, and public profile URL. Most of these tips hold keys to being found on LinkedIn. You must have keywords that people are searching for, and you must have them in the right places. You must have a robust network of at least 500 people. You must have a photo that engages your readers. And you would be smart to get your profile to All-Star status, or something close to that!

Completing the organizations, job titles, degrees, and dates in your Experience and Education sections is also essential to having a respectable profile, but since I have not seen many profiles that don't have this information filled in, I don't address it specifically in this section.

You may want to address the items in this section before moving on and getting creative with your About and Experience sections. However, some people like to wait until they have a KILLER LinkedIn profile before they start sharing it with the world, so you could opt to complete your entire profile, including your About section, Experience, and more, before building your network. It's up to you!

MISTAKE #1

Selling Yourself Short: Lack of Keywords and an Ineffective Headline

The Problem

There are nearly 800 million professionals using LinkedIn, about 24% of whom are in the United States; and the site is growing exponentially with more than two new members joining every second (check out LinkedIn's About Us page,[24] Wikipedia,[25] and these stats from Omincore[26] for more information). How will you possibly be found amongst all these people if you don't optimize your keywords? The answer is: You probably won't.

LinkedIn has become the go-to website for research on people and companies. When users do their research, they type keywords into LinkedIn's search box—words and phrases important to them that hopefully match the keywords in your profile. So if you want to be found as a "Sports Writer," you'll want that keyword in your profile multiple times and in the right places.

In your Headline, brief titles such as "IT Consultant," "Project Manager," or "Sales Professional" don't distinguish you from every other person with the same title in a pool of hundreds of millions of LinkedIn profiles. You must distinguish yourself in your Headline to stand out—with both keywords and an attention-getting statement if possible. Otherwise you won't get to the top of LinkedIn search results and you won't capture your readers' attention.

The Tune-Up

To a certain extent, the more often a particular word or phrase shows up in your profile, the more likely it is that you will appear in people's searches when they look for that word or phrase.

The basic strategy here is to put yourself in the position of the people who are searching for you, whether they be clients, recruiters, or other partners. Identify the keywords and keyword phrases they would be searching for. These keywords might include job titles, core competencies, geographical regions, technical skills, soft skills, languages, and more.

If you are a job seeker, look at job advertisements for your target position and count keywords that show up repeatedly; if you like cool online tools, put the copy from a few listings into a keyword analyzer like Visiospark[27] and you will easily see which words come up most frequently. Use those keywords.

You know your profession better than anyone, so simply brainstorming commonly used words in your field can reap the perfect keywords. Here are some other ways you can find your best keywords:

- Look at profiles of other people with similar backgrounds or positions to yours.

- Use the Skills section and scan through the drop-down menus there to see what keywords LinkedIn suggests for your profession. For more about adding skills, see Mistake #12.

- Review job postings that interest you to see what words and phrases they're using. Pay attention to different forms of words. You might need both "program manager" and "program management," for instance. With some Applicant Tracking Software systems, only exact matches will be found.
- If you own a business, look at company pages of top competitors to see what language they're using.
- Follow thought leaders in your industry to see what taglines, words and phrases are trending right now.

As Catherine Byers Breet, longtime recruiter and early adopter of LinkedIn, advises, "The first hurdle is to get found (to make sure you come up in the right kind of searches by recruiters). Making sure you have industry-relevant job titles and keywords is mission-critical. If you don't, you will never come up in their searches."

Once you have identified your top keywords, add as many of them as possible in the following sections: **Headline (most important!), Current Job Title, About section,** and **Additional Job Titles**. The LinkedIn search tool searches entire profiles, so insert your keywords throughout! Use them early (at the beginning of your profile) and often, while keeping your language natural (i.e., don't overload to the point of offense just for the sake of keyword optimization).

Before I knew the power of keywords, my Headline read: **Founder and Senior Editor, The Essay Expert.** Note the lack of keywords in that Headline! Now it reads:

Brenda Bernstein

Resume & LinkedIn Profile Writer, Author, Speaker ★
Executive Resumes ★ C-Level Resumes ★ Executive LinkedIn
Profiles ★ College Essays ★ Law School Admissions Essays ★
MBA Admissions Essays

The new Headline has a lot more keywords. When I changed my Headline, as well as added more keywords to my current job title, About section, Specialties, and other job titles, I went from being almost invisible in searches to coming up first in the search rankings on queries for "Executive Resume Writer" in my geographic area.

Craft a Headline for your profile that tells us what makes you unique and that includes as many keywords as possible. Here are some examples:

Dave Stachowiak (He/Him) · 1st
Host of the Coaching for Leaders podcast, downloaded 20 million times · Helping leaders discover wisdom through insightful conversations

---

Carole (Heinze) Mendoza (She/Her) · 1st
VP OF BENEFITS & GLOBAL BENEFITS EXPERT | Advocating for Employee Retirement Readiness, DE&I, and Benefits Equity in Partnership with Fortune 500 Companies and Advocacy Groups

---

> **Jill M Bornstein, ACC** · 1st
> Leadership & Executive Coach for Rising Professionals, New
> Leaders, New Executives and Budding Entrepreneurs | Senior
> Executive | Fortune 50, NGO, Government Leader | Culture Builder
> & Connected Leadership Champion

> · 2nd
> Fortune 10 Senior Executive | One of the Most Influential Women
> in Corporate America, *Savoy Magazine* | Global Strategist &
> Business Partner | Cross-Border Legal Expert & Risk Navigator |
> D&I Champion

See the advantage of the above examples over Headlines like "Consultant," "Senior VP" or "Project Manager"? More explicit Headlines give spark and color to your profile as opposed to just listing your job title; and they contain keywords to help you appear at the top of search results. They can also hint at your personality, the results you produce, and some of your "soft skills."

It might not be obvious that your zip code is a type of keyword in a way, especially if you are a job seeker. Recruiters look for job seekers by location! You will be asked to enter your zip code when you first create your account, and you must do so carefully. Adding your location makes you 23 times more likely to be found in LinkedIn searches.

▶ **Zip Code Tip:** Use a zip code that is close to the area where you want to work. If you are able to work in Chicago but live 25 miles away in the suburbs, for instance, consider using a zip code halfway between the two locations that will capture searches looking for someone within a 10-mile radius of either downtown Chicago or your suburb. If LinkedIn has your area listed incorrectly, find out how to change it here.[28]

▶ **Including proper keywords does not guarantee your profile will appear at the top of searches.** Search results are unique to the member searching for your keywords, and there are other factors that go into search rankings, most notably your number of connections, profile completeness, and activity level on LinkedIn. (For more on how LinkedIn's search works, see LinkedIn Search Relevance - People Search[29]; in addition, one industrious job seeker wrote a comprehensive article[30] on this topic.) Even with all these factors, without keywords, your profile is likely to remain at the bottom of the pile.

▶ **Prioritize Keywords: Use your most important keywords in the first 50 characters or less**. When connections search for you on their phone, via "U,"[31] or via their list of followers,[32] only the first part of your Headline is visible:

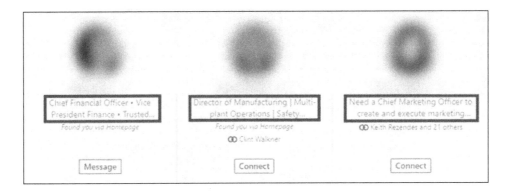

LinkedIn tells you how some viewers found your profile and who your common connections are, so you can strategize your marketing and understand the power of your network.

Pronouns

LinkedIn acknowledges that people have a range of gender identities and preferences for their personal pronouns. There is now a field where you may choose from She/Her, He/Him, They/Them, or create a custom pronoun. Here's how:

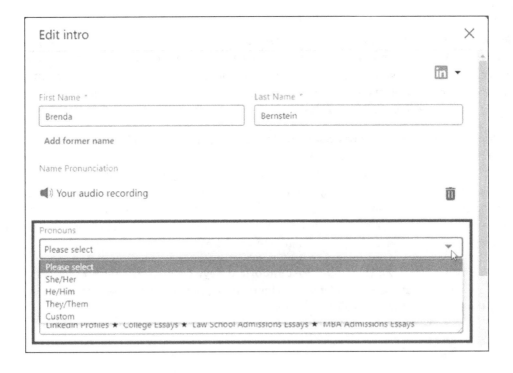

Your pronouns will look like this:

Maiden/Former Name

If you want your old elementary school friends to know for sure they have the right person, you can also add your maiden name or former name. Your former name can only be seen when viewing your profile and is not visible in LinkedIn search results.

To add a former name, click the pencil to edit your intro:

Then click on Former Name and insert up to 50 characters. You can also choose who can see your former name.

This is how your former name will appear on your profile:

Name Pronunciation Audio

Do you have a name that's difficult for others to pronounce? LinkedIn now allows you to record your name! This new feature can reduce the occurrence of having your name mangled, which will be a relief not only to you, but also to your connections who meet you over the phone or (in a post-COVID world) in person.

Sharing your voice will also add some interactivity and fun to your profile. You might be surprised how much an audio from someone's profile adds dimension to who they are—so listen to other people's names and share yours. And maybe even record your name if you have an easy name to pronounce!

Currently, this tool is only available on the mobile app. The example below uses screenshots from an Android device, but instructions for iOS are the same.

To record your name, go to your profile and click the pencil icon to the right of your photo:

Click on "ADD NAME PRONUNCIATION":

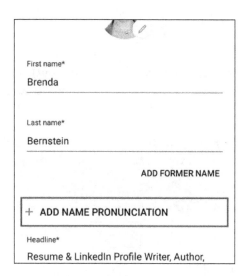

Hold the blue microphone button to record your name. It must be less than 10 seconds long.

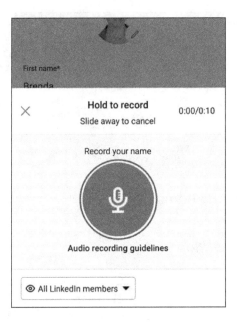

Once you've spoken your name, click the button again to preview it. If necessary, "Retake" the recording until you're satisfied. Then choose whether only your first-degree connections or all LinkedIn members will be able to listen to your name. Finally, click "Apply" to accept.

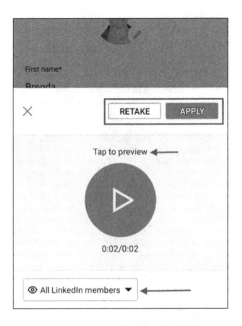

If you ever want to change or delete your pronunciation, click on the pencil icon.

When you're done adding your pronunciation to your Introduction Card, don't forget to hit Save in the upper right.

This is what your profile will look like when your recording is live:

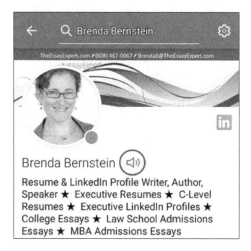

I personally appreciate when people with unusual names, and names with multiple pronunciations, use this feature. I want to pronounce people's names correctly when I talk to them, plus it's an extra bonus to "get to know" someone through their voice, even if they have an easy-to-pronounce name.

Career Gaps

Restrictions created by the pandemic resulted in over 2.5 million women and 1.8 million men leaving the workforce due to furlough or family demands. To accommodate this new status—and to help eliminate the stigma around these career gaps—LinkedIn has created new "career break" option.

To utilize this function, click the plus sign in your Experience section and select "Add career break":

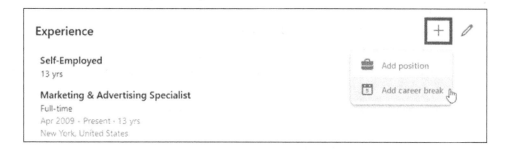

You will have the following options to choose from:

Insert dates and description just as you would any other position.

LinkedIn also offers "stay-at-home" job titles to help caregivers more accurately relay their current position. Choices currently include Homemaker, Stay-at-home Mom, Stay-at-home Dad, and Stay-at-home Parent.

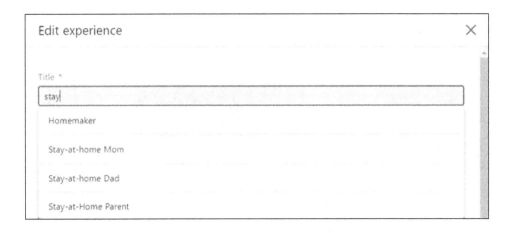

"On Leave" is another option that will populate if you type "On Leave" or "Sabbatical."

In the future, LinkedIn may be providing new options for work gaps such as parental leave, family care, and sabbatical.

Should I say "Open to Opportunities" or something similar in my headline?

When you're a job seeker, the most important thing you can do to appear in recruiter and hiring manager searches (in conjunction with expanding your network) is to have the right keywords in your Headline. Use your 220 characters well! Whenever possible, also include a unique selling proposition in order to increase interest once people find you (See Mistake #1).

In the past, some people have benefitted from putting "Seeking Opportunities" or "Open to New Opportunities" in their Headline. Some recruiters used to search for the word "Opportunities" and approach people they knew are looking for a job. However, most recruiters will find you regardless of whether you advertise that you are looking for work. Plus, with the "Open to Work" feature at your disposal, it makes more sense to use the precious characters in your Headline for keywords and for conveying your USP (Unique Selling Proposition).

What if I've never held the position I want to be found for?

If you are seeking a position as VP of Finance, and you have never held that position before, consider creative ways of including the keywords VP and Finance. For example: VP-Level Finance Executive or Available for VP of Finance Position at Growing Company.

Of course, you need to make sure not to misrepresent yourself, so you might need to say "Poised for . . ." or something similar. Note that if you have performed the functions to match a job title, you can put the job title in your Headline. I say if you've done the job, you can claim the job title!

Should I include a tagline?

People will get a true sense of your value if you include a tagline or "unique selling proposition" (USP) in addition to straight keywords in your Headline. Best strategy: Use keywords to increase the frequency with which you are found in searches; include a tagline or USP to generate interest so people click to read more. Once you have decided on your most effective Headline strategy, here's how to add it to your profile—and some pitfalls to avoid:

Click on the pencil icon to the right of your profile image.

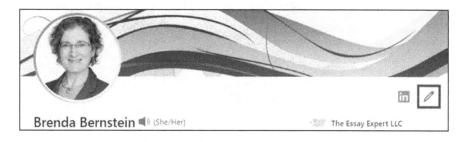

You will then have an opportunity to edit your Headline. On the non-mobile and Android versions of LinkedIn, you have 220 characters to use. Note that when creating your headline on desktop and iOS, you can enter 220 characters, but for Android, it's currently limited to 120 characters.

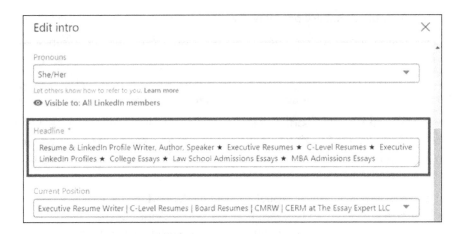

Displaying Your Education

If you're proud of your alma mater, you can make it one of the first things members see. Click the pencil icon to the right of the more button to edit your intro. Then check the box next to "Show education in my intro." By default, LinkedIn will show your most recent education. Click the drop-down to select another option.

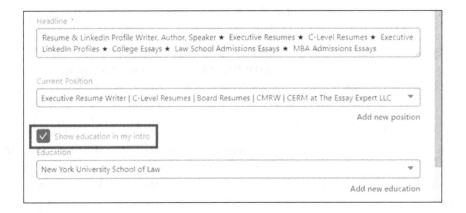

Your education will be displayed here:

How Do I Include Keywords in My Job Titles?

The job title fields are extremely important places to include keywords. Don't forget them! Pay attention here. This is the most common tip that readers don't pay attention to and it's essential to your search rankings!

You might think you have to put your exact job title in the "Job Title" field. You don't. You have 100 characters to play with, so use them. Put keywords in your job titles that people who are searching for you will care about. If you are a job seeker, use words that come up frequently in job descriptions for positions you want. If you are a businessperson, use keywords to get you found for what you do best. Here are some examples of job titles that are keyword optimized:

Example #1: Senior Legal Manager / Counsel

Senior Legal Manager - EMEA ▶ Trusted Legal Counsel | International Deals | Compliance Regional Senior Legal Counsel Middle East ▶ Contract Management | Due Diligence | Project Execution

Example #2: Technology Sales Executive

Sales & Channel Account Manager, Major Accounts | Enterprise Technology | Channel Strategy Business Development / Sales Manager | Cloud Computing | Technology Storage Sales Executive | Technology Solutions | OEM Business / Sales Development Manager | SaaS Technology | Channel Sales Executive | Technology | OEM

▶ **Note on Search Functionality:** LinkedIn searches for multiple-word keyword *phrases* such as "mortgage lending" will turn up results for profiles that include those words—"mortgage" and "lending"—separately as well. So be sure to intersperse your sections with both.

▶ **Special Note on "Keyword Stuffing"**: Some people have attempted to "stuff" keywords in their profile by adding them to their Name field. This strategy is against LinkedIn's Terms of Service and will not help you. LinkedIn has spam detection software that will filter out your profile if you overdo it!

If you have questions about what you can and can't include in the Name field, see LinkedIn's Help Center article, Adding a Suffix or Certifications to Your Profile Name.[33]

Results to Expect

Using more keywords in your Headline means you will rank higher in searches: *more people will find you.* And with an effective tagline, people will be sufficiently intrigued to read more. An increase in page views means more potential job inquiries or business for you. Keywords are your key to success. Here's an example.

Let's say you have a special credential of security clearance. If someone searches for "Security Clearance" using LinkedIn's search function, something like this will appear:

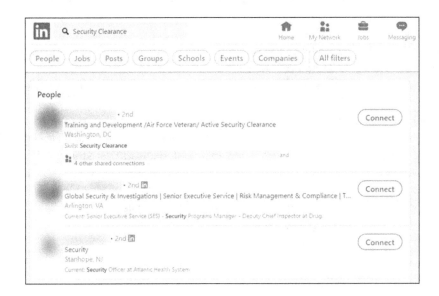

You'll see a list of people who have the keyword Security Clearance in their profile. Don't you want to appear on lists like this for your target keywords?

A strong LinkedIn presence will help you appear in Google searches as well. LinkedIn is the social network that most often appears at the top of Google search results, ranking "higher than all other profiles including all other social networks and website builders."[34] So even if you don't care about showing up in LinkedIn searches, if you want to rank on Google, make sure to optimize your keywords on LinkedIn.

▶ **Option:** If you need professional assistance with crafting your Headline, contact The Essay Expert.[35] All of our LinkedIn packages[36] include a custom Headline that will help you move up in LinkedIn search rankings.

MISTAKE #2

Unprofessional/Distracting Profile Photo, No Photo, or No Background Image

The Problem

Having no LinkedIn profile photo means your profile will be ranked lower in status. It also leaves your audience with only words to go on, and your profile will likely be skipped in favor of those with professional photos. According to LinkedIn,[37] profiles with photos receive 21 times more views and 9x more connection requests than those without. Think about it: If you were to look at two profiles side by side, and both people had the same qualifications, and the only difference was that one person had a photo and the other did not, which one would you look at first? You might even wonder whether the profile without the photo could be a fake (there are plenty of those on LinkedIn).

Photos are particularly important for job seekers, since recruiters report they like to see photos in profiles. People remember only 20% of what they read . . . but 80% of what they see; and you want to be remembered. A study by The Ladders[38] revealed that when recruiters review your profile, they spend one fifth of that time looking at your photo. If your photo includes your dog, cat, husband, or a lot of unnecessary objects in the background, viewers might think you're immature or unprofessional, or simply be distracted; and it will be hard to focus on YOU. If you are not looking at the camera, people might not be inclined to trust you as a capable businessperson.

Similarly, having no background image leaves you with no visual branding, not to mention with a profile that lacks the simple magnetic power a stunning banner image could add. Here's what the standard LinkedIn background looks like:

Boring right?

The Tune-Up

Photos

Get a professional headshot with a plain background. If possible, find someone who does "branded photo-graphy" which is a way you can ensure your personality comes through your photo. If a professional photo is not an option, stand outside on a bright day, in an open space, and get a friend to take a close-up. Use natural light (not a flash, which can create shadows). Smile and look directly at the camera. Make sure you portray yourself as you want to be seen by your intended audience.
If your photo is too small for the new image size, update it!

LinkedIn's official profile photo guidelines:

- Format should be jpg, gif or png.

- Photos should be square.

- Ideal pixel size is 400 x 400, and should not exceed 20,000 pixels.

- File size should not exceed 8MB.

▶ **Tip:** For all LinkedIn image dimensions, see Appendix C.

Here are what I believe to be some effective profile photos on LinkedIn:

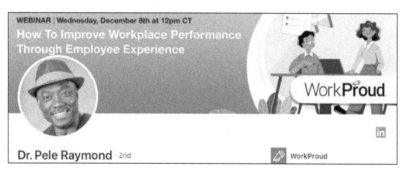

▶ **Note:** Depending on your industry, you might choose to post a more or less formal photo. If you work in the music industry, perhaps you might choose a more colorful pose than you would if you were an insurance broker.

Bright, solid colors can help you stand out among a sea of other connections, as well as an interesting backdrop.

If you have an image with a plain background, try using online tools like Profile Pic Maker[39] to help you create a more interesting backdrop for your image. You don't have to be a graphic artist to edit your photo! (Note: You might run into challenges if your hair is curly and whispy like mine. Here are some options using the image of my amazing assistant!)

Before:

After:

This image was chosen from the following options:

Once you have the perfect pic, view this quick video on how to enhance your profile photo using LinkedIn's editing and photo filtering tools.[40] Learn how to zoom in and crop your photo to the perfect size every time, plus add a variety of filters for a more modern look.

A Note About Harassment

You might have a concern that people could start harassing you due to your public photo. I myself have had a few people contact me under the guise of a professional connection when they seemed more interested in flirtation.

As an alternative to posting your photo publicly, you can change your photo settings to be visible only to your connections or only to your network (see Appendix H). This step may deter someone from asking for a connection based on visual interests alone. However, the downside is that you lose the very important advantages of having a profile photo. Also, keep in mind that your network circle consists of 1st-degree, 2nd-degree, and 3rd-degree connections and can reach farther than you think.

To set the visibility of your profile photo, go to your profile and click on your photo. Click on "View or edit profile photo":

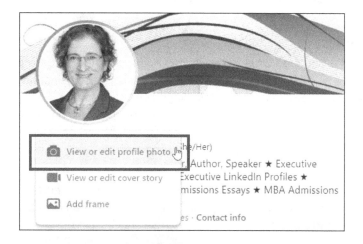

Then click Visibility and select who can see your profile: just your 1st-degree connections, just your network, everyone on LinkedIn, or everyone—on or off LinkedIn.

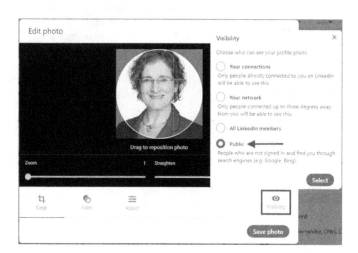

If you don't want your photo to be visible in web searches (or to anyone not logged into LinkedIn), do not choose the "Public" option.

For more information on privacy concerns, see Mistake #5.

A Note About Discrimination

Some people do not post a photo on LinkedIn because of concerns about age or race discrimination. Note that I can't give you legal advice. What I can say is that the reality is discrimination happens even though of course it is illegal. My question for you would be: Would you want to work for a company that doesn't contact you because of something they see in your picture? If they are going to discriminate, chances are they will do it in the interview if they don't have a chance to make judgments based on your photo. And the fact is, you will almost certainly be discriminated against for not posting a photo at all, since people are naturally more interested when they have a visual picture of the person they are contacting.

That said, if you are 50+ and concerned about age discrimination, it can't hurt to post a photo that makes you look as youthful as possible. Age is just a number, and your photo can give a sense of your energy and enthusiasm about your life and career!

Background Image

LinkedIn allows you to add a background image to your profile. To create a unique background, begin with a 1584x396 pixel image that depicts your brand.

Go to your profile page by clicking on your profile preview in the left column:

Or you can click on "Me" in the upper right of your menu bar and select "View profile":

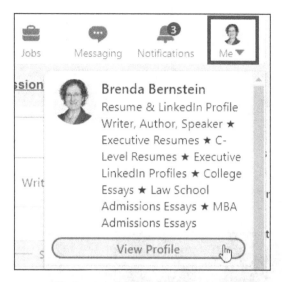

Click the pencil in the upper right of the background image area to access a pop-up window where you can upload your image and edit it.

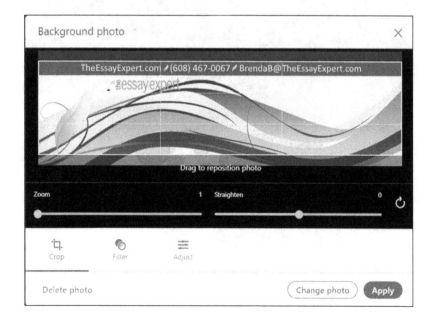

Here are what I believe to be some effective profile backgrounds on LinkedIn:

Videographer & Photographer | Graphic Artist

Personal Injury/Civil Litigation

✦ Executive Level Program Manager ✦ Problem Solver ✦
Tactical Execution ✦ Leads Technical & Security Teams to
Deliver ✦

Creating a Custom Background Image

There are several methods for creating a custom background image for your LinkedIn profile. Here are a few that I've discovered:

1. Canva[41]

Canva is a handy tool for creating professional-quality social media graphics, including custom banners for LinkedIn. Many of their ready-made LinkedIn banner templates[42] are free to use and are highly customizable. Add your name, logo and even embellish a bit more depending on the template you choose. Signing up is free.

2. Fotor[43]

Fotor Photo Editor is a free online designer and editing tool and collage creator. Go to https://www.fotor.com/templates/linkedin-background[44] to see all of the templates they have to offer. Or, create your own by clicking the "Collage" option on the home page. In the left sidebar, click "Create New Work" and select the Classic style of collage.

LinkedIn's background image dimensions are 1584 (w) x 396 (h) pixels. To change the size of the collage, click the lock icon to unlock the dimensions and Apply. From there you can create a tiled background using your own images. Here's an example:

3. Adobe Spark

Adobe Spark works much like Canva and Fotor to create a banner. Sign up for your account, then go to https://spark.adobe.com/sp/design/post/new[45] to select your banner size. Spark's free version does contain a watermark in the lower right corner; however, their premium is only $9.99/mo.

4. Free LinkedIn Backgrounds[46]

This site has a nice variety of photo backgrounds to choose from. You can start with one of these and use Canva or Fotor to add your logo.

5. Visme[47]

Currently, Visme only offers ten free templates, but they're quite versatile, allowing you to change out the text, font, and background image so you can fully brand your profile.

In case you're noticing the similarities, here's the difference between Canva and Visme.[48]

There are also many free photo editing software platforms out there that will allow you to create an image, including paint.net,[49] GIMP,[50] and Pixlr.[51]

What's the right image for you? You get to choose. For stock images free from copyright, Unsplash[52] pixabay,[53] Pexels,[54] and freepik[55] are great sources for photos and vectors.

Results to Expect

According to LinkedIn,[56] "Members with a profile photo on LinkedIn can get up to 21 times more profile views than members without." While there are no statistics available at this time about customized background images, I'm willing to bet more people will be interested in you if you have one.

An engaging profile photo and background create a personal relationship with your viewers and help to brand you. You will be more likely to be contacted by your target audience because people will see you as friendly and professional and will be encouraged to take you seriously, whether as a job candidate or a business partner.

MISTAKE #3

Not Creating an All-Star Profile

The Problem

Although LinkedIn has stopped telling you exactly what comprises a "complete" or "All-Star" profile, and although you're the only person who will be able to view the strength of your own profile, it's clear that if your profile is missing certain information, you will not rank as highly in LinkedIn searches. Plus, LinkedIn will keep bugging you with questions, egging you on to strengthen your profile every time you view it. This is one of the easiest items to handle, so why not take action?

There are five levels of profile strength, based on your level of completeness: Beginner, Intermediate, Advanced, Expert, and All-Star. I'd like you to be an All-Star by the end of this book!

The Tune-Up

The most basic way to move your strength meter up is to fill in all the sections of your profile. The meter will increase as you add more content (e.g., a photo, a location, an education entry, an industry, or a position) until you receive an "All-Star" profile rating.

You can view your profile strength meter in the upper right-hand corner of Your Dashboard, which you'll find just below your About section.

Below your dashboard, LinkedIn will give you some advice on any sections of your profile that need improvement. Answer the questions posed by LinkedIn to strengthen your profile.

▶ **Note:** that if you've created a custom Headline (see Mistake #1) and you add a new position to your Experience section, you must uncheck the "Update my Headline" option or LinkedIn will replace your custom Headline with this position.

▶ Similarly, if you add a new position to your Experience section, be sure to uncheck the "Update my Headline" option or LinkedIn will replace your custom Headline with this position title.

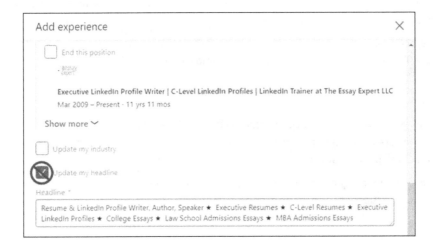

Completing the following items will give you a good start on increasing your LinkedIn strength:

- Your industry and location (More than 30% of recruiters search by location, and according to Link Humans, "adding an industry could get you 15 times more profile views." LinkedIn reports that more than 300,000 people search by industry on LinkedIn every week!)[57]

- An up-to-date current position (with a description)

- At least two past positions (According to LinkedIn,[58] your profile gets up to 29 times more views if you have more than one position listed in your Experience section.)

- Your education, including the details requested by LinkedIn (According to Link Humans, "members who have an education on their profile receive an average of 10 times more profile views than those who don't" as well as 17 times more messages from recruiters.)

- Your skills (minimum of 3)

- A profile photo

- At least 50 connections

What should I put in my current Experience section if I'm not currently working?

Perhaps the most controversial of the profile completion items is "current position." What should you put here if you are not employed? There is no definitive answer to this question. The fact is, if your profile is missing this item, yet you have taken all the other advice in this book, you will still have a strong profile and do quite well in searches.

Yes, we all know that despite the clear fact that unemployment does not truly indicate lack of talent or skill (especially during a pandemic), many employers prefer to hire people who are currently employed. Ultimately, there will often be no perfect way to hide the fact that you are not currently working. However, you have many choices of how to approach this situation in your LinkedIn profile.

Following are some of the most common ways to handle your current experience section. Note that before changing your current job title, you should turn off "Share profile updates with your network" in your Privacy Settings. Be aware that when you change your current job title, LinkedIn will ask if this is your current title. Say "NO" to avoid having your Headline replaced by the new title. You will be tempted to click "YES" but don't do it! This way your Headline will remain the way you wrote it, with all the keywords you worked so hard to put in there (also see Mistake #1).

Here are some options for how to populate your current job title when you are not employed full time:

1. **"Consultant."** Some job seekers establish consulting companies in the interim while they are looking for their next permanent position. Others write "Consultant" in their current position because it sounds credible. *Please, *only* write Consultant as your job title if you are truly doing consulting work and have at least one client (or proof of marketing) to prove it!* Otherwise it will look like you are hiding something. And always include keywords for what you are consulting *about* to help your SEO.

2. **"[Job Title] at Seeking Opportunities."** Some recruiters might respond negatively to this current experience description, and there's really no reason to put this in your headline, especially since you can use the "Open to Work" feature instead.

3. **Volunteer.** According to Link Humans, "42% of hiring managers surveyed by LinkedIn said they view volunteer experience as equivalent to formal work experience"! If you are participating significantly as a volunteer and have major accomplishments to report, putting a volunteer role in the current experience section may be appropriate. You don't necessarily need to specify that you are a volunteer; you can list your title and leave it at that. If the position is not worthy of the Experience section, use the Volunteer Experience section instead.

4. **Part-Time.** If you are employed part-time, there is absolutely no requirement that you reveal that fact. Complete the section as if the position were a full-time job. Enter the company name, your job title and accomplishments, and leave it at that.

5. **Parent or other gap.** See Mistake #1 for details of how to handle a leave or stay-at-home position. LinkedIn has made some advances in this arena!

6. **Blank.** This strategy is recommended by many recruiters. Their philosophy is that if you're not employed, honesty is the best policy.

▶ **The good news:** Your LinkedIn profile is a living document and you can always handle something one way for a month or two, then switch it up. I invite you to try different ways of presenting yourself in your Headline, About section, and job titles. Just remember to take control of your privacy settings when you make any changes.

▶ **More good news:** I can say with confidence that being unemployed does not have to be a dealbreaker! If you stay active on LinkedIn and represent yourself as an experienced professional, you can absolutely attract the attention of recruiters and hiring managers.

Results to Expect

Completing your profile is one of the easiest paths to a KILLER LinkedIn profile.
With a strong profile, you will rank more highly in searches, and, according to LinkedIn, your profile will be 40 times more likely to be viewed. Your profile ranking will increase, perhaps as high as to All-Star, a status you'll see when you view your own profile.

The chart in the Introduction section of this book bears repeating and shows clearly that the more comprehensive your LinkedIn profile, the more likely you are to be contacted by recruiters:

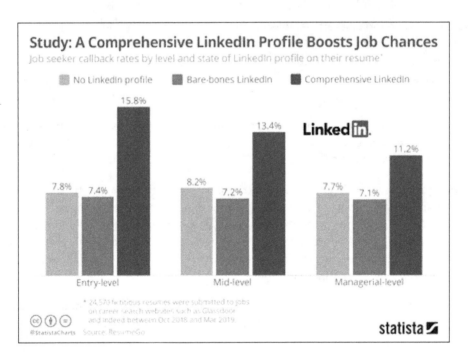

A comprehensive LinkedIn profile can give you from a 4.1% to 8.4% better chance of a callback over a bare-bones one.

Not only that, but the more complete your profile is, the more likely you are to rank highly in Google searches (be sure to have your profile set to "Public" so that people can Google you).

Including your contact information means that the people who want to connect with you will be more likely to reach out.

Have fun going for the stars!

MISTAKE #4

Missing or Outdated Information in Contact and Personal Info

The Problem

In your Contact and Personal Info section, found on the right side of your Introduction Card, visitors can view your LinkedIn URL and up to three websites of your choice, plus your phone number, email, Twitter handle, and birthday. If you fill in your birthday, be prepared to get happy birthday messages galore on LinkedIn. If you don't complete your contact information, well, people might not be able to reach you privately if they want to. And since this is a networking site, don't you want to make it easy for people to find you?

Your Public Profile URL is the first thing people see in this section. It's the link that brings people to your LinkedIn profile page.

LinkedIn creates a Public Profile URL for you that contains lots of slashes and numbers at the end. All this gobbledygook (to use a technical term) prevents brand recognition. If you leave your Public URL as LinkedIn's default, your readers will be left with letters and numbers instead of your name. "http://www.linkedin.com/in/brendabernstein/13/72a/a64" just isn't as memorable as "https://www.linkedin.com/in/brendabernstein/" It takes up a lot more room on your resume or business card too.

The Websites section of LinkedIn is even more important than you might think. Google ranks web addresses on LinkedIn very highly, so if you don't list your company website(s) on LinkedIn, you're squandering a valuable SEO opportunity.

The Tune-Up

Contact Information

I can't emphasize enough how important it is to include your contact information, including your email address and phone number, in your LinkedIn profile. I am constantly shocked at how many people do not include this information and thus make it difficult for anyone to contact them.

I'm also shocked at how many people do not look up my contact information simply by clicking on the "Contact info" link, and who request my email address by IM when they could easily obtain it from my profile. If you're asking people for information you could find easily yourself, you're not truly a LinkedIn superuser.

Click and you shall receive!

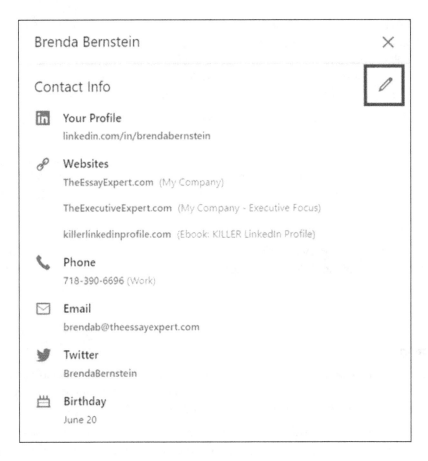

It's easy to edit your contact information on LinkedIn. Simply click on "See contact info" in your own Introduction Card, which will bring you to a window where you can click on the pencil (edit) icon:

Should I include my personal details?

If you're comfortable receiving phone calls from LinkedIn connections, include a phone number. If not, don't. But be aware that you could be skipped over if you don't include it.

I have my phone number listed and have rarely gotten any inappropriate calls. That said, I would recommend posting non-personal numbers here that only ring during business hours.

I would also recommend creating a separate email account for your LinkedIn emails. When you accept a connection request, that person can obtain your email address (if your Privacy settings allow) and put you on a list without your permission. So be aware that you could be opening yourself up for spam by including an email address in the Contact Info section. I think it's worth the hassle, but the ultimate decision is up to you.

To make sure your contact information is easily accessed by the people who want to reach out to you, go to your Settings & Privacy and scroll down to Visibility. You'll want to consider the following four settings:

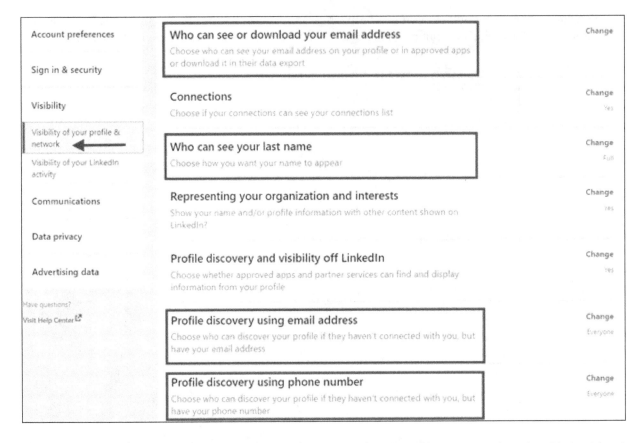

For the first option, "Who can see or download your email address," I recommend setting this to at least your 1st-degree connections. If you're in job search, I would set this to "anyone on LinkedIn."

▶ **Note:** I do not recommend allowing connections to download your email. This is an open invitation for spam/abuse.

Set "Who can see your last name" to Full and both "Profile discovery using email address" and "Profile discovery using phone number" to Everyone. This will give you maximum find-ability!

You can also get great mileage out of including your contact information in your About section. Recruiters are in a hurry, so the easier you make it for them to contact you, the better. (If you are worried about privacy, create an email address that you use just for LinkedIn contacts, and/or a free phone number through a provider such as Google Voice.)

Finally, the question of birthdays. I'd say they're not that important, and there's definitely no need to include a year. If you want happy birthday messages on LinkedIn to add to the host of good wishes you probably receive on Facebook, go for it! If you want more peace and quiet, you can omit this piece of personal information.

> ▶ **Birthday wishes from The Essay Expert:** If you are connected with me on LinkedIn and you have your birthday listed, expect a birthday message from me each year! If you don't get a message, it probably means the notification feature on LinkedIn isn't functioning properly.

Profile URL

There's simply no reason to have a LinkedIn URL with lots of letters and numbers at the end. It's easy to change your URL to a "vanity" URL that ends with your name.

> ▶ **Before you start take note:** You may only change your LinkedIn profile URL five times every six months, so I would not recommend randomly plugging in options without a good idea of what you want first. Once you've tried your fifth option, you'll need to wait another six months before you can change it again.
>
> Once you know what URL you want, click on "Edit public profile & URL" in the right sidebar of your profile.

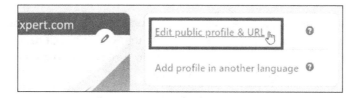

Then click on your Profile URL and you will land here:

At the top of the right-hand column, you will see "Edit public profile URL." Click on the pencil icon to reveal an entry field where you can customize away! You have 100 characters to make your LinkedIn profile a memorable—and searchable—one. Remember that it has to fit on your resume and other career documents, so you might choose to make it succinct.

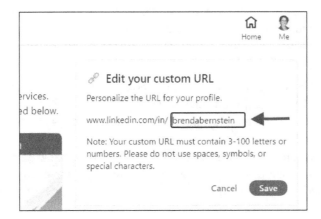

Is the name you want unavailable? Try your last name followed by your first name; or use a credential or keyword. Find a solution that works for you! Keep in mind that the custom ending to your URL must be between 5 and 30 characters and may not include any spaces or "special characters" which include dashes, dots and other symbols.

LinkedIn recommends using a variation of your name and/or your professional brand so your URL is memorable. The customizable portion of your URL is not case-sensitive, so BrendaBernstein and brendabernstein will both point to the same profile.

Once you test/use a URL it will be unavailable for use by other users for six months; however, it will still be available to you. URLs that are in this limbo state will redirect to a "Profile Not Found" page holder.

▶ **Important URL Note:** If you have your original Public Profile URL on your resume, business card, email signature or any other materials, that old URL will redirect to your new URL. However, if you change the customized URL to a different customized URL, the first customized URL will not redirect to the second one!

If you close your account, your custom URL will be up for grabs to other users after a 20-day grace period.

▶ **Keyword Tip:** If you have room to add keywords at the end of your profile URL, you can get search engine optimization (SEO) mileage out of adding your top keyword directly after your name! For instance, john-jones-corporate-counsel or jane-smith-it-director. Adding these keywords will not affect your search rankings within LinkedIn itself, but it will provide some leverage in Google searches.

▶ **Resume Tip:** I credit this tip to a client who told me he had purchased his name.com domain and then pointed the domain to his LinkedIn page. If you don't already own yourname.com for other purposes, such as a blog or other job search marketing materials, this option might be a good one for you. For example, instead of listing your profile at the top of your resume as "https://www.linkedin.com/in/brendabernstein," you could write "LinkedIn profile: www.brendabernstein.com," which looks much cleaner and also shows that you are tech-savvy.

Website URLs

Speaking of websites, have you listed yours in the Contact and Personal Info section? As we demonstrated above, start by clicking on the pencil icon in the Contact Info section:

Then you can edit your website info:

Type in your information and select the type of link you are adding. Then from the drop-down, select the appropriate choice. If you don't like the choices, no problem: just say "Other" and you'll be able to enter anything you want in the "Type (Other)" box that appears.

If your company has a special landing page you want LinkedIn users to see, feel free to list that page as one of the three websites.

Another great option for sharing websites is to post them in your Publications or even your Projects section. See Mistake #14 for more information on the ever-important Special Sections.

Results to Expect

With a customized LinkedIn URL, your name will stand out and provide a cleaner image on your resume, business cards, or anywhere else you are sharing your LinkedIn URL. Your Google search rankings will improve based on the inclusion of your name as well as keywords if space allows.

Updating your websites and other contact information will give your viewers more ability to find out who you are, and to contact you if they want to. The easier it is for people to discover and reach you, the more results you'll get from LinkedIn.

Finally, if you work for or own a company, putting a link to your company's website on LinkedIn will boost the company's Google page rank. Here's how The Essay Expert shows up with a Google search for "theessayexpert. com":

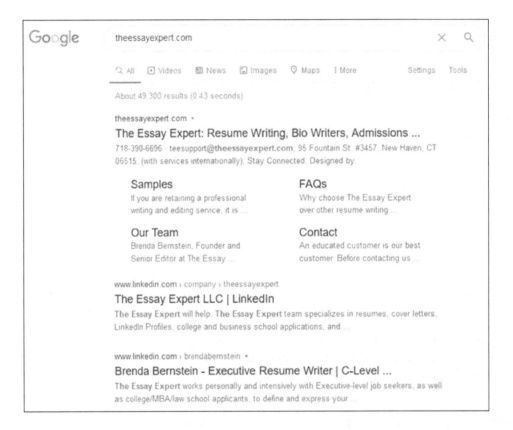

As you can see, LinkedIn shows up as the third and fourth results on the page. That's the kind of SEO you want for your company.

MISTAKE #5

Fewer than 500 (or even 1,000) Connections

The number of Connections in your LinkedIn network appears to the right of your location:

The Problem

LinkedIn claims that the average number of connections per regular user is 400, and if you count companies with millions of connections, the average number of connections is 930. In my experience, serious LinkedIn users consistently have between 500 and 900 connections or more.

Depending on your intention with your profile, you might be putting yourself at a big disadvantage by having fewer than 500 connections—and I would assert that you really need more than 1,000. With a smaller network, your updates will go to a limited audience; the people who view your profile might see you as "unconnected"; and, perhaps most important, you will often not appear in searches if you are not connected on at least a second-degree level to the people conducting the search.

> ▶ **Someone could search for you by your actual name and not find you** if you do not have at least a second-degree connection to that person! So it is absolutely critical that you increase your number of connections.

There are admittedly some advantages to having fewer connections, or at least to having carefully chosen connections. For instance, if you want to increase your ability to obtain referrals, as opposed to just job leads, you must have a strong network of people who know you well. Or if you are in a field like Venture Capital, it does not look good to have a sprawling, unfocused network. However, in most cases, I would suggest that a large network and a strong network are not mutually exclusive, and that almost every LinkedIn user would benefit from building both.

Another reason to expand your network is that LinkedIn has made it more and more difficult to communicate with people who are not first-degree connections. You've probably experienced searching for someone and having results come up that suggest you must send InMail or subscribe to LinkedIn Premium in order to write to the person you're trying to reach. Perhaps the Connect button is nowhere to be found! This is certainly a bind you want to get out of.

The Tune-Up

There is a balance to be struck between expanding your network as aggressively as possible and expanding it with quality connections. Your strategy will be different depending on your situation. If your title is CEO or Corporate Counsel or VP of Asset Management at a hedge fund, you will make different choices than if you are an internet marketer or a resume writer. Choose your connections based on the image you want to project as well as your goal with your LinkedIn profile.

As a general rule, the more people you are connected with within your field or client base, the more leverage you will get from your connections. Additionally, the more connections your connections have, the more rapidly your network will grow.

▶ **The network size limit for LinkedIn members is 30,000.** If you're getting close to that number, it's time to look at the quality of your connections and start disconnecting as appropriate.

Passive Network Building

One easy way to expand your network is to accept connection requests from people you know or whom you would want to know. LinkedIn used to display a warning about not connecting with members you don't know, but they have (smartly) removed it. However, do make sure when you receive invitation email notifications to check the sender address so you don't become a victim of phishing! Read this article[59] and this article[60] for more about how fake emails have been used and what they look like (they can be hard to spot!).

You may get some connection requests directly by email, or you can view them by going to the upper right-hand corner of your LinkedIn page and clicking on "My Network":

On the resulting page, you can accept or ignore the connection requests you've received.

If you see a message below the invitation, that means the person has taken the good advice of many LinkedIn experts and sent you a personal note along with their request. Click on the "Reply to [connection's name]" below the message to respond.

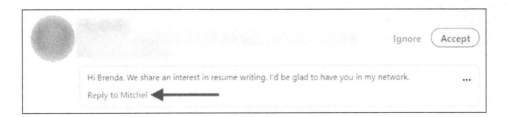

By writing a message in response to invitations, and not just accepting them, you can make a more personal connection that spurs dialog and may even lead to new job or business opportunities.

My favorite response from a LinkedIn connection read, "Thank you, thank you! Tonight I'm going to read your book to my kids. It's never too early to start building your LinkedIn network."

Whenever someone reaches out to connect with me, I give them a few tips on their profile. This practice has built trust with my network and even attracted some clients. Likewise, when people have offered me advice after connecting with me, I've been spurred to speak with and even hire some of them!

Some professionals have a rule that they will only connect with someone after a phone call or in-person conversation. This practice is a great way to meet people in an authentic way and to create valuable alliances.

> ▶ **Note:** Don't send your visitors to someone else's profile! The "People also viewed" feature allows your visitors to see a list of people others searching for you have found—i.e. your competition. To turn off this feature, go to your Settings & Privacy and under "Account Preferences" and "Site Preferences" turn the toggle button under "People also viewed" to off.

Following are some suggestions of ways to expand your network responsibly. Choose the options that work best for you.

Active Network Building: 9 Ways to Find People to Add to Your Network

There are two categories of people you can reach out to in order to grow your network: people you already know, and people you don't know yet! These tips will help you connect with both new and old connections.

1. LinkedIn Search

If you know the name of the person you want to connect with, simply type that name into the search bar. Let's say you're looking for Jane Smith. You'll get a list which you can then narrow by People, Jobs, Posts, Companies, Groups, Schools or Events. Note, however, that if the person does not have 500+ connections, it's possible that you can type in their name and they will not show up in your search.

If you type "jane smith photographer" you'll get a different results list:

Boolean logic is available to refine your search. For more details on how to use this method, read LinkedIn Help's article, Using Boolean Search on LinkedIn.[61]

Of course, you don't always need to use Boolean search logic to expand your network. Many potential connections are right in front of your nose: friends and yes, even family. Do not discount your family! You truly never know who might know someone who will lead you to your next job or your next client.

2. Your Address Book

One easy way to build your LinkedIn network is by sending requests to people in your address book. If they are already LinkedIn members, they will accept your invitation almost 100% of the time. If they are not members, many will join LinkedIn at your request, because they trust you and they've probably been thinking about joining for a long time anyway.

Before I share how to get a list of your contacts, let me say that I do NOT recommend having LinkedIn invite everyone in your address book to become members! Many of them might be outdated, and they could reject your invitation, creating some issues for you with the LinkedIn powers that be. However, you can use this feature to get a list of people you might want to invite personally.

In essence, you'll proceed **as if** you're going to add your contacts, but you won't do it. Here's how:

Click on the "My Network" tab. In the left sidebar click "Contacts" (not Connections).

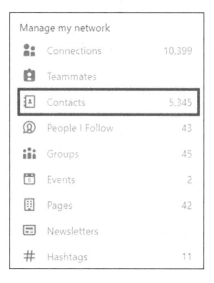

Click on "Add more contacts."

If you're not already logged into your email account, and you have a web-hosted mail like Gmail, Yahoo, Comcast, etc., enter the email address you'd like LinkedIn to access and click "Continue":

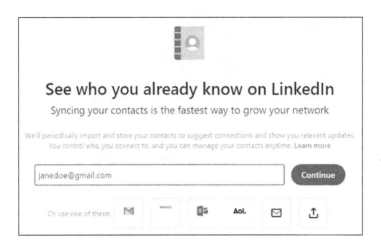

Once logged in, you'll be taken to a screen similar to this (it will vary depending on your email program) where you can grant LinkedIn permission to access your email:

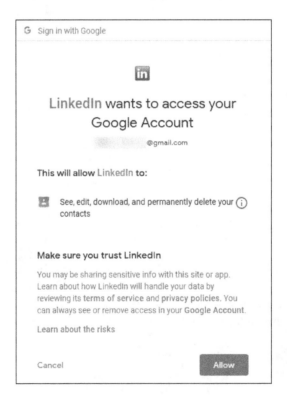

Click "Allow" and you will get a list of people in your email address book who are current members of LinkedIn.

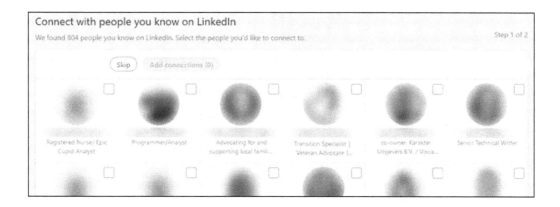

▶ This is so important I am going to say it again!! I do NOT recommend sending invitations to your contacts using this feature! They will receive an invitation with no message, you will risk getting an unacceptable number of rejections, and LinkedIn will temporarily limit you from requesting more connections. If this happens, you'll need to manually withdraw as many invitations as possible.

If you do need to withdraw an invitation, go to your My Network tab and click on "See all #."

Then view your sent connection requests click on the "Sent" tab.

To avoid this unnecessary hassle, instead look at the list and note the people with whom you would like to connect. Then visit each profile, click "Connect," and send them a personal message. Since they are in your address book, you most definitely have their email address, which you may need to provide.

3. Alumni

I recommend connecting with alumni from your educational institutions. To find alumni, put the name of your school in the main search bar and then click on your school from the drop-down.

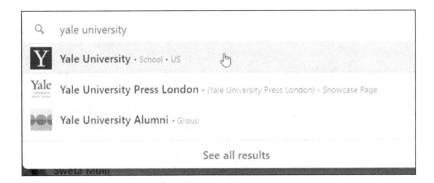

You'll be taken to a page where you can then click on "Alumni."

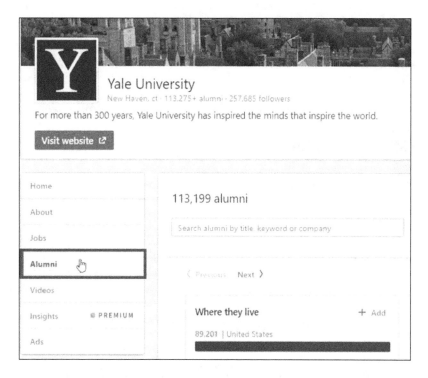

With this feature, you will have the opportunity to send invitations with personalized messages to each of your desired connections. You can invite a new connection to your network, or find those who are already first-level connections.

Use the "Next" button to scroll to the "How you are connected:

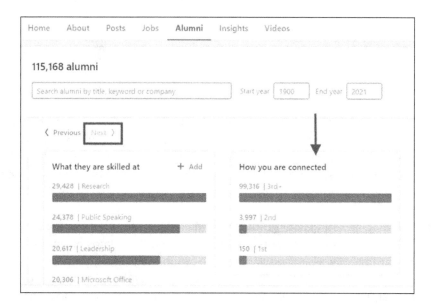

Then click the "1st" row to reveal all of your first-degree alumni connections:

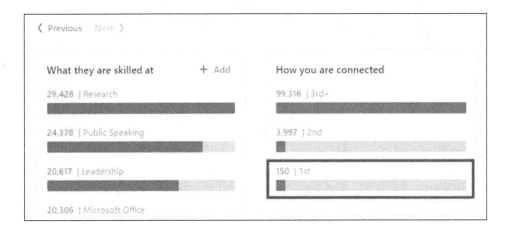

Scroll down to see all of the alumni you can connect with. Then click on "Message" to send a message.

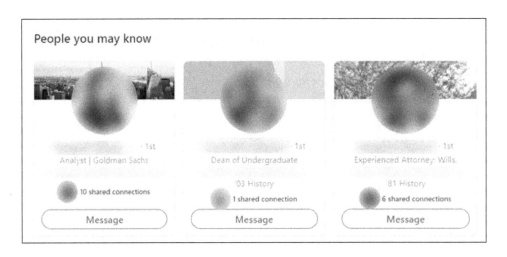

For more information on connecting with alumni, go to The Best Way to Network with Alumni on LinkedIn[62] and Tuesday Tip: Get your Foot in the Door with the Alumni Tool.[63] This feature is quite robust, allowing you to sort alumni by date, location, company, career, field of study, skills and connection level. Don't miss out on this opportunity to start up conversations with your fellow classmates; you have an automatic connection with them and they are likely to want to help you!

> ▶ **Word of warning on listing your graduation date—especially for older job seekers:** If you search for alumni by date and the person has not entered their dates of school attendance, you will not find them by searching with a date range. Similarly, if you do not enter your dates of education, you will not be found by your classmates if they search by date. You need to consider the benefits of hiding your age vs. the benefits of connecting with alumni from your class.

▶ **Important! If you want to be found as an alumnus or alumna of an educational insti-
tution, you must enter a school that LinkedIn recognizes.** Here's what to keep in mind:
When adding a school to your Education section, you want the logo of the school to appear
if possible, since that is what will link the school to the Alumni feature on LinkedIn. The first
field to complete will be the school name. Begin typing the name to reveal a listing.

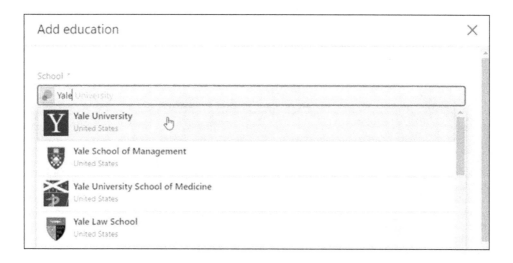

Select the correct school and once you have saved your entry, the school's logo will appear on your profile.

If the entity you want doesn't appear in the drop-down list when you begin typing the name into that field,
you may have some luck searching for the school on the web. If you search for "Yale University LinkedIn,
you'll get a link to the school's page.

Or you can go to the school's website directly to get social media links. Here's an example from Yale:

Stay Connected to Yale University

FIND US EVERYWHERE   VIEW BY ORGANIZATION   VIEW BY SOCIAL MEDIA ACCOUNT   GET LISTED ▸

Yale University   9 Accounts

Facebook
https://www.facebook.com/YaleUniversity ☐

Twitter
https://twitter.com/yale ☐

Instagram
https://www.instagram.com/yale/ ☐

Flickr
https://www.flickr.com/photos/yaleuniversity ☐

LinkedIn
https://www.linkedin.com/school/yale-university/ ☐

Sina Weibo
http://weibo.com/yaleuniversity ☐

Soundcloud
https://soundcloud.com/yaleuniversity ☐

YouTube
https://www.youtube.com/user/YaleUniversity ☐

YouTube
https://www.youtube.com/user/YaleCampus ☐

The same goes for "alumni" of past companies.

Don't underestimate the power of employer alumni networking! If you want to be found as a past employee of a company, and I assert that you definitely do (see Secret Networking Powerhouse: Employer "Alumni"),[64] make sure you enter a company name in your Experience section that LinkedIn recognizes. The surest way to do that is to use the name that generates a logo automatically on LinkedIn.

4. Group Members

Another potential source of connections are your LinkedIn groups. If someone posts an interesting conversation or comment, compliment the person in your request to connect. The people in your LinkedIn groups are likely to be interested in connecting with people like you. And you can message them without needing to be officially connected first! Note that LinkedIn limits the number of 1:1 group member messages you can send to 15 per month.

5. Find an Expert

If you want to connect with someone in the service area of Accounting, Coaching and Mentoring, Design, or Marketing, you're in luck. In September of 2019, LinkedIn rolled out a new mobile app feature to help members find connections based on recommendations from their network. Here's how it works:

1. Click on the + icon to start a new message/update

2. Choose "Find an Expert" from the bottom menu

3. Click "Ask your network."

4. Choose from four current "quick list" of categories provided: Coaching and Mentoring, Consulting, Design, Marketing, or Other

5. If you choose Other, you'll be able to select from a more comprehensive list

6. Select your location

7. Provide a description of the type of service you're looking for (LinkedIn provides some samples)

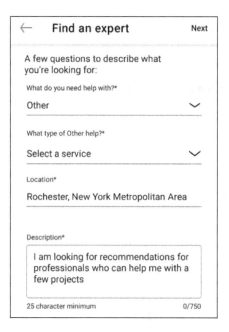

8. Click Next in the upper right corner

9. Select who you'd like to see your request: anyone on or off LinkedIn (+ post to Twitter), connections only, or group members only (you can select multiple groups)

10. Click "Connections" in the lower right to select whether you want to allow comments on your post

11. Review your message, add relevant hashtags for better exposure, and send

12. Wait for recommendations from your network

The Find an Expert tool is meant to get recommendations for service providers, but you might discover other creative ways of using the feature. For more information on how to use the Find an Expert tool, read "Tap Your LinkedIn Network to Fill Your Project Needs."[65]

6. Requesting an Introduction

Because you see not only your 1st-degree connections' posts in your feed, but also comments and reactions to *their* connections' posts, this can be a great place to "meet" new people. The same applies to groups and more. Here's an example of what I mean:

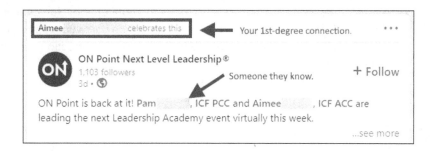

If you feel comfortable, you can ask your 1st-degree connection to introduce you to someone they know using the "Mutual Connections" link. Here's how:

Find a member you'd like to meet, click to visit their profile, then scroll down to the Mutual Connections section.

Clicking the link will take you to a list of 1st-degree connections you have in common.

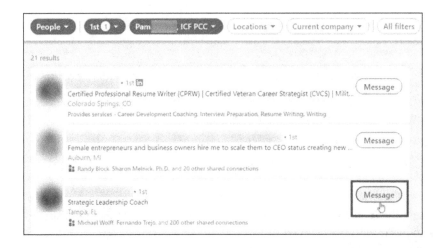

Click on the messaging button next to the person's name who can introduce you and **send a message with your request**. Paste in the contact's profile URL, so your introducer knows who you want to be introduced to.

Requesting an introduction may seem intimidating, but if your first-degree contact knows both you and the person you would like to meet, they will likely be happy to make the connection. However, it's also possible that they don't know them, in which case, your request may be denied. Don't give up! You can try the other first-degree contacts from your "Mutual Connections" list. Remember, the more connections you have, the easier it will be to connect with almost anyone on LinkedIn.

7. Who's viewed my profile?

A great source of connections—including, if you are doing business development or sales on LinkedIn, potential customers—can be the people who visit your profile. But who are they?

Occasionally, LinkedIn will send a notification to your email like this:

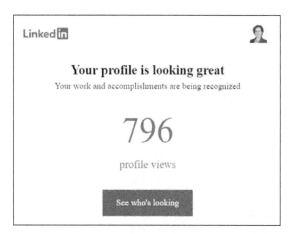

But don't wait for LinkedIn's logarithm to send you something. For valuable information on your visitors anytime, go to your homepage and look below your About section to see how many people have viewed your profile in the past 90 days and the number of times your profile appeared in search results in the last week.

If you click on the box with the number of people who have viewed your profile, you will be brought to a screen with a list of your most recent visitors and a graph of how often people viewed you over the past 90 days.

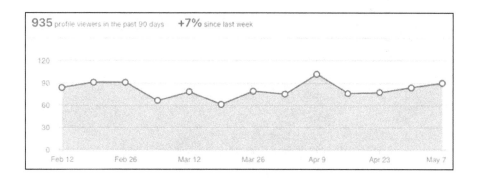

Seventy-six percent of LinkedIn members[66] said the "Who's Viewed Your Profile" feature was one of the most helpful tools on LinkedIn (paying members get much more value from this feature). If you are a job seeker, knowing which employers or recruiters have been visiting your profile can guide you to follow up with those individuals. You might say something like, "I noticed you viewed my profile. I am very interested in x and would like to have a conversation with you this week or next. Are you available next week to connect?"

Unfortunately, information on your viewers is extremely limited without a LinkedIn Premium membership. But you can get some details. For example, try clicking on "Search appearances" from your profile page:

Then you'll see all this:

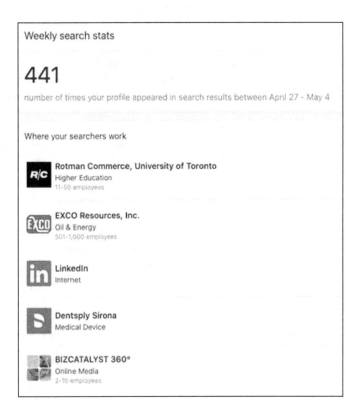

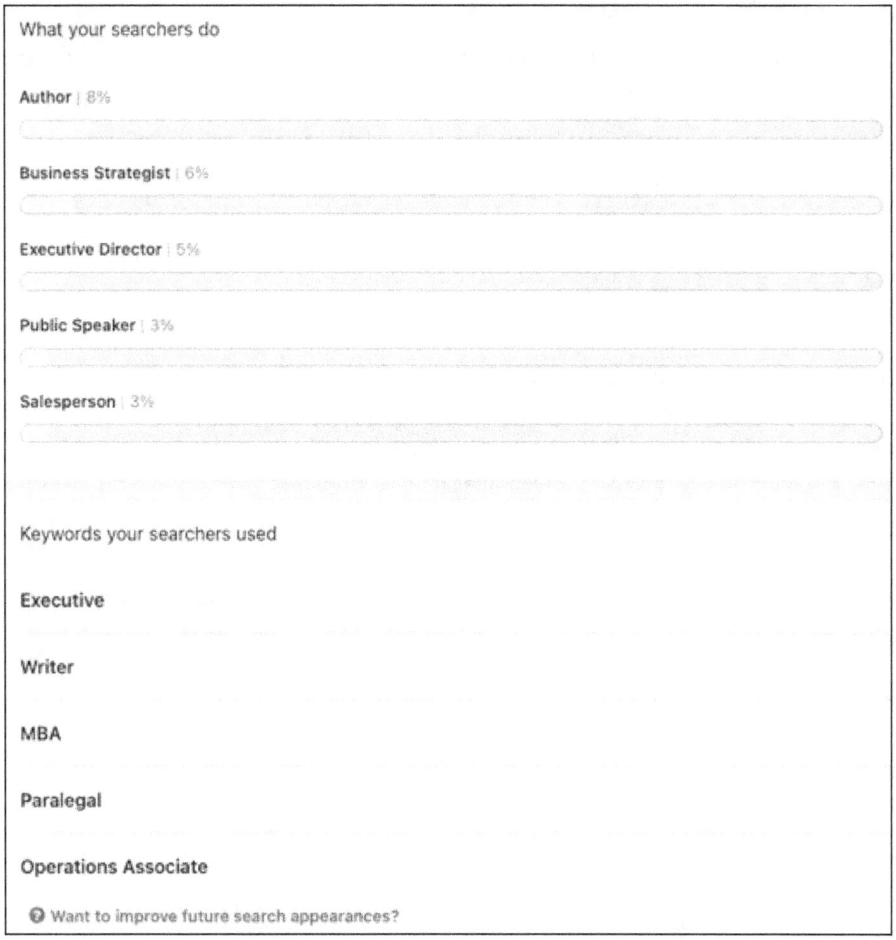

What your searchers do

Author | 8%

Business Strategist | 6%

Executive Director | 5%

Public Speaker | 3%

Salesperson | 3%

Keywords your searchers used

Executive

Writer

MBA

Paralegal

Operations Associate

❓ Want to improve future search appearances?

Have you wanted to know what search terms other members use to find your profile? Or did you think you needed a Premium subscription to be privy to that information? Here's some good news: at the bottom of your Search appearance[67] page, you'll see a section called "Keywords your searchers used."

This list shows the top keywords members were searching when they found and clicked on your profile in the past week. Keep in mind that most of the people who viewed your profile may not have been looking for your particular expertise, but LinkedIn's algorithm landed you into their search results.

Also, look in the "What your searchers do" section to find out the most common professions of people viewing your profile.

If you're not happy with the breakdown you see, it might be time to adjust your keywords!

Troubleshooting Connection Challenges

Now that we have some good ideas of who could be in your network, let's cover some strategic issues that might arise.

Challenge #1: LinkedIn's Commercial Use Limit

The first challenge you might run into is simply being able to conduct a search. If you have a free membership and you perform a lot of searches, you might run into this when you're looking for people on LinkedIn:

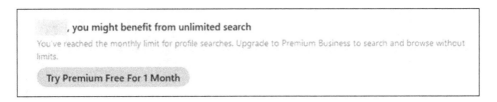

You can learn more about LinkedIn's Commercial Use Limit here.[68] Thankfully, you have options. LinkedIn suggests other ways to search for connections that don't count towards the limit, such as searching by name (rather than industry or title) and using the jobs page. There is also a workaround for this issue in Google—a secret weapon for any LinkedIn search! If LinkedIn won't let you search for Jane Smith in Atlanta, search on Google for "Jane Smith Atlanta LinkedIn" and you might find her. This trick works better for people with unusual names.

Assuming you make it to someone's profile and click to connect with them, you may very well run into your next obstacle: a page like this, where your only option is to provide the connection's email address:

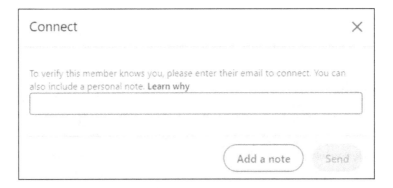

According to the LinkedIn Help Center,[69] an email address is needed for an invitation when

- The recipient's email preferences are set to only receive invitations from members who know their email address.

- Several recipients have clicked "I don't know this person" after getting your invitations. (To limit the number of people who claim they don't know you, send a personal note to remind them who you are and explain why you want to connect).

When you want to connect with someone and don't have the person's email address, try the following:

1. Look in the person's LinkedIn profile. You might find an email address somewhere if you look carefully!

2. Search for the person's name and title on Google. They may have a bio page listed with a contact email.

3. Look up the person's company on Google and see how the company addresses are created. If you see other people with addresses like SamA@ABC.com or PaulaD@ABC.com, you can be pretty sure of the address for your targeted contact.

▶ **Important:** Do NOT enter a random email address and think you have beat the system! If you do not enter an email address that matches an address associated with the LinkedIn member, your request will not be sent and you will not be notified.

Challenge #2: Address Blocker

Remember that other people are trying to connect with you too! Make it easy for them by setting your privacy settings so people don't need your address to connect with you (see Appendix H for how).

If you decide to require people to list your email address, put as many of your email addresses in the LinkedIn system as possible. Some of your connections might have an old email address or one you do not use very often. Listing multiple email addresses in your contact information will increase the possibility that your past contacts will be able to connect.

To enter additional email addresses for your account, go to your Account tab. Under "Login and security," click on "Email addresses":

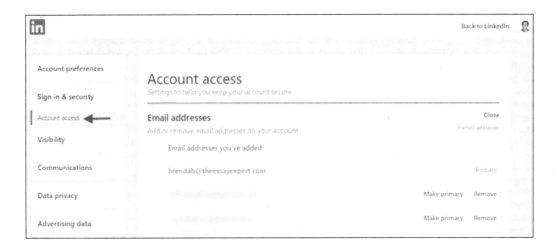

Scroll down and click on "Add email address." You will then need to verify the address. Adding as many email addresses as possible will make it easy for people to contact you, no matter where they know you from.

Challenge #3: "No InMail Credits"

You might not be able to message some Premium users if they only accept InMail and you have no InMail credits. In this situation, you might need to be a Premium member to message them.

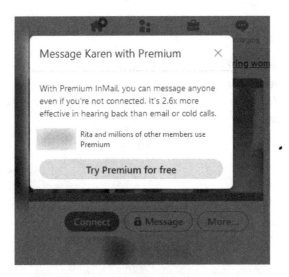

Or, you could try to connect with them outside of LinkedIn and ask them to send you an invitation.

Even in this situation, if you receive an invitation from someone with a Premium account, after you accept it you might see this message:

I believe LinkedIn does this to persuade you to purchase a paid membership. However, if you simply click on the person's name in the left-hand column, you'll be able to send a message.

Similarly, if you try to connect with someone and it looks like your only option is "Message" with a lock icon (indicating you need InMail capabilities) or no message option at all, there might be a workaround. Try clicking on the "More" button to see the menu, which will sometimes give you an option to connect.

Note that some members have set their privacy settings to block InMail. With those members, even having InMail credits will not allow you to send them InMail.

Challenge #4: Who's Viewed Your Profile

With a free LinkedIn account, you're limited in how many people per day you can see who have viewed your profile.

For more detailed information about your viewers, as well as the ability to sort them in various ways and discover exactly how they found you, you must upgrade to LinkedIn Premium (LinkedIn Corporation will encourage you in multiple ways to do so).

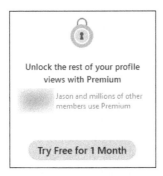

Be forewarned that due to limitations members put on their profiles with their privacy settings, you might still run into roadblocks in trying to find out who has been visiting your profile; but you might get some information you would not otherwise be able to access.

Once you know who has been "checking you out," you might want to reach out. Is it a recruiter? You might be able to find out what interested them in your profile and why they didn't message you. Is it a potential client? Ditto.

Choose carefully whether you want the people who viewed your profile to be part of your network. You don't want to connect with people who might end up spamming you.

Challenge #5: Removing a Connection

If you add someone to your network and start to question the wisdom of that connection (e.g., the person starts spamming you with advertisements or, shall we say, "love notes"), LinkedIn makes it easy to report a message as spam.

Just click the three dots in the upper right corner of your inbox message to open a "Message action" menu. Then select "Report" and follow the prompts detailing why you want to report that person:

You'll receive a message from LinkedIn letting you know next steps:

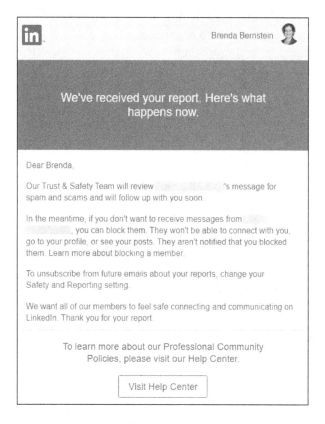

This is what I received after they reviewed my case:

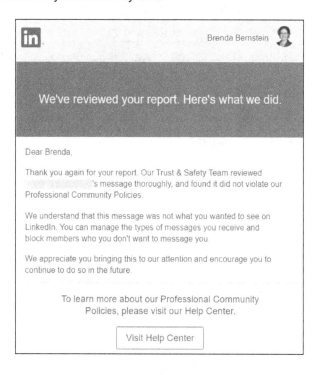

If you don't want to report the person and just want to remove them as a connection, an easy way to do this is to click on their name to be taken to their profile, then hover over the arrow next to the Send a message button.

From the drop-down menu, select "Remove connection":

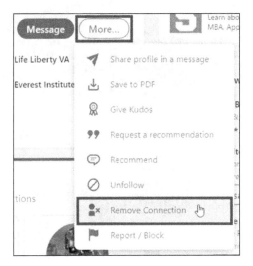

Alternatively, you can click on My Network.

From the left sidebar, click on Connections:

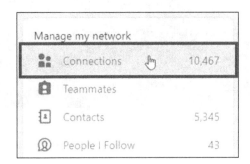

Use the search bar to find the connection, then click the three dots to the right of the Message button and "Remove connection":

Challenge #6: Connecting with the Wrong People?

If you want to make sure the person you're about to connect to is legit, you might like to try some of the following detective-style methods recommended by my colleague, Rabbi R. Karpov, Ph.D.:

First, check out the photo.

1. Click on any profile image. This opens the image in your browser. Then copy the image location/address. If you're using Chrome as your browser, you can select "Search Google for image" and skip step 2 below. In Firefox, choose "Copy Image Location."

2. Next, run that photo through Google Images.[70] You can also find it by typing "google images" into your browser. Click the camera icon and paste in the image URL.

Now you can find some things out. Look for red flags:

a. Stock photo. That wholesome-looking woman, it turns out, wasn't *really* an Apple Computer VP— nor was that her profile!

b. Or worse: The photo is real, but it was stolen, either from someone living, such as a Miss World Philippines contestant, or from someone *deceased* (hey, that's *the late President of Zaire!*)

Next, check out the rest of the general "picture":

1. Run the email address you find under the connection's Contact Info through Google.

 Did it come up as a known email address associated ONLY with a scammer/spammer? If so, don't connect—or disconnect!

2. Run the connection's name through Google. What turned up?

3. Run the name AND the email address through Google. Sometimes that is what turns up information that will make you glad you took this extra 5 minutes.

Challenge #7: Privacy Concerns—Keeping LinkedIn Safe

Once you connect with anyone on LinkedIn, your new connection has access to viewing people you know (if your settings are set the same way as 63% of LinkedIn users); reading every activity update you post; and sending items to your inbox. In rare instances, you may discover that you accepted an invitation you wish you hadn't. Or you might want to block a user from seeing your profile and updates for some other reason. Blocking a member allows you to completely remove your profile from that connection's view, and theirs from yours. In addition, says LinkedIn:

- You won't be able to message each other on LinkedIn.

- You won't be able to see each other's shared content.

- If you're connected, you won't be connected anymore.

- You won't see each other under **Who's Viewed Your Profile**.

- You won't be notified about any of their upcoming LinkedIn Events. **Note**: An attendee can only block the organizer of an event after they **leave the event**.[71]

- If you block a member who is subscribed to your Newsletter, they will no longer receive it.

- We'll remove any endorsements and recommendations from that member.

- We'll stop suggesting you to each other in features such as People You May Know and People also Viewed.

- Only you will be able to **"unblock" the member**[72] and in most cases, we won't notify the member that you blocked them.

To block someone, visit their profile and click on the "More" button below the person's Headline (or on the three dots if on mobile). From the drop-down menu, select "Report / Block" and you'll be able to choose to block this person, report them, or report the image.

If you choose to report them, you will need to provide a reason for doing so.

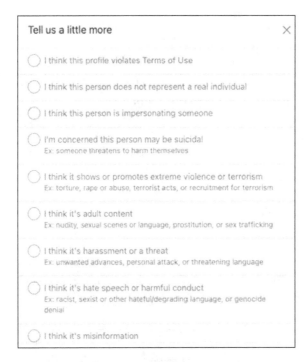

After you file a report, LinkedIn will confirm via email and follow up regarding the action they have taken.

If you choose to block a LinkedIn user instead of reporting them, this action will automatically disconnect you. When blocking, you do not need to provide a reason.

To unblock someone, click on the Visibility tab, and scroll down to "Blocking" in the left menu and click "Change." From here you can unblock members, should you choose to do so.

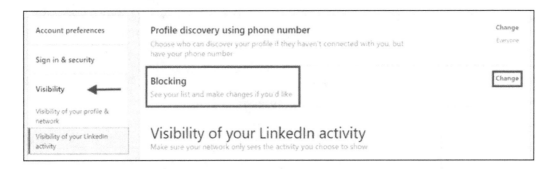

Once you have blocked someone, their name will appear on your block list. You can view the list by visiting your Settings & Privacy management area under Visibility > Visibility of your profile & network > Blocking.

For more information on how the blocking feature works, including how to block from within a group environment, read "Block or Unblock a Member."[73]

Of course, ideally we would never want to have to block anyone, so here are a few things you can do to protect your privacy in the first place:

1. Only accept connections from people you know. LinkedIn is a great supporter of this philosophy; however, there is a trade-off between maintaining a small number of reputable connections and broadening your network (and thus increasing your leads) by connecting with people outside of your circle.

2. Change your settings under Settings & Privacy so that only those who know your email address or are in your imported contacts list can send you invitations (Go to Settings & Privacy, Communications > Who can reach you > Invitations from your network. (For more details on how to find the Settings & Privacy section, see Appendix H.)

3. To protect the privacy of your connections, go to Settings & Privacy, Visibility > Visibility of your profile & network > Connections and you will have an option to prevent others from seeing your network. Toggling to No will block your first-degree connections from seeing exactly how many connections you have; otherwise they will be able to get past the "500+" and see both your exact number of connections and who those connections are.

None of these alternative actions is a perfect solution. If you encounter unwanted attention on LinkedIn, it is your prerogative to block them. You may also want to report any harassment to LinkedIn® Corporation; and if necessary, please seek legal counsel.

Results to Expect

By increasing your number of connections (preferably to 1,000+), you will be much more likely to appear at the top of searches. You will also appear more frequently in "people similar to X" when potential customers or recruiters search for people comparable to others that interest them. You will have more views of your page each day and each week. More people will request to connect with you because of whom you know. And you'll eventually be able to impress your viewers with that coveted "500+" connections listing on your profile!

If you are a job seeker, according to Greig Wells of BefoundJobs.com,[74] you will get one job offer for every 300 views to your account. That means if you get 10 views a day you will likely receive a job offer within one month!!

Here are some of the results readers produced by implementing the suggestions in this book:

"My WHO'S VIEWED MY PROFILE is up 324% in just a week."

— **Joe N.**, Graphic Designer, San Francisco, CA

"Since incorporating many of the suggestions in your book, my average daily views have more than doubled!"

— **David Goren**, National Account Manager, Atlanta, GA

"My profile views went from 2-3 a week to 197!"

— **rquiles**, Amazon Reviewer

"I am already receiving more targeted profile views prior to updating my profile under your recommendations. Huge thanks!"

— **Gary Wilson**, Sales Manager, England, UK

"My profile views and new connections have skyrocketed applying your tips and I'm only on page 83."

— **Darcy Locke**, Sales Executive, Louisville, KY

Do you want results like these? Start (or continue) growing your network now!

MISTAKE #6

Sending the Dreaded Generic LinkedIn Invitation

The Problem

LinkedIn allows you to request a connection without a personalized message, resulting in a pre-written introduction that says something like, "Hi Brenda, I'd like to join your LinkedIn network." DON'T DO IT!! This generic LinkedIn invitation is a pet peeve of most LinkedIn experts and business people on LinkedIn, prompting such snarkily written articles as Why I Didn't Accept Your LinkedIn Request.[75]

Take the time to write a personal note to anyone you want to connect with. Wouldn't you appreciate the same courtesy?

This problem is especially prevalent on mobile phones, where LinkedIn has made it extremely counterintuitive to send a personalized message. But you can do it! (I'll tell you a secret: I once did this myself. Okay, maybe twice. Clicking that little connect icon is oh-so-tempting!!)

The Tune-Up

Initiating a Connection the Right Way

On your desktop, when you click "Connect" on someone's profile or next to someone's name in a search results list, you will receive the option to send a customized invitation.

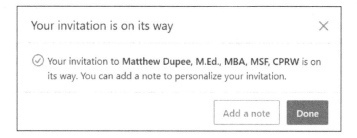

You may note at the top of the box that it says "Your invitation is on its way" and think, "Woops! Did I just send a blank invite?!"

No reason to panic—the invitation was not actually sent. You will still enjoy the option to "Add a note" before your invitation reaches your connection.

I strongly urge you to choose "Add a note" (even though, for some strange reason, it's less prominent on the screen) and write a message here. Clicking "Send" without customizing sends an email invitation containing a generic message. Here is what your contact will see:

On their "My Network" page, they will see a notification like this, containing no message at all:

What would someone's incentive be for accepting such a generic invitation? Probably not much.

Instead, click "Add a note" and a popup will appear:

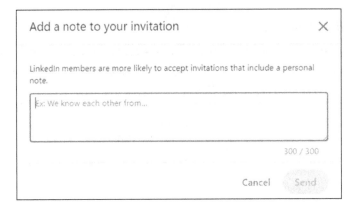

You cannot click "Send" until you have written something personal. Make an impression!

The Mobile Challenge

To send a customized invitation, go to your contact's profile and click the three dots (do NOT click on CONNECT!!):

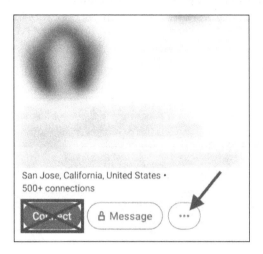

Then (for both Android and iOS) click "Personalize Invite":

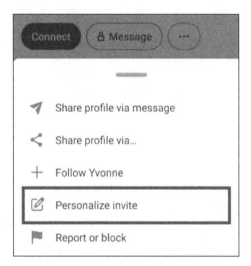

And write your message.

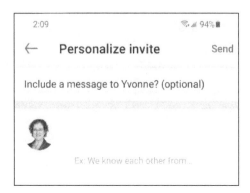

Oops!!

If you accidentally connect with someone without including a message, you can always cancel the invitation or, if you miss the window for cancellation, you can send another message with a customized invitation later. Note that this second solution will only work for people who accept non-InMail messages, or if you are able to, send InMail.

To rescind your invitation before it's accepted, click on the "My Network" tab:

Next, click "See all [#]" in the upper right-hand corner:

On the resulting page, click on Sent and you'll get a list of pending invitations. You can click on Withdraw to cancel that message you sent accidentally.

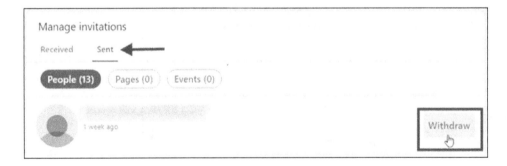

For mobile users, click on "My Network" in the toolbar at the bottom of the screen, then click on "Invitations":

On the next page, under the Sent tab, click Withdraw.

Note that you will not be able to send an invitation to that member again for up to three weeks (their Connect button will show as faded and "Pending" until the restriction is lifted).

Now that you know the basics about LinkedIn invitations, here's a chance to practice: connect with me on LinkedIn![76]

Results to Expect

You won't get reported for spam or blocked by users, and you will have a much higher quality LinkedIn network. People will like you a **lot** more!

MISTAKE #7

Ineffective or Inappropriate Communication with Your Network

The Problem

Once someone accepts your connection request, you have a golden opportunity to communicate with that person. Consider this a privilege not to be taken for granted. It's easy to connect with someone and then forget about them, in which case you will not get value from the connection. The other possibility is that you can communicate inappropriately and be seen as a spammer. This chapter will help you to get the most value out of your LinkedIn communications.

The Tune-Up

We're connected. Now what?

Once you're connected with someone, the most important thing is to communicate with them—and not succumb to apathy, lethargy, entropy, or any of those addictive downers. And you must communicate in a way that inspires people to respond.

What should you say in your LinkedIn messages?

Whenever you're communicating on social media, it's paramount to avoid sounding like a spammer. Social Media Today polled over 5K LinkedIn users,[77] and unwanted messages and spam topped the list of things they found most annoying about LinkedIn. To that end, I do not recommend sending emails to all your connections stating that you are a job seeker and asking them if they know of any openings, or that you have the best new app since TikTok. This type of email will be quickly forgotten at best, and result in a spam report at worst. Here's an example of a connection request I would consider spam:

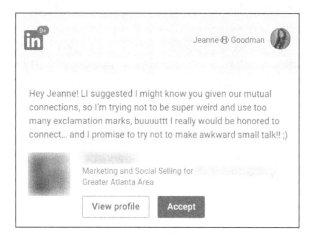

That's one example of what not to do; the message along with the job title Marketing and Social Selling raise red flags galore. Instead, I've provided some tips below on how to approach new connections.

Job seekers:

> ▶ **Do not, under any circumstances, have your first communication to a stranger be to ask them if they know of any jobs.** I promise you, you will not get a positive response.

As an alternative, you might want to ask your new connection, very respectfully, for advice on steps to take to have the most effective job search. If they engage with you, perhaps you can escalate to asking them whom you might approach to further your search.

If you connect with someone at a company where you would like to work, and if they respond favorably to an initial message, try offering to take them for coffee or lunch, or even to meet for a virtual coffee or lunch. Let them know you're interested in finding out more about what it's like to work for their organization. Again, at no point is it appropriate to ask for a job, unless this is a connection you already know well. If they like you and see an opportunity for you, they will raise that possibility.

You need to have a very high level of rapport to ask directly about job opportunities at an organization. If you already know about a job there, you could ask for advice on how to best position yourself to apply for the job.

Business owners:

Do **not** send out unsolicited requests for business to your contacts. Instead, thank them for their connection, and perhaps send them an article you think they will like, comment on something you were impressed by in their profile, ask them a great question about their business, or even mention someone in your network with whom they might want to connect.

> ▶ Stats on Unwanted Messages: As mentioned above, Social Media Today found clearly that[78] unwanted messages and spam were the things they found most annoying about LinkedIn. Please don't add to that annoyance!

If you have something to offer them that is not spammy, offer it. (I always give free advice to my new connections on their LinkedIn profiles, and many people write back either thanking me or asking me for more information about my services.) If you think it would be useful, go ahead and set up a phone or in-person meeting to get to know your new connection.

I have had success reaching out to executive coaches to let them know who I am and ask if they find it useful to have executive resume writers in their network. If they are members of the Forbes Council, I mention that in my message to them. The majority of coaches I reach out to accept my connection request, and many of them set up meetings with me. Here are some messages that have worked for me:

> Hi [first name], I see you're a member of the Forbes Coaches Council. I'm an executive resume writer and think we could be valuable connections for each other! I look forward to having you in my LinkedIn network.

Or, even simpler:

> Hi [first name], thank you for your contribution to the recent Forbes article about the future of Executive coaching. I'd love to connect!
>
> Sincerely,
> Brenda Bernstein
> Executive Resume Writer
> Owner, The Essay Expert LLC
> Author, How to Write a KILLER LinkedIn Profile & How to Write a STELLAR Executive Resume

If they accept my request, I follow up with this:

> Thanks for connecting with me, [first name]! I'm wondering, do you find connections with Executive Resume Writers to be valuable? I have some Executive coaches in my network who send clients to me, and I'd love to be a resource to you. Let's chat about how I can support your clients!
>
> Best,
> Brenda

My aim is not to be pushy but to provide value. So far it's working. A couple of the coaches I've reached out to have hired me themselves. The main lesson here is that as long as you use your networks wisely and politely, your approach can reap big rewards!

Receiving Messages

Be sure you set your email frequency under Settings & Privacy > Communications to receive individual emails for each message you get from a connection. On the Communications tab, under "How you get your notifications," click on Email:

On the following page, choose "Conversations":

On the Conversations control page, you'll be able to set the frequency or turn off a variety of communications.

It's unclear what the "Recommended" frequency is, but you can also opt for individual (as messages arrive) and weekly.

Note that messages coming from LinkedIn might sometimes get caught by your spam filter, and if you use Gmail, messages from connections can get filtered into the "Social" category, so be sure to check these places often and don't miss that next opportunity. And sometimes, the notification system simply fails, which means you won't get notifications of your messages. So check your actual LinkedIn inbox regularly. Put it on your calendar.

LinkedIn Communications in Your Email Inbox

Unfortunately, LinkedIn has slowly been making it more difficult to read messages that were not sent by InMail. In October 2018, for non-InMail messages, they stopped including the full message text in the email notification. The message "[Jane Doe] just messaged you" is frustrating at best and you need to click through to LinkedIn to read its content. In addition, even these skimpy messages are unreliable at best. Occasionally, you will discover a message in your LinkedIn inbox without receiving any email notification at all.

▶ **You will only receive email notifications reliably when a message was sent via InMail.**
That leads us to a conclusion I wish I did not have to make: If you want to get reliable notifications and the full text of messages by email, as well as make sure your connections

receive messages from you, LinkedIn Premium is the answer. Unfortunately for those who don't want to add a $19.99-$47.99 monthly expense to their budget, LinkedIn Premium is becoming more and more necessary for a positive LinkedIn experience.

▶ **Check your LinkedIn inbox on the site or app at least once/day;** and check more frequently if you're engaged in an active job search or doing business development, where a quick response can make the difference between winning or losing a sale.

Let's Get Personal!

Two great ways to keep in touch with your connections are by congratulating them on their successes and wishing them a happy birthday. A simple human connection often leads to a deeper conversation.

Start by checking up on what's happening in their lives using the Notifications tab:

On this page, if notifications are working properly, you will see the recent happy events in your connections' lives. You can customize which notifications you want to see. Just click the three dots and turn that type of notification off if you don't want it.

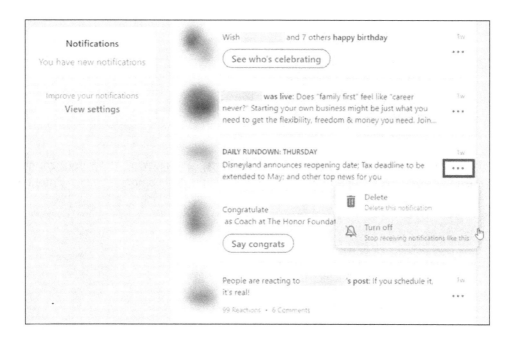

If you change your mind, turn them on again at any time by clicking "Edit" in the left sidebar.

When you see an announcement that you want to respond to, go ahead and reach out! Just click the message link to "See who's celebrating" and say happy birthday or "Say congrats," etc.:

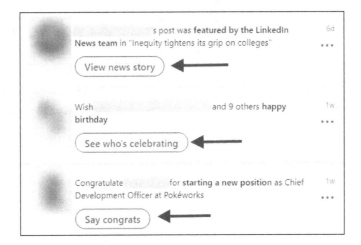

Add your customized note and send.

Other notifications you can respond to are the emails you receive letting you know your connections were mentioned in the news. What a great opportunity to congratulate them or comment on the content of the article.

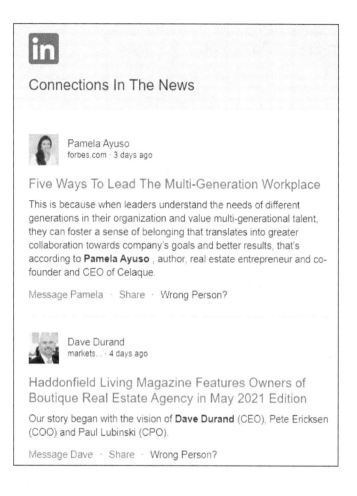

Auto-Away Messages

If you're a Premium LinkedIn user, you can set up an away message so you can take a vacation from business emails without worrying that people will think you are ghosting them. Anyone who sends you a LinkedIn message while you're taking a break will receive your own personalized preset response.

To find the "away message" setting, click your Messaging tab, then the three dots in the upper right. From the dropdown menu, select "Set away message":

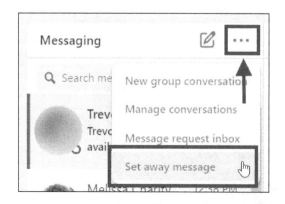

In the resulting pop-up window, set the dates and customize your message (up to 300 words). You must toggle the switch to "On" before you can make any changes.

The canned response is already entered, but as always, I encourage you to customize your LinkedIn messages. If you're a job seeker, let recruiters and potential employers know when they can expect a response. If you're attending a training, what a great way to announce what you're up to and that you're expanding your skillset. If you own a business, tell clients you appreciate them and will get back to them as soon as you return.

Unread Message Badge

To make addressing your unread messages easier, LinkedIn has added a numbered badge. Prior to the badge, unread LinkedIn messages were indicated by bold type in the left column. Now they are also accompanied by a blue dot with the number of unread messages from that contact.

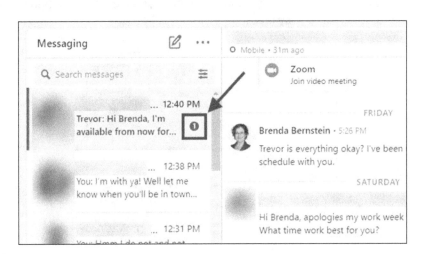

Emojis Hover Function

Sometimes as an exchange winds down with someone and you want to let them know you read their last LinkedIn message, a thumbs up or smile emoji is the perfect way to acknowledge that you appreciated their response. LinkedIn has provided a quick and easy option: hover-over emojis.

When you hover directly over your contact's message on desktop, or click and hold on the message on mobile, you'll see a preset row of the five most popular emoji responses. To choose one not listed here, click the gray emoji to open the full keyboard.

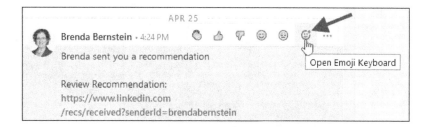

Did you know you can change the skin tone of your emojis? First click the gray emoji face below the LinkedIn message window. Then click the hand icon next to the search box and select the tone you prefer.

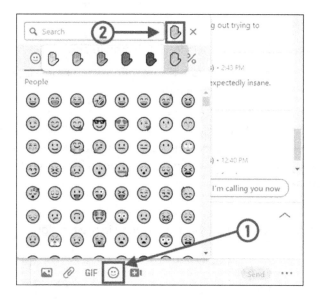

Messaging Options

When you send a message through LinkedIn mail, you can attach files to your reply, so if you are a job seeker, you might choose to forward a copy of your resume or other marketing materials. If you are a business owner, you might attach a brochure or PowerPoint. You can also ask the person you're messaging to send something to you. I frequently request people's resumes through LinkedIn, since I offer resume writing services. Here's what the interface looks like:

Desktop View

Mobile View

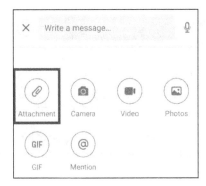

Voice Messaging

LinkedIn's new Voice Messaging feature is available in the mobile app.

In theory, this tool is a very useful way to make sure the intention of your message is understood, avoiding the potential miscommunications of written communications.

The voice messaging feature does have its downsides. One author makes a good point stating, "When someone sees a voice message, there's no way to discern the content. They have no idea what they're about to listen to . . ." Therefore, connections who don't know you might not take the time to listen to your voice message. Then again, curiosity is a strong force. It might be a good idea to preface your voice message with a written message just to be safe.

To use the voice message feature, click on the Messaging icon in the top right.

Click the plus icon to begin composing a message, then select the microphone icon at the bottom of your message window.

Hold down the microphone/record button while speaking. When you're finished you will have the option to send or cancel your message. Unfortunately, previewing your recording is not currently an option, so make sure you feel confident with your message before hitting send.

To learn more about voice messaging, read LinkedIn's blog article.[79]

Taking it Off-Line

▶ **Don't be afraid to pick up the phone or get on a video meeting** to talk to your new connections in real time.

By clicking on the video icon (from either mobile or desktop versions), you can connect to Microsoft Teams, Zoom, or BlueJeans and initiate or schedule a meeting.

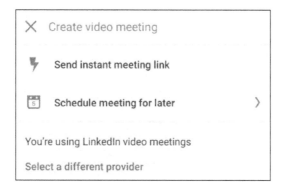

Start up a conversation with a new connection, and you will learn much more than you could ever gather from their static profile.

Results to Expect

Once you start using LinkedIn messages effectively and your network starts to grow, you will see an increase in the number of conversations you're having on LinkedIn, on the phone, and over coffee. People will like you because you are treating them with respect, being curious about them, and letting them know you care about them as a person.

It goes without saying that by engaging more effectively in your LinkedIn communications, you'll also see a big increase in the results you achieve. Your calendar will be as full as you want it to be. Plus you might end up feeling good about yourself and the new relationships you are creating!

Writing and Presentation Tips for Your KILLER LinkedIn® Profile

I'm about to make suggestions that might inspire you to change some sections of your profile. While not all changes are announced to your network, if you don't want changes to your Experience and Education sections shared with all your connections, you need to take control of your settings.

To turn off your Experience and Education section change announcements, go to Settings & Privacy:

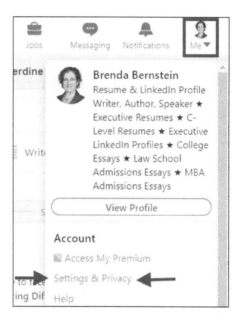

You may be required to enter your password again before proceeding. You will then be taken to the Settings & Privacy page. Click on the Visibility tab, and under "Visibility of your LinkedIn activity," you will see the option "Share profile updates with your network":

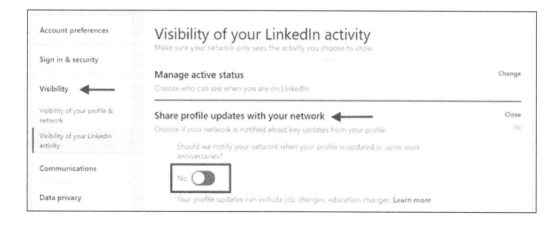

Move the switch to Yes or No depending on your preference. Then edit away!

MISTAKE #8

Blank or Ineffective About Section

The About section (previously your LinkedIn Summary) is your first opportunity to write a bio or other statement about who you are. It will get people interested in you and what you have to offer. This section is your chance to show what makes you unique and desirable. It's also your chance to give context to the rest of your profile. As of January 2020, you have 2,600 characters to work with in this section, the first 200-230 or so of which will appear when people view your profile on desktop, and the first 100 or so of which will appear on the mobile app.

The Problem

If you don't catch your reader's attention in the first few lines of your About section, you've lost the game. If you've done all the work to appear in a search, what's the point if you lose the attention of the people who are actually interested in reading your profile?

Leaving the About section blank leaves your readers with no background, and maybe no reason to read further. According to LinkedIn spokesperson May Chow, if your About section is less than 40 words, it won't even be included in searches! Even if you use the 2,600 characters, writing long blocky paragraphs or a generally dull About section will bore your readers at best, and turn them off at worst.

Did you copy your summary paragraph from your resume directly into your LinkedIn profile? When you do this, you miss out on a chance to tell your story in 2,600 characters. A copy and paste job will look exactly like a copy and paste job. I invite you to see some samples of how to do it differently on my LinkedIn About Section Samples Page.[80]

Another common mistake I see people make in their LinkedIn profiles is that they do not distinguish who *they* are from who their *company* is. I call this "conflating" yourself with your company.[81] It leaves your readers confused.

And then there are the drab, boring About statements that turn the reader off in the first sentence—the most important sentence in your entire profile!

> ▶ **A note on keywords:** If your About section does not utilize all the characters allotted, you limit your opportunities to include keywords that can make you appear more frequently in searches. Don't let that opportunity pass you by!

The Tune-Up

To hold the attention of your readers, write not only a keyword-rich About section, but also one that makes your audience want to know more about you. It can be an engaging bio or other well-written statement about your strengths, skills and accomplishments and what you have to contribute to your intended audience. Make sure you gear this statement toward your targeted readers. If you aren't sure of your target audience, it might be because you are unclear of your direction, or because you have two very disparate audiences—in which case you might not be ready to write an About section at all.

My only rules about the LinkedIn About section, if you choose to write one, are to write it with your intended audience in mind and make sure it expresses who you are and what you have to offer. Or, in the words of Catherine Byers Breet, "Who are you, and why should I care?"

Some questions you might want to answer in your LinkedIn About section include:

- How did you get to where you are professionally?
- What are your top 3 accomplishments?
- What is the most important thing your audience should know about you and/or your company?
- What makes you different than others who do the same type of work?
- What action do you want people to take after reading your About section?

Again, and I can't emphasize this enough: Direct your About section to your audience! You would write something very different to target a potential employer than you would to target a potential client.

I quote Byers Breet again here:

> "Dare to have a little fun! Times have changed, and people love to see a little personality and humor jump off their screens when they are learning about you. Keep it light, clean and professional . . . but dare to let a little of your shine through."

Following are some issues that might come up as you are writing your LinkedIn About section, and some ideas of how to address them.

1st or 3rd Person?

Most LinkedIn About sections are written in the first person ("I"), which makes them more personal and conversational. Some higher-level executives prefer to write in the 3rd person ("He" or "She"). In the end, this decision is up to you. Look at some profiles similar to yours and see what you like best!

Regardless of whether you write in first or third person, your About section must express who you are as a *person*. Your company website, your LinkedIn Company page, and even the LinkedIn Experience section are available for reporting information about your company. Your About section is there for LinkedIn members to learn more about *you*.

How to Start?

With the new interface that LinkedIn rolled out in early 2017, only the first 200-230 characters (including spaces) are visible when you initially view someone's profile. This means that whatever you consider the most important information for viewers needs to be in your first few sentences.

About

✳ Stop struggling to write about yourself! And start looking great on paper.

The Essay Expert works personally and intensively with Executive-level job seekers, as well as college/MBA/law ... see more

---

It also means that contrary to older-style LinkedIn Summary Sections, you don't want to start with a line across the page. "---------------------------" Graphics here will just take up valuable real estate.

If you attract enough interest in your opening lines, people will click on "See more" to read the rest of your About section.

I often choose to start clients' About sections with a sub-Headline or introductory line re-introducing the person. Even though you have a Headline for your profile, attention spans are short so it can't hurt to remind people of who you are. Don't use the exact wording from your Headline; instead create something new that includes keywords and a tagline. While this is not a rule, it's a trick to put in your toolbox.

If you're up against writer's block, try looking at other profiles of people in your industry. You might get inspired! Don't copy their profiles word for word of course (that would be plagiarism) but you can use them as jumping-off points.

Example #1: HR Executive

Headline:

VP OF BENEFITS & GLOBAL BENEFITS EXPERT | Advocating for Employee Retirement Readiness, DE&I, and Benefits Equity in Partnership with Fortune 500 Companies and Advocacy Groups

About Section Intro:

SENIOR BENEFITS EXECUTIVE & INDUSTRY THOUGHT LEADER with 20+ years' experience developing innovative, progressive solutions in benefits, human resources, and healthcare planning at global companies like Voya Financial, IBM, and Amgen.

Example #2: Global Executive

Headline:
Global Business Architect, Marketing Strategist, Investor & Advisor | Senior Non-Profit Leader | Multi-Hundred-Million-Dollar Revenue Generator | D&I Change Agent Enabling Daring Women to Develop Transformative Companies

About Section Intro:

As a Global Business Leader, Marketing Strategist, Investor, Advisor, D&I Champion, and Multilingual Entrepreneur who was born and raised in India, I've built businesses that generated hundreds of millions in revenue, funded and mentored Women Business Enterprises (WBEs) in sectors ranging from AI to fashion and hospitality . . .

Example #3: Chief Communications Officer

Headline:

Founder, Original Strategies | Chief Communications Officer | Storyteller | Crisis Management | Strategic Communications | Public Affairs

About Section Intro:

GLOBAL CORPORATE COMMUNICATIONS EXPERT partnering with multinational brands to improve communications through storytelling, crisis management, executive communications, and strategic messaging.

Following your Headline, you have many choices.

You might choose to demonstrate your knowledge of your field and your strategic approach. For example:

CONVERTING DATA INTO INSIGHT THAT FUELS BUSINESS TURNAROUNDS AND ACCELERATES GROWTH

Businesses can only succeed in line with the caliber of their data and their ability to interpret and translate that data into informed strategy and decision-making.

Or you might choose to dive right into your history:

I am a Ph.D. candidate in Computer Engineering with 12+ years of systems architecture design, software development, and process enhancement experience in the US and abroad. A strategic and informed risk taker, I am an effective project manager and the "go-to" choice to analyze complex problems and identify actionable processes.

OR, if using 3rd person:

EXECUTIVE LEADERSHIP OF ABC GROUP - A *Leading Provider of Products and Services for the Pharmaceutical, Medical Device and Biotechnology Industries*

25+ Years of C-Level Life Sciences Leadership Experience
John Doe, Founder and CEO of ABC Group, has led the company to become a trusted advisor to 250+ pharmaceutical, medical device, and biotechnology companies worldwide.

I have seen effective profiles that begin with a quotation. For instance, this one from Eric Schmidt, VP of Business Technology at Spacesaver Corporation:

"You need to be constantly reinventing. You need to challenge things. You need to try different ideas, different technologies, different creative approaches. Because the world is changing." Miles Nadal. That quote is very representative of my career . . .

There is no hard and fast rule about how to start your profile. Choose a strategy and style that works for you!

Run-On Sentences

Run-on sentences can leave the reader out of breath and confused. It's worth taking some time to write an About section that comes across clearly and concisely. Use powerful language and correct grammar. It makes a difference.

You vs. Your Company

One of the biggest mistakes I see in LinkedIn About Sections is the tendency for business owners to mix up who they are and who their company is. They might, for instance, write one sentence about the company followed by a sentence about themselves. The reader is left confused.

Here's an example from Michael Phelps (no, not the swimmer), who does a great job of distinguishing himself from his company, and who succeeds in selling both:

> I am a research professional and LinkedIn trainer with more than eight years of combined market intelligence, competitive intelligence and Internet recruiting experience. My focus has been on deep web sourcing, executive interviews and online networking through social media. I've spoken at more than 60 events to hundreds of business professionals about the power of LinkedIn!

See how this entire paragraph is about the *person* himself? It works! We're right there with him!

His second section reads as follows:

> Current Phelps Research Services Initiatives:
>
> • Selling and conducting targeted business research to help Wisconsin-based sales teams utilize market, competitive and prospect information to customize approaches to their clients.
>
> • Selling and conducting customized LinkedIn training to sales, marketing legal, HR, public relations, consulting, research and training teams.

Phelps clearly makes a switch from talking about himself to talking about his company. We understand, since his last name is Phelps, that he is the principal in the company and that he is behind these initiatives. We stay engaged and want to read more.

Here's another example of a business owner who writes about himself while still making it clear what his company offers:

> ■ **LEADERSHIP DEVELOPMENT** ■ **BUSINESS STRATEGY** ■ **MANAGEMENT CONSULTING** ■
>
> Is your business poised to blast above your current expectations? Are you ready to take action to heighten your leadership performance?
>
> For more than two decades, I have helped executives improve success ratios, productivity, ROI and ROE. My clients include Fortune 500 companies such as Crown Holdings, IBM, and Time Warner, as well as many smaller business entities.
>
> When problems and obstacles go unsolved, they prevent optimal operations and results. Asking and answering precisely the right questions is sometimes all it takes to develop a leader's ability to identify and resolve a business dilemma.
>
> That's where I step in. In addition to consulting and mentoring executives and entrepreneurs, I

have served as CEO of four companies, where I have improved leadership practices, implemented significant efficiencies, increased lines of credit, and preserved relationships through pragmatic and compassionate management.

My unique and confidential approach of guided dialogue and best practices teaches leaders to lead themselves so they get their careers back on track. Work with me to work smarter. Reduce stress by conquering challenges such as . . .

- Distractions
- Low Productivity
- Employee Retention
- Overdue Work
- Out-of-control Budgets
- Mismanaged Projects

Leaders who manage these issues in turn drive their company to solve problems and create higher levels of individual and organizational productivity. Most important, they become free to enjoy business again.

For more information about my company [Company Name], please visit [Web address] or read my book, Stop Telling . . . Start Leading! The Art of Managing People by Asking Questions.

When you are ready to take action to improve your leadership performance, call 555.555.1234 for a conversation about your requirements.

Confidential Job Search?

If you are engaged in a confidential job search, it is essential that your LinkedIn About section does not make you look like a job seeker. I am unable to share specific examples of profiles for confidential job seekers, for obvious reasons. However, here are some things to keep in mind and some guidelines to follow:

1. Remember, recruiters love passive job seekers! If you write a profile that sells your current company well, makes it clear you are happy and thriving in your current position, and includes effective keywords, guess what? You WILL be contacted by recruiters (assuming you follow most of the other advice in this book). And you could make your current employer happy as well—maybe even attract new clients and alliances.

2. Turn off your activity broadcasts before making any changes. Please see Appendix H for instructions on how to change your privacy settings so that you do not announce to the whole world that you have changed your profile. Many employers see changes in your profile as a sign that you might be looking; so if this is not cool with your current employer, turn off your notifications!

3. You might want to stick with talking about what you do for your current company. The more emphasis you put on what you're currently doing, the more you will benefit your current employer.

4. You can also go with a general bio format. Just talk about where you've come from and how you got to where you are now.

5. Limit the number of "accomplishment" bullets in your About section. Bullets of accomplishments scream out "resume" and might raise suspicion.

Be cautious about using LinkedIn's Open for Job Opportunities feature. All recruiters will be able to see that you are open for opportunities, so word could potentially make it back to your current employer. See Mistake 16 for more details about this LinkedIn Jobs feature.

Let's Get Personal

Some of the best profile About Sections highlight the personalities of the people writing them. Following are some samples that stood out to me for their creative approach.

Example #1: Anna Wang, Diabetes Sales Specialist (check out her last line!)

Quota Beating, Award-Winning Sales Rep

I am an extremely effective communicator, and an incredibly fast learner. I enjoy rising to new challenges, and I thrive in a competitive sales environment.

I close deals.

I have an innate ability to read between the lines and identify the needs of my customers, allowing me to consistently exceed quotas with my high close ratio and high rate of account retention. I am a creative problem solver who thinks outside the box. One of my greatest strengths is the ability to turn a cold call into a sale and a warm invitation back.

When training reps in the field, I can quickly spot their weaknesses, and devise an immediately actionable plan to increase their close ratio.

As an ADM at American Marketing & Publishing selling four days a week, I broke $300K in revenue in 2013 to rank in the top 5% of reps nationwide in 2013.

I achieved a rating of "Outstanding" at GSK in 2015.

Currently, I am a diabetes sales specialist at Abbott Diabetes Care and was recently promoted to District Sales Trainer.

Example #2: Jess Hornyak, Marketing Director

When I was little, I boldly claimed to anyone who'd listen I wanted to drive a garbage truck when I grew up. Then, I moved to Wisconsin & declared I would be the next Green Bay Packers QB once Brett Favre retired.

No one ever told me "No" (or that girls don't play in the NFL), but soon after I found the Arts; hopes of being the next big name in football were passed along to Aaron Rodgers.

Ever since I've been immersed in creativity. Weekly weekend watercolor lessons and hand-made gifts for friends' birthdays filled any spare time. And falling in love with writing equaled a 150 page novel in 8th grade and eventually a minor in Creative Writing from a Big Ten school.

I've filled just as many notebooks with poems and free writing exercises as I have canvases with brush strokes and color.

I'm also practical . . . I make lists for my lists. I've played three sports since age three, and learned from a young age how to manage my time. Not to mention I hated losing . . . & still do; saying I'm competitive is an understatement.

I want to give my best all the time, in hopes of inspiring others to be better too. And not only am I a team player as a result, but I've come to believe that being a team player is at the center of any success. Because it's true when they say that two minds are better than one.

Therefore, it's safe to say I don't fit into a traditional bubble. I'm an art director, but I'm really so much more. I'm a strategist. A writer. An artist. A competitor.

It's why I'm looking for people who could use a little more non-traditional in their everyday lives.

Plus, it means I'm never bored. And definitely not boring.

Specialties: adobe photoshop, advertising, brand management, brochure design, budgeting, closing, coaching, concept development, customer service, development, dreamweaver, illustrator, indesign, microsoft excel, microsoft powerpoint, microsoft word, persuasion, web site production

How would you express your true self in your LinkedIn About section? It might not look like either of the above examples, and, in fact, it shouldn't! If you're inspired to get creative, find your own expression and go for it! Remember to include as many keywords as you can in the process.

What Makes a Good Call to Action? And Should I Include Contact Info?

If you want readers of your profile to take action, then tell them so! Ask them to contact you if you want to enter into conversations about a particular topic. Tell them that you can create results like the ones reported in your profile for their company.

If you are in a confidential job search, your best call to action would be something relating to your current company—perhaps an action for a potential client to take.

Example #1:

If you would like to connect with a top-level cross-functional leader on the forefront of global business technology, particularly the industry shift to Cloud Services and Channel Incentives models, send me an invite!

Example #2:

I am available for a leadership role where I can leverage my expertise to build new brands and transform businesses for rapid growth.

Video "Cover Story"

If you want to convey more of your personality and value than is possible in a static profile (and I hope you do!), post a 20-second video cover story on LinkedIn. **This feature is available only on your mobile app.**

Look for the plus sign near your profile image. Here's what it looks like on my assistant's smartphone:

When you create your video cover story on LinkedIn, be sure your appearance, lighting and background all convey your personal brand. This video is now the first thing most people will notice when they open your profile page. So you want to make a good impression here!

If a script helps you, great—and whether or not you use a script, please speak naturally and be yourself. Introduce yourself and the most important thing you want people to know about yourself. An elevator pitch has never been so important!

When you're ready to create your video, log into your app, click the plus sign by your profile image, and then "Add cover story":

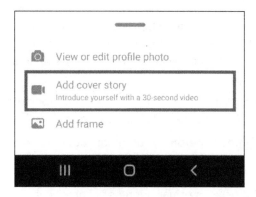

Take a deep breath and tap the camera icon to begin recording. You can then add stickers and select whether everyone or just your connections will be able to see it. Always preview your recording before adding it to your profile.

When you're done, your profile photo will have an orange frame. When someone visits your profile, they will see a short, muted preview of your recording to entice them to click and watch.

I invite you to view my cover story here.[82] I'll admit I resisted creating it, but once I started, it took about 10 minutes and was totally worth it! I plan to update my story in a few months to keep things fresh, and I encourage you to do the same. Have fun!

Should you include contact information in your About section?

If you are a job seeker wanting recruiters to access your contact information readily, or if you want people in general to be able to contact you easily, then consider including your contact information in the first 50 words of your About section. Why? Because the list view generated by LinkedIn® Recruiter displays the beginning of your About section. If your contact information shows up in the list view, recruiters won't have to work hard to reach you.

You can also put your contact information at the conclusion of your About section, which is where people will look if their interest was sparked enough to read through to the end.

You can use cute Unicode symbols before your email address and phone number, like this (see Mistake #11):

Contact me: ✆ 123-456-7890 or ✉ my.email.address [at] gmail.com.

If you do include your email address, consider writing [at] instead of @ so that spambots won't be able to find your address easily.

Remember, you also have the option to include your contact details in the Contact Information section and making that information visible to your network or to everyone.

Name with Common Misspellings?

If you have a commonly misspelled name, include common misspellings in your About section. So if your name is Izabela Tomkins, include in your About section a line that says "Izabela Tomkins, AKA Isabella Thompkins." That way you will appear in searches for common misspellings of your name!

Other Special Issues?

For samples from the LinkedIn® Official Blog of possible ways to approach career changes and other gaps on your LinkedIn profile, see their presentation on SlideShare, Representing your unique career path on your LinkedIn profile:[83]

Even with all these topics and suggestions addressed, you may have a career history that requires individual attention. Don't be afraid to ask friends, colleagues or other professionals for assistance and feedback.

Results to Expect

A well-written or even creatively written About section tells the world that you are taking control over your personal brand. By powerfully stating who you are and what you have to offer up front, you will encourage more people to read your full profile. Add to that a solid showing of keywords and a robust network, and more people will not just find you but also read your profile. A well-directed and well-placed call to action is the final ingredient and is likely to inspire more people to pick up the phone or send you an email.

According to Link Humans, "a summary [now known as the About section] of 40 words or more makes you more likely to turn up in a future employer's search." And LinkedIn® Small Business states that profiles with [About sections] get 10 times more views. Your [About section] CAN be the section that gets you a job or a new customer! It is not a section to be ignored.

SAMPLES

For samples of LinkedIn About sections from The Essay Expert's clients, see my LinkedIn About section samples page. You might also like my blog article, 3 Reasons NOT to Copy Your Resume Summary Into Your LinkedIn About Section![84]

Following are some LinkedIn Profile About sections by The Essay Expert. These samples are geared toward the U.S. job market where a strong sell is appropriate; adjust accordingly based on your target country.

Example #1

Leron Grossman, Real Estate Broker

About

One of the most sought-after and respected Realtors in Philadelphia, according to *Top Agent Magazine*, I'm an experienced, trusted, and premier Real Estate Broker and Investment Expert.

I've built my success on the singular vision of providing an unrivaled customer experience—one that leverages top research and deep local expertise, enabling clients to make informed decisions and realize stellar results.

Why Leron Grossman?
⭐ **Experienced**. Closed 100+ transactions over past 5 years
🏆 **Trusted**. 100+ Reviews! Rated 5/5 on Zillow, Trulia, REALTOR.com; secure 75% of business from repeat clients & referrals
◎ **Successful**. Own and operate several established real estate companies
∞ **Full-Service**. Offer A to Z transaction guidance
⬤ **International**. Experienced with investors across Asia, Europe, Middle East, US

Specialties
☑ Multi-family and Residential Real Estate
☑ Purchaser, Seller, Leaser, Investor Representation
☑ Real Estate Negotiation
☑ Property Portfolio, Construction & Remodeling Management
☑ Real Estate Coaching, Mentorship, Strategic Sales

Global Experience and Boutique-Level Service
When you work with me, you'll be drawing upon world-class experience, rigorous research practices, and a proven track record, while having boutique-level attention.

Path to Victory
I am a PA Licensed Real Estate Broker and active member of the National and Greater Philadelphia Association of REALTORS®. I was a former member of the Special Forces, Israeli Defense Force, and hold a BA in Management from Derby University (Top 3% of Class).

Ready to Talk?
Whether you are a newly minted real estate agent, enthusiastic first-time home-buyer, middle-market seller, motivated investor, a combination of these, or anywhere in between, I'd love to help create your roadmap to victory and fast-track the realization of your goals. Contact me today for a free consultation!

Leron Grossman

Victory Real Estate
With us it's always a win!
✉ Info@VictoryRealEstateLLC.com
📞 215-709-0909
🌐 www.VictoryRealEstateLLC.com

Grossman Group LLC
Real Estate Intelligence
✉ Info@GrossmanGroupLLC.com
📞 267-223-7788
🌐 www.GrossmanGroupLLC.com

Example #2

Anonymous, Global Benefits Executive

About

BENEFITS LEADER with deep technical expertise in designing and delivering employee-focused global benefits programs.

--

For 20+ years, I have been developing innovative, progressive solutions in benefits, human resources, and healthcare planning at global companies like ▮▮▮ ▮▮▮ ▮▮▮. As a global benefits leader, I strive to reach solutions that positively impact the lives of my employees, addressing their complex needs while also driving efficiencies and cost savings for some of the world's leading organizations.

As the current Director of Global Health Benefits & Well-Being Strategy for ▮▮▮, I've worked to overhaul the US benefits program, which resulted in simpler and better benefits for ▮▮▮ with no employee cost increase for the first time in 8 years.

Global Benefits Expert
✓ Implemented a global brokerage arrangement for ▮▮▮, realizing 10% in initial annual savings.
✓ Developed a new governance process outside of the US for health and well-being program delivery.
✓ Saved $17M+ in annual benefits savings over the course of career at ▮▮▮ ▮▮▮ ▮▮▮.
✓ Was an early adopter of HSA-compliant high deductible health plans (HDHP) in 2005 and promoted the full-replacement HDHP plans in 2010, earlier than other industry leaders.

Organizational Executive
✓ Provided internal thought leadership to C-suite regarding employer plan sponsors' role in US medical/pharmacy benefits.
✓ Supported the commercial organization in leading a migraine awareness campaign for internal and external audiences.

Industry Thought Leader
✓ Spoke at HLTH Conference, National Business Group on Health, CEO Roundtable on Cancer, and the Conference Board Health Care Conference.
✓ Participated in the International Foundation of Employee Benefit Plans and the Health Transformation Alliance.

My aim is to make ▮▮▮ and each one of my companies a top place to work. To learn more, please contact me here on LinkedIn or at ▮▮▮.

Example #3

Morgan Woodruff, Managing Partner, Strategic Partnerships & Growth Executive

About

DRIVING GROWTH AT THE INTERSECTION OF TECHNOLOGY AND REAL-WORLD SOLUTIONS.
My core leadership strength is to spur growth for companies. Bringing C-level insights, 15+ years of battle-tested capital-raise experience, and an undying passion for technology, I partner with companies in startup, reinvention, or rapid expansion mode. Together we architect a unified vision and strategy, secure investment relationships, navigate M&As, and build and scale operations.

I recognize that culture can make (or break) any company, so I make it a priority to inspire and mentor teams of top performers to rally around a unified mission.

I have propelled exponential revenue growth for companies offering technology solutions such as Omnichannel, Commerce, SaaS, Cloud, POS, and VoIP. Industries include Specialty Retail, Hospitality, Data Centers, Finance, Communications, and Security.

Notable projects:
- Co-founded and spurred 8x growth for a SaaS commerce startup in retail.
- Secured Fortune 500 partnerships (AWS, GCP, SFDC) for a relaunch of a hybrid cloud business unit.
- Drove capital raise and provided CEO oversight for reinvention of a cloud-based SaaS Product Information Management (PIM) solution.
- Built a high-profile customer portfolio for a VoIP company, leading to its ultimate sale to Google.

I formalized my advisory projects under the umbrella of Slinger Group, which I founded in 2016. We deliver hybrid advisory and fractional C-level management services, including talent recruitment, for high-potential ventures. I contribute as evangelist and champion for a Direct-to-Consumer (DTC) home furnishings eCommerce company, a fin-tech startup for the gig economy, a Data Management Platform (DMP) company, and a cybersecurity provider.

Example #4

Debra Keenan, Senior Organizational Consultant

About

Brief Overview
EMPLOYEE ENGAGEMENT LEADER with 20+ years of success driving diversity initiatives, strategy, revenue growth, and operational excellence at global organizations.

Career Narrative
Over the course of my career, I've operated in the private and non profit sectors, led teams in large firms, launched a startup, and held employee and business development roles. In diverse environments, I have gained a deep understanding of workplace demands and how to engage others across functions and levels. My experiences have enabled me to consistently engage employees to drive quality, productivity, and profitability. They have also sprouted a lifelong fascination with how to inspire professionals, break down limiting beliefs, and empower people to realize their full potential.

Representative Achievements:
► Architected first global employee engagement program for BNYM's Treasury Service Technology arm, which staffs 600 across the US and India.

► Co-founded an executive leadership coaching company, DKBWave, which served 500+ executives across the NGO, government, and private sectors, including Fortune 500 firms.

► Oversaw $100M+ P&L and 80+ employees as SVP of JPMorgan's Institutional Trust Services (ITS). Served on Corporate and ITS' Diversity Councils; raised $2M as UNCF Campaign Co-Chair.

My Vision
As technology connects the world more closely, engagement has likely never been more important. I'm excited to continue to inspire people at all levels, help firms create positive employee experiences, and accelerate collaboration, innovation, and revenue growth.

If you would like to collaborate with a high-level leader at the forefront of global employee engagement and leadership development, I'd love to connect!

Specialties
► Employee Engagement Strategy
► Global Program Design
► Diversity and Inclusion
► Surveys and Data-Driven Initiatives
► Business Development Strategy
► Executive Coaching

Example #5

Robb Delprado, Senior Consultant & Trainer

About

Passion for Our Clients and What We Do • Thirst for Knowledge • Empowerment of Others • Straight Talk with Everyone. These core values guide our training and consulting services at New View Strategies (NVS) and deeply align with my own. So when NVS co-founders and fellow D365 Business Central/Dynamics NAV User Group "All-Stars," Kerry Peters and Kim Congleton, invited me to join their team in 2020, I didn't hesitate!

Battle-tested
As senior advisor and trainer at NVS, I bring over 2 decades of leadership in ERP, Finance, Operations, and Business Integration across diverse industries, from retail to GPS technology, to help our business partners turn around problems, save costs, and navigate change. I'm most energized when empowering clients to grow their knowledge and maximize use of Microsoft Dynamics 365 Business Central/NAV platforms.

After having led teams as President, COO, Controller, and Project Manager through multiple M&A transactions and over 50 successful NAV ERP implementations, I'm still guided by the age-old principle that "Attitude is Everything." Teams can triumph through turmoil when they're inspired to persevere and remain mission-focused.

Milestones
▪ I'm a champion for the D365 Business Central/NAV User Group (BCUG/NAVUG) community of 26K+ (since 2011), and in 2019, my peers honored me with "All-Star" recognition, the organization's highest award. I founded and chaired the Houston and Dallas chapters, and I've served nationally as Advisory Board Member, Committee Chair, and YOY conference presenter.
▪ As COO and then President (2008–2017) of Western Data Systems, a survey technology equipment distributor, I navigated our teams through sales growth and tax audits, laying the foundation for successful acquisition.
▪ In my formative years as Project Manager on behalf of a Navision U.S. channel partner, I drove the success of 50+ end-to-end NAV implementation projects.
▪ For a 450+ store retailer, I collaborated with store operations to establish better Loss Prevention processes, and we reduced shrinkage by over $20M during an 8-year period.

If you're a member of the BC/NAV community, need help with training, or are just getting started with the platform, please reach out:

🌐 https://newviewstrategies.com
✉ robb@newviewstrategies.com

New View Strategies
Training • Consulting • Contract Controller/CFO • Microsoft Dynamics 365 Business Central/NAV • Relationship Management

Example #6

Anchie Kuo, Founder, Thalos

About

"Thousands have lived without love, none without water." – W.H. Auden

If I had a superpower, it would be the ability to solve the climate and environmental issues that we are facing in our world. I believe part of that solution begins with water. Accessible clean water is critical and necessary for individuals to thrive.

Contaminated drinking water impacts billions of people and is the leading cause of death globally. I founded Thalos to address this crisis and reduce our plastic bottle footprint.

Academic and Medical Background

Originally an economics major, I was in the midst of a surgical residency when I realized that I had a bigger mission than medicine and a passion to contribute to human health on a much larger scale. I spent many years investing and acquiring technologies at Pfizer and Bank of America Ventures. Most recently, I spent eight years owning and growing a China-based international healthcare company. These experiences proved to be the foundation I needed to take on the challenge of delivering clean safe drinking water to the world.

Did you know....
- Over 2.1 billion people do not have access to clean safe drinking water.
- Over two thirds of the world's fresh water supply is contaminated.
- Over 100 million people in the US will be exposed to unsafe water.
- Bottled water is less regulated than the US public water supply.
- In the United States, 50% of all bottled water comes from the tap.
- Over 200 billion plastic bottles are produced per year and less than 20% are recycled.
- According to the World Health Organization, half of the world's population will be living in water-stressed areas by 2025.

Mission-Driven Solutions by Thalos

What we eat and drink is intimately intertwined with our health and well-being. Thalos utilizes NASA technology, proven effective through its use by the US military, that offers a drinking water filtration system capable of improving the health of people and communities everywhere. Our products remove more contaminants, including viruses, metals, and chemicals, than any other portable system on the market.

My goal with Thalos is to create products that put the control over clean, safe, and affordable drinking water in the hands of families and communities across the globe.

Anchie Kuo

Thalos

✉ info@thaloswater.com

🌐 www.ThalosWater.com

Example #7

Anonymous, Senior Operations Executive

About

Delivering Results, Outperforming Customer Expectations, and Leading Award-Winning Teams.

I am an unstoppable **Senior Operations Executive** and fearless challenger of the status quo. As a visionary leader with a passion for running large field organizations, I have contributed to the sustainable growth of a $6.5B global relocation service provider with 2,700 worldwide employees.

Running global enterprise-level operations in a highly regulated industry—where delivery of five-star, direct-to-consumer service is demanded—requires rapid-fire decision-making and stealth communication skills, which I have mastered over a multi-decade career.

Beyond having direct accountability for financial control centers (client services, accounting, and audit/quality control), I have earned successive promotions for the strategic implementation of many complex initiatives. I am a strong collaborator with proven ability to resolve challenging problems involving infrastructure, talent management, technology, and process improvement.

CAREER HALLMARKS:
▲ Drove integration of $2.8B acquired company, a process involving data, systems, staffing, and client management.
▲ Orchestrated $6M urgent relocation of 2,000 government-agency employees displaced by Hurricane Katrina.
▲ Managed the first fully outsourced government relocation of >1,200 employees with revenue of $3.1M.
▲ Saved $1M by consolidating six international locations into one U.S.-based processing center.
🏆 Awarded **Support Department of the Year** and received **Global President's Award**.
"Your work has been critical in positioning us for future success. I can't thank you enough." –   CEO

SPECIALTIES:
Operations Management | Customer Experience | Account Management | Continuous Improvement | Budget Administration | Audit & Quality Control | Strategic Planning & Implementation | Project Management | Change Management | Regulations & Compliance | High-Performance Teams | Sales | Business Development | Marketing

I am interested in expanding my network of executive operations leaders and thought leaders. Please reach out to connect with me at 📧

Example #8

Ross Dabrow, VP & Co-Founder, Catch & Release

About

LAUNCHING / TRANSFORMING BUSINESSES DOMESTICALLY AND INTERNATIONALLY

✔ Building #1 sales organizations.

With a servant leadership philosophy, I have repeatedly proven that when sales executives invest in assembling and training teams of emotionally intelligent strategic thinkers aligned with the company vision, revenue & sales performance follow.

After 13 years of driving explosive growth in digital / online media—including 7 years as N.American Sales Director for Getty Images, as well as the VP of Sales at Corbis, a Bill Gates company, a global photography & video licensing leader—I know what it takes to build and develop sales organizations, launch new products, and guide startups to market dominance in E-Commerce & B2B environments.

✔ Applying high-velocity, decisive business leadership when organizations need to power launches or overcome a crisis.

After delivering historic-level sales at Getty Images, I was recruited by Wazee Digital and positioned this no-name startup to ► overpower the top 2 industry players and ascend to market leadership in our initial 24 months sales-startup. After 5 years at other firms, I was re-recruited and ► transformed their troubled Eastern sales operation into the highest-performing region in 1 year.

✔ Channeling forward-thinking creativity into YoY revenue growth.

At Framepool, a German content licensing company with no U.S. brand awareness, I optimized tight resources to pioneer a product that offset flatlining sales and attracted formerly elusive ad agency business. We converted every single customer-facing meeting into revenue, ► outdistanced 4 formidable competitors to earn "preferred vendor" status and ► realized triple-digit growth in 3 years.

Example #9

Brenda Bernstein, Resume Writer & LinkedIn Expert

About

✺ Stop struggling to write about yourself! And start looking great on paper.

The Essay Expert works personally and intensively with Executive-level job seekers, as well as college/MBA/law school applicants, to define and express your essence. We create powerfully written resumes, LinkedIn profiles and bios that spark the interest of hiring managers and universities.

If you are not getting the results you want with your Executive resume, LinkedIn profile or application essay, contact us for professional writing and coaching services--and start moving your career to the next level.

BRENDA BERNSTEIN & THE ESSAY EXPERT TEAM

Brenda is one of a handful of Certified Master Resume Writers (CMRWs) and Certified Executive Resume Masters (CERMs) worldwide. She holds an English degree from Yale and a J.D. from NYU, both with honors. Her team of certified, award-winning writers insert the "wow" factor into every writing project!

OUR PROFESSIONAL WRITING SERVICES

✍ **Resume Writing | Executive & Board Resumes**
Your resume is your first opportunity to impress a potential employer, a board, and your network. We make sure you stand out from the competition. No templates! Executive Resume Specialist.

✍ **LinkedIn Profile Writing & Coaching**
If you want your target audience to find and contact you, work with a company led by the best-selling author of How to Write a KILLER LinkedIn Profile.

✍ **College | MBA | Law School Application Essays**
Applying to college, law school or business school? We coach you to write essays that give you the best possible chance of acceptance to your target school.

Clients report unprecedented results from working with The Essay Expert. Contact us now ... because you need to "look great on paper."

Specialties: Executive Resumes | Board Resumes | Executive Cover Letters | Executive Bios | Executive LinkedIn Profiles | LinkedIn Training | College Admissions Essays | College & Law School Application Essays | MBA/EMBA Admissions Consulting | Personal Statements

You might still want assistance writing your LinkedIn About section. After all, writing about yourself is one of the hardest things you will ever have to do! The Essay Expert offers professional services to create an About section that is uniquely about you. We ask you questions, interview you, and write the About section for you, complete with graphics that you can cut and paste into your profile.

As an e-book reader, you can get special discounts on The Essay Expert's LinkedIn services.

Go to Appendix K for coupon codes
and to read what clients are saying about our LinkedIn Profile Services.

You are now halfway through your 18 steps to a KILLER LinkedIn profile! Like us on Facebook[85] for more suggestions and to join a community of like-minded readers. Please share your comments . . . online!

MISTAKE #9

No Descriptions or Weak Descriptions of Job Duties and Accomplishments

The Problem

People are looking at your LinkedIn profile to find out what you've done professionally. If you don't tell them, they might be left wondering what you are hiding, or whether you're just too lazy to write something. You are also losing out on opportunities to insert keywords into your profile.

The Tune-Up

For an effective Experience section, provide robust descriptions for your most recent and relevant jobs. Note: You are not required to match your resume exactly to your LinkedIn profile. Since you have the option of *attaching* your resume to your profile (see Mistake #15), you can use the Experience section on LinkedIn to complement rather than duplicate what's on the resume.

To add a position to your Experience section, go to your profile page, scroll down to find your Experience section, and then click the plus icon:

Note that when adding a new position, you can choose whether or not to notify your network:

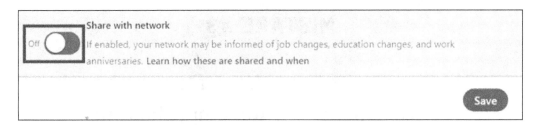

When you fill in your company, if the entity has a LinkedIn Company Page, that listing should appear as you begin typing the name.

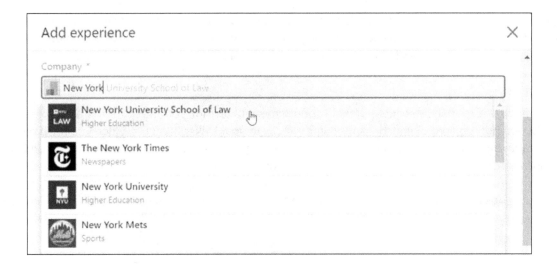

Once you have saved your entry, the company's logo will also appear on your profile beside the name. Companies that are established on LinkedIn add credibility to your work history.

A recent LinkedIn study[86] found that members with current positions get up to 5 times more connection requests. So be sure to complete a current position.

You can rearrange the entries within your Experience section by dragging and dropping the four black bars to the right of the entry. These bars will appear when you hover over the position. Note, however, that not all entries can be reordered. For instance, if you have 2 positions that are [date] to Present, you can rearrange them. If there are no black bars, the item cannot be moved.

How should I show multiple roles at the same company?

There are two ways to list your promotion in your Experience section:

1. Create a new entry for each role you've held at a single company, listing them as separate positions. Remember to include keywords in your job titles!

2. Use method one, plus add another entry. In the second entry, list the full date range of your employment at the company and include as many of your positions as fit in the job title field, plus the phrase "and other positions"—for example, "Senior Product Manager, Product Manager, and other positions"; then list all your job titles in the description if they did not fit in the job title field. Your positions will technically be represented twice; however, readers will also get a sense of your full time at the company. Option #2 also gives you an opportunity to maximize the keywords in your job titles and descriptions.

3. When adding consecutive positions at the same company, LinkedIn groups them into a single section to show your progression. In other words, instead of showing several different entries for the same company, the company will only be listed once, and your subsequent positions will appear in that section. Here's an example:

Should my Experience sections be copied from my resume?

I like to say that your LinkedIn Experience section should be completed as if you were talking to someone at a networking event. After all, LinkedIn is one big networking event! I generally prefer these sections to be written in the 1st person ("I") and to be fairly conversational, with some bullets of your accomplishments to make it clear what you're capable of achieving.

Don't forget that every section of LinkedIn is a repository for keywords! You can even put a Skills list in each of your Experience sections to beef up your search results. Sometimes, including a description of each company is an easy way to include keywords.

If you happen to be applying for a job using your LinkedIn profile, usually there is an option to attach a resume. If there is no such option, then it will be necessary for you to include all your resume bullets in your LinkedIn Experience.

For any resume-like bullets, start your phrases with verbs whenever possible (past tense verbs for past positions, present tense verbs if appropriate for present positions). Rather than state your job duties, state what you accomplished or how you helped the organization you work(ed) for. The more concrete and quantifiable you are, the better (include keywords!) If you are struggling with how to write effective resume bullets, you might like my books, *How to Write a WINNING Resume* and *How to Write a STELLAR Executive Resume*.

Some examples of great bullets are as follows:

- Secured record $5 million order from Varian Medical that was the largest single order taken in North America. Obtained trust of Management Team to implement key strategies for success.

- Improved team effectiveness by 25% in six months by redefining sales strategy and message, developing and documenting a formal sales process, and training the group in sales skills and use of new strategy.

- Teach 4 separate LinkedIn training courses
  - LinkedIn 101: Learning the Basics of LinkedIn
  - The Top Ten LinkedIn Business Development Strategies
  - Sourcing and Recruiting Top Talent Using LinkedIn
  - Tactical Research and Intelligence Gathering on LinkedIn

Note how these bullets leave you thinking, "It sounds like this person might be able to accomplish something for me."

Here's an example of a well-crafted LinkedIn Experience section, from The Essay Expert's client Ross Dabrow. Note that here, I break my own rule of using "I"; I break my own rules a lot!

> Vice President Sales | Startup & Sales Growth Leadership | Strategy Development | Change Management
> Wazee Digital
> Dates Employed Mar 2013 – Mar 2014
> Employment Duration 1 yr 1 mo
> Location Greater New York City Area
>
> Dates: 2013 to 2014; and 2006 to 2008 (3 Years)

▶ Wazee Digital is an industry leader in digital content licensing and asset management.

Originally recruited in '06 by this industry startup to launch sales operations across 3 major U.S. media markets. Exerted strategic authority as VP of Sales, North America to achieve 112%+ YoY revenue growth and overtake top global market leaders in less than 2 years.

After expanding international business expertise for 5 years with other companies, received an exclusive invitation from T3Media's CEO and Head of Global Sales to return to the company, revive challenged Eastern sales division (Eastern U.S. and Canada) and restore market credibility.

▶ SUCCESS HIGHLIGHTS ◀

✔ Turned lowest-ranking region to highest company-wide performer within 1 year of turnaround by restructuring and leading sales organization to deliver 31% global licensing revenue.

✔ Improved monthly sales pipeline 27% via lead generation strategy.

✔ Slashed operating expenses 16% YoY by introducing efficiency controls across the region.

Sometimes lackluster bullet content or descriptions in your LinkedIn profile are an indication that your resume needs an overhaul as well. If you are a job seeker, consider hiring a professional resume writer to make sure that your entire presentation—resume and LinkedIn profile—are optimized to get you interviews. The Essay Expert offers resume writing services[87] for people at all stages of their careers and we would be happy to work with you.

Again, note that while you want your resume and LinkedIn profile to be consistent with each other, you do not want your LinkedIn profile to look *exactly* like your resume. To engage the reader in a more creative way, consider writing a compelling paragraph followed by some select bullets on LinkedIn. If you are a job seeker, remember that many of the people reading your LinkedIn profile will have already seen your resume; so give your viewers something a little different to read! Also, there might be items on your resume that are too confidential to share in the public space of LinkedIn. Rather than automatically copying your resume bullets into your LinkedIn profile, consider how you want to craft each section for your audience.

Results to Expect

Your readers will be able to understand something about your experience that they would not know from reading your resume. They will feel more of a human connection with you. And they will be impressed by your accomplishments, which are an indication of what you could offer them. By learning more about you, employers or potential customers can determine whether you're someone they want to contact for further discussion.

MISTAKE #10

Lack of Consistency/Discrepancies in Format and Structure—and Spelling, Grammar and Punctuation Errors

The Problem

Lack of consistency makes information harder to absorb because the reader starts to expect a particular format or grammatical construction—and instead gets something else. A mixed-up format also appears unprofessional; people might think you did not take the time or know enough to put care into the details.

Spelling and grammatical errors will turn many of your readers off and absolutely do not project the professional image you want on LinkedIn. You can send away employers, customers and clients with a single—and **avoidable**—error. Don't let this happen to you!

The Tune-Up

Be consistent. If you have a list of items that start with verbs, make them ALL start with verbs. If you are writing in the third person (e.g., *Ms. Bernstein is* an expert writer. *She holds* an English degree from Yale University . . .), write everything in the third person; if you're writing in the first person (e.g., *I teach* people how to use LinkedIn effectively; *I work* with job seekers and business owners), stick to the first person. If you use periods at the end of your bullets, do it everywhere. If you have a heading under one job description that says "Major Accomplishments," use the heading in all positions where you had major accomplishments. Whenever you add a new position to your profile, make sure you use the same structure and format as you used for past positions. If it's a new position, people will understand if it's a little shorter than positions you've held for years; but then remember to update it! Once you've been in a position for 2-3 years, you need to add accomplishments so it doesn't look like all your great achievements happened in past jobs. Staying current with your accomplishments is key.

To make sure you are staying consistent, find a good editor to review your profile! Use your friends and family if they have skills in this area.

Another effective tool is Grammarly's extension for Chrome. Grammarly will tell you the number of "errors" it finds in your writing. This number will be in a red circle in the bottom right of the box you are working in.

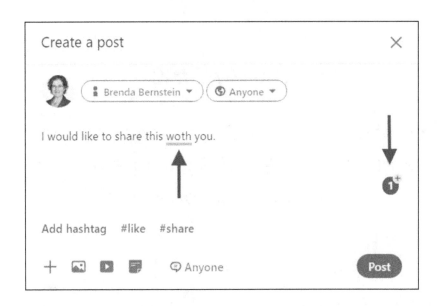

Grammarly is currently available for Firefox, Safari, Edge, and Chrome. To learn more about Grammarly's browser extension and to install it, visit their support page[88] and search for your browser + "extension."

Be careful! Grammarly often identifies as "errors" some things that constitute perfectly good English. The program is not a substitute for your own (or an editor's) discernment.

Results to Expect

Your consistency will demonstrate that you are organized, detail-oriented, and capable of clear communication. And your viewers will easily read your entire profile. An error-free profile will have people saying, "Wow what a great profile! It's so well put together! This person presents himself/herself really well. I'm ready to take action."

MISTAKE #11

Unattractive Formatting

The Problem

Unattractive formatting can be boring at best, and unprofessional at worst. At the very least, you want to make your profile easy to read. And preferably, you'll make it fun!

The most common formatting problem I see is with bullets. Does the following look attractive to you?

> • Directed $3 million dollar product division which developed solutions for FTSE 100 companies and others.
> • Successfully managed OEM technology relationships with HP, Lennox, Kyocera, Citizens and Brother.
> • Brought in new products and evaluated software development needs to maintain company's leading position in the technical world.

Even if your eyes don't hurt reading these bullets (mine do), you will probably notice that these tiny dots do not draw your attention to each statement. They are a weak formatting choice.

The Tune-Up

One easy bullet format to use on LinkedIn is the arrow: ▶

Look at the difference:

> ▶ Directed $3 million dollar product division which developed solutions for FTSE 100 companies and others.
> ▶ Successfully managed OEM technology relationships with HP, Lennox, Kyocera, Citizens and Brother.
> ▶ Brought in new products and evaluated software development needs to maintain company's leading position in the technical world.

Now my eyes are easily drawn to each of these notable achievements rather than straining to read them. (Unfortunately, hanging indents are still not an option on LinkedIn.)

I'll get to some fancier options in a minute. First, though, let's cover the basics of where to find these common symbols. They do not always translate correctly from word processing programs! So feel free to copy and paste these, or any other graphics you like, from my profile. "Steal" away!

Here are some other common bullet choices in Unicode:

Symbol	Unicode (Arial Unicode MS)
▣	25A3
■	25A0
◈	25C8
✦	2726
▶	25B8

If you want to experiment with different geometric shapes, or even letters in different languages, try copying and pasting your favorites from Wikipedia's List of Unicode Characters[89] or (for foreign languages) use Google Translate.[90]

Websites like copychar.cc[91] are an excellent source for mostly internet-friendly symbols. Just click to copy to your clipboard and CTRL+V to paste into your profile.

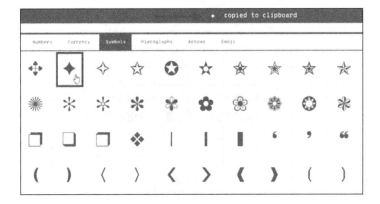

There's one easy symbol that doesn't require anything but your regular keyboard: the "pipe" symbol (|). Perhaps you've seen this one and wondered how to insert it! The pipe is a useful formatting tool that you will usually find right on your keyboard, on the same key as the backslash (\ ). The pipe is most useful in your Headline, e.g., Executive Resume Writer | C-Level Resumes | Board Resumes. It's clean and efficient.

Use it well!

Bored of the Black & White? Add Color to Your Profile with Emojis!

At long last, here's the fun stuff! There are several sites on the internet that list emojis that you can paste into documents, emails, subject lines, and even your LinkedIn profile. Two of my favorites are Emojipedia.org[92] and getemoji.com.[93]

Here's a taste of what you'll find:

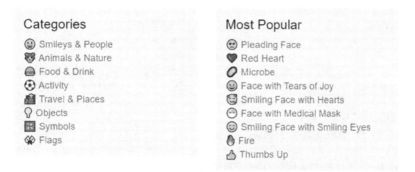

What does a LinkedIn profile look like that takes full advantage of these resources? Here's an About section, created for our client, Leron Grossman, that utilizes emojis and other creative visual elements:

About

One of the most sought-after and respected Realtors in Philadelphia, according to *Top Agent Magazine*, I'm an experienced, trusted, and premier Real Estate Broker and Investment Expert.

I've built my success on the singular vision of providing an unrivaled customer experience—one that leverages top research and deep local expertise, enabling clients to make informed decisions and realize stellar results.

Why Leron Grossman?
☆ **Experienced.** Closed 150+ transactions over past 5 years
Trusted. Rated 5/5 on Zillow, Trulia, REALTOR.com, and secure 75% of business from repeat clients and referrals
Successful. Own and operate several established real estate companies
Full-Service. Offer A to Z transaction guidance
International. Experienced with investors across Asia, Europe, Middle East, US

Specialties
☑ Multi-family and Residential Real Estate
☑ Purchaser, Seller, Leaser, Investor Representation
☑ Real Estate Negotiation
☑ Property Portfolio, Construction & Remodeling Management
☑ Real Estate Coaching, Mentorship, Strategic Sales

Global Experience and Boutique-Level Service
When you work with me, you'll be drawing upon world-class experience, rigorous research practices, and a proven track record, while having boutique-level attention.

Path to Victory
I am a PA Licensed Real Estate Broker and active member of the National and Greater Philadelphia Association of REALTORS®. I was a former member of the Special Forces, Israeli Defense Force, and hold a BA in Management from Derby University (Top 3% of Class).

Ready to Talk?
Whether you are a newly minted real estate agent, enthusiastic first-time home-buyer, middle-market seller, motivated investor, a combination of these, or anywhere in between, I'd love to help create your roadmap to victory and fast-track the realization of your goals. Contact me today for a free consultation!

Leron Grossman

Victory Real Estate
With us it's always a win!
📧 Info@VictoryRealEstateLLC.com
📞 215-709-0909
🌐 www.VictoryRealEstateLLC.com

Grossman Group LLC
Real Estate Intelligence
📧 Info@GrossmanGroupLLC.com
📞 267-223-7788
🌐 www.GrossmanGroupLLC.com

Here's another sample of creative use of emojis:

About

HIGH PERFORMANCE EXECUTIVE LEADERSHIP, CRISIS MANAGEMENT, COMMUNICATION, NEGOTIATION & PRESENTATION SPEAKER, AUTHOR, FACILITATOR & COACH

WHAT I DO:

☑ I help organisations put in place holistic, ALL-hazard (rather than haphazard!) crisis management & critical incident plans, policies, procedures and protocols to ensure they are crisis response ready & resilient.
☑ I also help organisations incorporate the well-tested real-world skills, tools & techniques used by crisis & hostage negotiators worldwide to develop high performance leadership, communication, negotiation & presentation skills that will help accelerate decision-making, credibility, authority, confidence & trust.

SERVICES PROVIDED:

▪ Review of your existing crisis management & critical incident policies & plans
▪ Crisis response readiness programs (strategic & scenario planning, awareness briefings, red-team seminars & multi-level exercises or drills)
▪ Group or team workshop programs to develop high performance leadership, communication, negotiation & presentation skills, particularly for high-stress, high stakes situations
▪ Conference & corporate event keynotes & Conference Chair
▪ 1-to-1 strategic brainstorming sessions

MY STORY:

With over 38 years of leadership experience in both law enforcement and the security industry, I have responded to countless emergencies & incidents. I was also a hostage negotiator for 24 years and a Crisis Negotiation Unit Commander for 12 years. I've had guns pulled on me, almost been killed by a machete wielding mad-man & hold the record for Hong Kong's fastest successful hostage negotiation (30 seconds!).

WHAT OTHERS SAY:

👤 "Peter can always be relied on to give an engaging & thoughtful presentation that provides plenty of key learning points & actionable takeaways. He shared a case study on the Hong Kong SARS outbreak & the audience really enjoyed & appreciated Peter's entertaining & lively delivery." Henry EE, International Organisation for Standardization

WHERE YOU'VE SEEN ME:

2019 – Keynote speaker: Asia Pacific Association of Threat Assessment Professionals, Hong Kong
2019 – Conference Chair: Corporate Travel Safety and Duty of Care Conference, Singapore
2019 – Keynote speaker: International Association of Emergency Managers Workshop, Hong Kong
2018 – Keynote Speaker: Global Security Conference, Philippines

READY TO TALK?

Contact me directly here on LinkedIn or email me at prmorgan@netvigator.com.

Be aware that emojis can look slightly different across operating systems, search engines, and social media platforms, so once you find one you want to use, I recommend viewing it in Emojipedia.org. For example, here's how the "speaking head" symbol (shown above on desktop Microsoft) looks when viewed on different devices and systems:

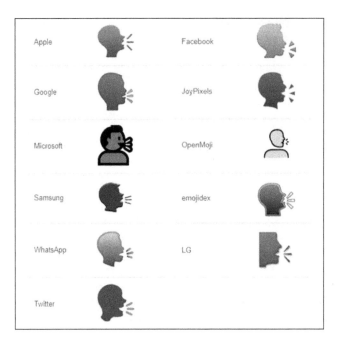

Leron Grossman's profile, displayed above, appears one way on the web (above) and another way on an Android device:

And here it is on an iPhone . . .

You may have noticed in the example above that in addition to all the really cool emojis, some of the text is bold and italicized. How **_did_** we do that? Here's how:

> To create bold or italicized text, use an online text generator, like fsymbols[94] or yaytext. Type your text into the box at the top, then copy and paste the version you like into your profile.

▶ **Important Notes:** There are 2 important things to keep in mind when using a text generator!

1. Bolded and italicized fonts take up more space than plain text, so while you gain pop, you lose character space. This should not be too much of a problem with the new 2600-character limit for the About section.

2. If you use a text converter, the resulting words will **not** be read as words by search engines! Therefore, do **not** convert text that you want to serve as a keyword. Bolded, italicized, or otherwise fancified words will look pretty, but they will not help with your LinkedIn SEO!

3. When you create a .pdf of your profile, your converted text will not translate properly. You will likely see some "&" signs and other glitchy bits. In my opinion, this imperfection is worth it for the style it gives your online profile.

Here's how I used bolding and emojis in my own profile:

iOS View

About

✏️

Stop struggling to write about yourself! And start looking great on paper.

The Essay Expert works personally and intensively with Executive-level job seekers, as well as college/MBA/law school applicants, to define and express your essence. We create powerfully written resumes, LinkedIn profiles and bios that spark the interest of hiring managers and universities.

If you are not getting the results you want with your Executive resume, LinkedIn profile or application essay, contact us for professional writing and coaching services--and start moving your career to the next level.

BRENDA BERNSTEIN & THE ESSAY EXPERT TEAM

Brenda is one of a handful of Certified Master Resume Writers (CMRWs) and Certified Executive Resume Masters (CERMs) worldwide. She holds an English degree from Yale and a J.D. from NYU, both with honors. Her team of certified, award-winning writers insert the "wow" factor into every writing project!

OUR PROFESSIONAL WRITING SERVICES

✍ RESUME WRITING | EXECUTIVE & BOARD RESUMES
Your resume is your first opportunity to impress a potential employer, a board, and your network. We make sure you stand out from the competition. No templates! Executive Resume Specialist.

✍ LINKEDIN PROFILE WRITING & COACHING
If you want your target audience to find and contact you, work with a company led by the best-selling author of How to Write a KILLER LinkedIn Profile.

✍ COLLEGE | MBA | LAW SCHOOL APPLICATION ESSAYS
Applying to college, law school or business school? We coach you to write essays that give you the best possible chance of acceptance to your target school.

Clients report unprecedented results from working with The Essay Expert.

Contact us now ... because you need to "look great on paper."

Specialties: Executive Resumes | Board Resumes | Executive Cover Letters | Executive Bios | Executive LinkedIn Profiles | LinkedIn Training | College Admissions Essays | College & Law School Application Essays | MBA/EMBA Admissions Consulting | Personal Statements

Windows View

About ✎

☼ **Stop struggling to write about yourself! And start looking great on paper.**

The Essay Expert works personally and intensively with Executive-level job seekers, as well as college/MBA/law school applicants, to define and express your essence. We create powerfully written resumes, LinkedIn profiles and bios that spark the interest of hiring managers and universities.

If you are not getting the results you want with your Executive resume, LinkedIn profile or application essay, contact us for professional writing and coaching services--and start moving your career to the next level.

BRENDA BERNSTEIN & THE ESSAY EXPERT TEAM

Brenda is one of a handful of Certified Master Resume Writers (CMRWs) and Certified Executive Resume Masters (CERMs) worldwide. She holds an English degree from Yale and a J.D. from NYU, both with honors. Her team of certified, award-winning writers insert the "wow" factor into every writing project!

OUR PROFESSIONAL WRITING SERVICES

✍ RESUME WRITING | EXECUTIVE & BOARD RESUMES
Your resume is your first opportunity to impress a potential employer, a board, and your network. We make sure you stand out from the competition. No templates! Executive Resume Specialist.

✍ LINKEDIN PROFILE WRITING & COACHING
If you want your target audience to find and contact you, work with a company led by the best-selling author of How to Write a KILLER LinkedIn Profile.

✍ COLLEGE | MBA | LAW SCHOOL APPLICATION ESSAYS
Applying to college, law school or business school? We coach you to write essays that give you the best possible chance of acceptance to your target school.

Clients report unprecedented results from working with The Essay Expert.

Contact us now ... because you need to "look great on paper."

Specialties: Executive Resumes | Board Resumes | Executive Cover Letters | Executive Bios | Executive LinkedIn Profiles | LinkedIn Training | College Admissions Essays | College & Law School Application Essays | MBA/EMBA Admissions Consulting | Personal Statements

---

Want to see what some other graphically designed profiles look like? See The Essay Expert's Sample LinkedIn Profiles[95]—these will be updated as we produce designs with these new tools.

Results to Expect

Your profile will have a professional, attractive and even creative look, and you'll be creating a brand with your graphic presentation. People will enjoy the experience of reading your profile, compliment you, and maybe even copy some of your ideas (the sincerest form of flattery!)

MISTAKE #12

Blank or Skimpy Skills Section

The Problem

The Skills section is a valuable opportunity to appear in recruiters' searches conducted for people with your skills. Forty percent of hiring managers use skills data to locate talent (spending an estimated 60 seconds in this section alone), and they are 60% more likely to find the right hire than those who don't review skills. In 2021, LinkedIn Learning helped 47 million members learn skills that were sought by almost 400,000 hiring companies.

Many people don't take the Skills section seriously because in the past, anyone could endorse you for a skill, even if they had no first-hand experience of your skill level. LinkedIn has made efforts to make skills more relevant and valuable, however, and recruiters do use this feature. If you do not complete the Skills section, you will lose leverage in your job search.

The Tune-Up

You'll need to complete a few steps in setting up your profile before LinkedIn will allow you to add skills, such as your location, current position, education, industry, and profile photo.

Once you've achieved Intermediate Level, you'll see a button to "Add a profile section." Select "Add skills" from the drop-down:

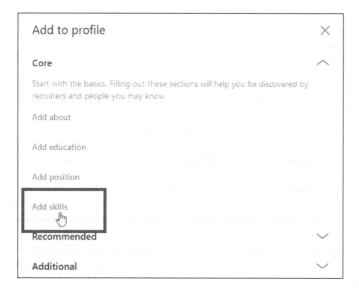

LinkedIn will suggest some skills for you based on the content of your profile:

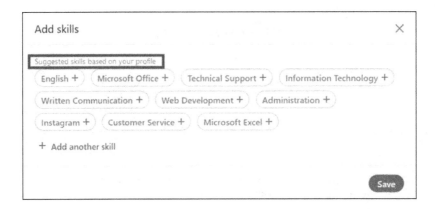

You can select the suggested skills that apply to you or add other skills.

To add a new skill, begin typing and you will be given a list to choose from; whenever possible, choose skills that auto-populate, since these are the skills most searched for, especially by recruiters. You can add up to 50 skills.

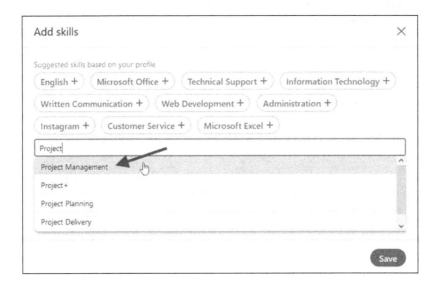

Not sure what skills to choose?

To choose skills, you can type your best guesses at keywords into the field in the "Add skills" box to see what shows up in the dropdown menu. You can analyze job descriptions (you probably thought of that). You can look at the Skills listed by other LinkedIn members who hold the role you are targeting. And, with the advent of LinkedIn's Future of Skills search tool,[96] you can research which skills are most popular for your position and industry.

Let's say you are a VP of Business Development in the U.S. You can search for VP of Business Development or for a title that most closely matches, like Business Development Executive. Results reveal that the skills for this position have changed over time:

Using this research tool can help you determine what skills to add (and update!) to optimize your views and endorsements.

Removing and Rearranging Skills

As your career progresses, some skills will become less relevant and others will become more important.

> To remove a skill, click the pencil at the top right of the Skills section, and then the pencil icon or number next to the particular skill's name. Click "Delete skill."

To rearrange your skills, click the pencil icon in the upper right of the Skills section, then on the three dots. Select "Reorder."

Grab the image with four lines to the right of the skill and drag and drop it to the correct spot so that your most pertinent skills are located at the top of the list.

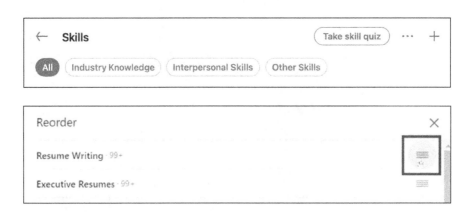

LinkedIn automatically categorizes your skills into Industry Knowledge, Interpersonal Skills, Tools & Technologies, and Other Skills. You do not have the ability to choose under which category your skills appear. When someone clicks on "See all ## Skills," these top tabs will appear for them to sort by the appropriate categories.

Managing Your Endorsements

To show or hide individual endorsements in the Skills section, click on the number next to that skill.

You'll then see a list of Endorsers. Note that your connections can also see the list of people who've endorsed you. Click the toggle switch if you don't want a specific endorsement to be visible—for instance, if you don't know the person and they don't truly know your skills and abilities.

If someone who endorses you has been endorsed by 99+ others for the same skill, they will be identified as "highly skilled." The more endorsements you receive from "highly skilled" members, the more your skill level will be trusted.

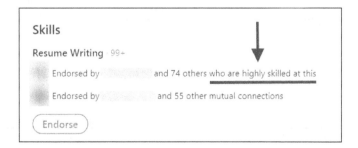

When you have 99+ endorsements and you endorse someone else for that skill, you will show up in their Skills section as the one who is highly skilled. If you are in job search, recruiters are likely to find you here.

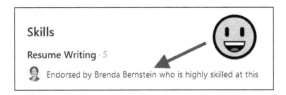

The Gift of Giving

If you're not getting as many endorsements as you'd like, try endorsing other people. You might be amazed at how quickly they return the favor.

Endorsing others can put you top of mind. Here's how:

If you come across a connection you'd like to endorse, click on their photo to be taken to their profile and scroll down to their Skills section. Next to each skill, you'll see an "Endorse" button (or, if you've already endorsed them, there will be a checkmark that says "Endorsed"). Click the button for to each skill you'd like to endorse.

LinkedIn might suggest endorsements for some of your connections. Don't be surprised if you get a prompt from LinkedIn asking if you'd like to endorse someone for a particular skill.

You have control over whether LinkedIn suggests endorsements for you to your connections, and over whether you receive endorsement suggestions from your connections.

To edit your settings, click on the pencil icon, then the three dots. Select "Endorsement settings":

Toggle the "Show me suggestions to endorse my connections" on or off.

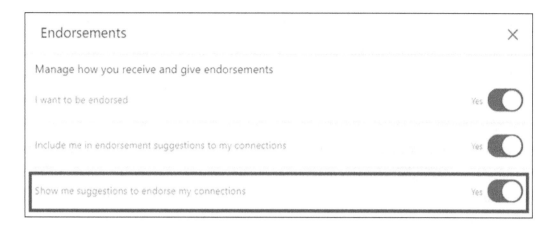

Here's the page from the LinkedIn Help section[97] that provides some additional information about giving and receiving endorsements. I recommend that you read it!

What if I don't want to endorse someone?

You don't have complete control over who sends you a request for endorsements. If someone sends you a message requesting an endorsement and you don't feel comfortable providing one, then don't! I have turned down many of these requests by writing something like this:

> "I appreciate your request. Unfortunately, since I have not worked with you in your professional capacity, I am not able to provide an endorsement at this time. I encourage you to ask your supervisors, colleagues, or others who are directly familiar with your work."

While it might not be comfortable to turn down someone's request, it's important and has integrity. And it's great practice in saying no!

Skills Assessments

Do you want to prove that you have the skills you're claiming in your Skills section? If so, you are in good company. According to LinkedIn, "69% of professionals think their skills are more important than college education when job-seeking, and more than 76% wish there was a way for hiring managers to verify their skills so they could stand out amongst other candidates." Enter: Skills Assessments, a way for LinkedIn members to validate the ubiquitous skills listed in their profiles.

Here's how it works:

1. Complete the assessment for the skill area in which you most want to demonstrate proficiency.

2. If you succeed, LinkedIn will issue a badge that will be displayed on your LinkedIn profile.

3. Immediately receive relevant job postings.

Of course, someone could fill out the assessment on your behalf; however, if you're not proficient in the skills you're being sought for, your deficiency is soon to be found out.

Take the Skill Quiz!

To begin, go to your profile, scroll down to your Skills section, and click the "Take skill quiz" button:

A pop-up window will suggest quizzes for you based on your current skills (and LinkedIn's available quizzes).

Each quiz takes between 15 and 20 minutes to complete. You must score in the top 30% of quiz takers to earn a badge.

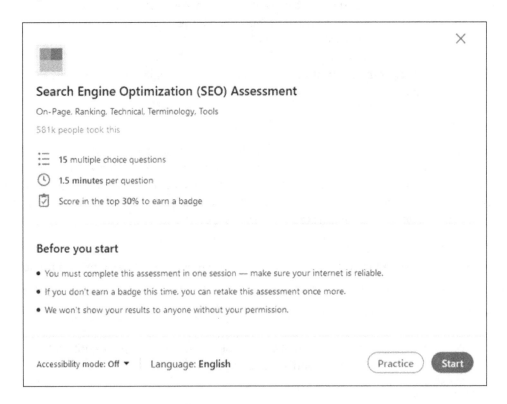

If you pass, you'll get the option to add the badge to your profile. If you don't pass, your results will not be displayed, and LinkedIn will recommend free courses in that skill category. You can retake the quiz up to once every three months.

Here's what your badge will look like:

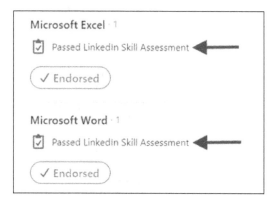

Results to Expect

LinkedIn states that "accumulating a high number of endorsements for a skill adds credibility to your profile, shows that your professional network recognizes you have that skill," and "contributes to the strength of [your] profile, and increases the likelihood [you'll] be discovered for opportunities related to the skills [your] connections know [you] possess."

Link Humans states that "members who include skills get around 13 times more profile views"; LinkedIn claims that this number can be as high as 17x. Furthermore, LinkedIn reports that members with more than five skills are 27x more likely to be discovered in searches by recruiters.

Even better, according to LinkedIn, candidates who complete Skills Assessments are almost 30% more likely to get hired. And a former global recruiter for Goldman Sachs' Investment Management Division asserts that skills assessments are "a game-changer in recruiting."

Regardless of the numbers, a robust Skills list helps people to understand where your skills lie; you will have more credibility; and recruiters will *find* you when looking for someone with your skills.

The more endorsements you have as a job seeker, the more likely you are to be contacted by a recruiter with a Premium account. If you can get 99+ endorsements for any skill, regardless of whether it's a technical skill that can be tested, it will be hard for potential clients and employers not to give you some credit. In contrast, having few endorsements for a skill can be a bad sign. Endorsements seem to be here to stay—so take them seriously.

MISTAKE #13

Not Staying Active through Activity Updates, Publishing, Comments, Videos and Kudos

The Problem

There are multiple ways to stay active on LinkedIn. More and more, your activity level plays a big role in how well you perform in searches. There are a multitude of options for engaging in activity on LinkedIn. Yet often I see people with well-written profiles who have done nothing but like other people's posts for months on end. I have even seen people in recruitment who have not shared any jobs in their LinkedIn posts. Clearly, opportunities are being missed.

If you don't post valuable information, conduct relevant searches, and participate in conversations, you won't be seen as an attractive candidate by recruiters—and you could be seen as a net taker (vs. a net giver) on LinkedIn.

The Tune-Up

The Share bar, which can be accessed from your homepage, is a good place to start when sharing information on LinkedIn. You might be familiar with this type of function if you spend time on Twitter or Facebook. Here's what it looks like:

This feature is your opportunity to let your readers know that you're active in your life and in your field. If you do not use this function, your name and updates will not appear in the ongoing activity feed found on your connections' homepages.

It's essential on LinkedIn to keep your updates current and to share valuable information consistently. Use hashtags to get your content in front of those searching for specific topics.

Don't stop at posting yourself. Read and comment on other peoples' articles. Write articles yourself! And explore the many tools available to help you collect and curate great information for sharing. Here are just a few:

- Pocket:[98] Save articles, blog posts, videos and images for later use.
- Feedly[99]: Follow blogs, podcasts, YouTube channels and publications, and access the content anytime.
- Google Alerts[100]: Get email notifications when Google finds new results on a topic that interests you.

• Listly[101]: Create lists of just about anything and let people contribute.

Once you know what's important for you to share and what articles you want to interact with, you have many ways to do so.

Creator Mode

LinkedIn has been rolling out something called Creator Mode, which is essentially a way for thought leaders to enhance their influence. Here's what Creator Mode currently offers:

• Follow will be the primary action shown on your profile and your follower count will be displayed

• Your content will be showcased more prominently on your profile

• You can show topics you post about on your profile

• LinkedIn Live Video

• LinkedIn Newsletters

Newsletters and Live Video are LinkedIn's latest methods for sharing content that I'll cover in more depth in this chapter (Option #3 and Option #5 respectively).

To find out if Creator Mode is available to you, go to your profile and scroll down to your Dashboard.

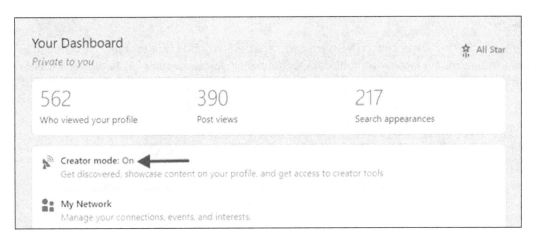

Whether or not you have access to Creator Mode, there are still six categories of good options for sharing content highlighted below.

Option #1: Post Updates

After accessing your Sharing bar from the Home tab, write something current about what you're learning, a project you're working on, even your latest favorite quotation. You have 3000 characters to show us you're alive and inspire us with your insight and success! You might even choose to reveal your sense of humor (keep it clean folks!) Some clients have gotten results from posting that they are seeking to relocate to a particular city—it is possible to catch the attention of recruiters that way. Did you just get a new certification? An interview offer or job offer? Why not report that to the world? News like this will likely make you attractive to another organization.

▶ **Note to Job Seekers:** I do not recommend posting anything about seeking opportunities in your activity updates. Doing so can make you look desperate and is unlikely to succeed. Instead, reach out individually to people in your network and ask them specific questions that will help you in your search. Take them to lunch and learn from them. Begging is not encouraged.

When you post updates, you can include articles, photos, presentations, and videos. Here are some examples of what you can share and tools to get the most bang out of each post:

▶ **Link Posting Hack:** According to Entrepreneur article, "How to Get Thousands of Views on Your LinkedIn Content,"[102] you can garner more clicks by not including a link in your status updates; put a link in the first comment instead. In testing this theory, author James Carbary "went from getting 100-200 views per post to getting over 5,000 views per post."

Another trick is to leverage people's curiosity, keeping in mind that LinkedIn only allows three lines of viewable text and makes people click to view more. Here's an example:

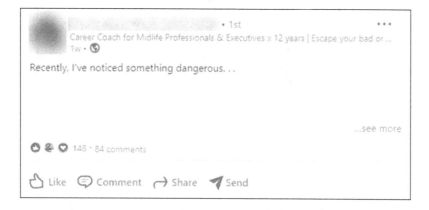

However you choose to share and stay active, keep it interesting and keep playing and experimenting with what works!

a. Include Images Using Alt Text and Tags

To share an image, for example, click the "Image" button and choose a photo from your files.

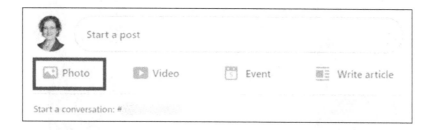

This is what your post will look like:

Don't forget to add "alt text" to your images—text that describes what's in the images. Alt text allows search engines to index the pictures you share, so be sure to include keywords to help you get found. Just click "Add alt text" and include a description.

You have up to 120 characters to describe your photo.

Your alt text will be visible if for any reason your image does not appear. This allows readers to understand what your photo was about even if they are not able to view it. Note that adding alt text is not available in the mobile app yet, as of April 2019.

If a LinkedIn connection appears in your photo, tag them! After selecting your image, click on the member you want to identify and a search field will appear. Begin typing in the name of your connection, then click their profile to tag them.

Tagged connections will be notified of your post and also have the ability to remove the tag if they wish.

There is some concern that spammers will use tagging to harass LinkedIn users. I haven't experienced this so far, though it certainly could happen in the future.

b. Share Videos—with Optional Stickers

If you really want to get attention, post a video. You can either paste your video URL, or if you want to share a file directly from your computer, click on "Video":

Videos posted from your computer will look something like this:

With LinkedIn's mobile app, you can add text and stickers to your videos and images.

There doesn't currently seem to be a way to search the available stickers, so you'll need to scroll through them to find one you like. Perhaps LinkedIn will improve that functionality in the future, as well as increase the limited number of options available.

c. Use Hashtags

Each time you draft an update to share, LinkedIn will suggest hashtags to use to help your post be found. Readers who follow those hashtags will see your post in their homepage feed, so selecting relevant and popular hashtags is key. Social Media Today suggests using hashtags that are as specific as possible, like #linkedintips instead of the broader topic #linkedin. Research trending relevant hashtags to break into the current stream of trending posts. You can also follow LinkedIn VP, Daniel Roth's newsletter "Creator Weekly"[103] for what topics and hashtags are trending.

See LinkedIn's Help article, "Using Hashtags on LinkedIn"[104] for more on hashtag best practices.

d. Don't Forget Mentions: Give Credit Where Credit is Due

LinkedIn's "Mentions" feature is a great little tool for crediting connections in your updates—or to simply include people and let them know you're thinking about them and want them to pay attention. If you type the "@" symbol, followed by the name of a connection or a company in your Update box or a comment field on the homepage, the field will auto-generate potential people or companies you can mention. (For more information, see this LinkedIn Help article.)[105]

To mention a connection, start typing the person's name and select the correct name from the drop-down. Then write your post and click the Share button. The person or company you mentioned will automatically be notified.

Here is an example of mentioning someone in a post:

You can also mention someone in a comment:

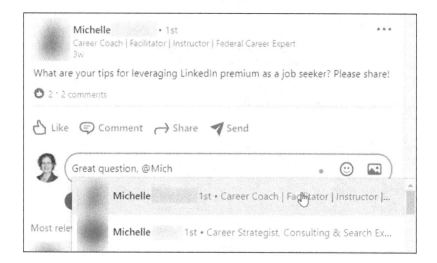

If you get mentioned and you don't want the publicity, you can remove the mention (see Removing a Mention or Tag of Yourself).[106] You can also control your settings to prevent mentions.[107]

In addition to first-degree connections, you can mention those LinkedIn members who are engaged in conversations about posts. This means you can essentially start conversations with people even if they are not in your network. You can also respond in real time in the comments section of a post when someone—even someone not in your network—initiates a conversation there with you.

Option #2: Publish Single Articles

Publishing industry-relevant original articles is a great way to get the attention of clients, recruiters and employers. According to LinkedIn's Official Blog post, The Definitive Professional Publishing Platform[108]:

> "When a member publishes a post on LinkedIn, their original content becomes part of their professional profile, is shared with their trusted network and [can] reach the largest group of professionals ever assembled. Now members have the ability to follow other members that are not in their network and build their own group of followers."

LinkedIn's total publishing platform includes: 1) sharing updates via your homepage and 2) publishing articles. Both are accessed from the same place on your homepage (although you can now publish articles from your company page too). Perhaps the coolest thing about publishing articles on LinkedIn is that they are searchable *outside* of LinkedIn. That means readers don't even need to have a LinkedIn account in order to view your work. Your articles will show up in Google searches!! Think of the reach you can have.

Are you concerned about copyright on the articles you publish on LinkedIn? Here's a message from LinkedIn regarding published content:

> At LinkedIn, we want to help you make the most of your professional life. Part of that is showing the world more about who you are and what you know by sharing ideas, starting conversations, and inspiring others with your work.
>
> So, that raises a question: who owns all of the content you post on LinkedIn? You do, and you always have. We've updated our User Agreement[109] (effective October 23, 2014) to reinforce our commitment to respecting what's yours. Whether it's an update, photo, comment, post, presentation, portfolio, or anything else, we want to make it clear that you're in control of your content.
>
> Here are some highlights:
>
> • **You're in the driver's seat.** We'll always ask your permission before using your content in third-party ads, publications, or websites. We've always done this, but now our User Agreement specifically spells it out.
>
> • **You decide when your content goes.** If you delete something from our platform, we won't use it anymore.
>
> • **Share wherever or whenever you'd like.** We don't own or have exclusive rights to your content. It's yours, so feel free to repost it anywhere, however you want.
>
> Thanks for being a member!
> The LinkedIn Team

Read this article for the fine print[110] about how LinkedIn protects your content.

All members of English-speaking countries have the ability to publish long-form posts; and LinkedIn plans to expand that privilege to all of the languages they support.

Over 130,000 articles are published weekly[111] on LinkedIn, and 45% of their readers are in upper-level positions (managers, VPs, Directors, C-Level). If you're looking to get the attention of that audience, you want to be posting! To create content, go to your homepage or company page and click on "Write an article":

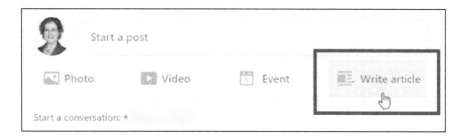

Select whether you want to publish the article under your name or via one of your pages.

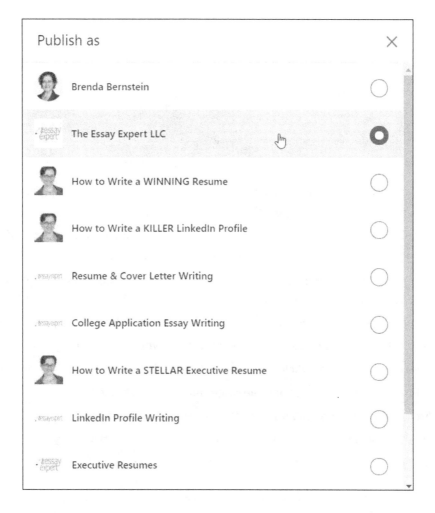

Click next and you will arrive at a page where you can create a new post. To publish an article, insert your content, along with images and pertinent links.

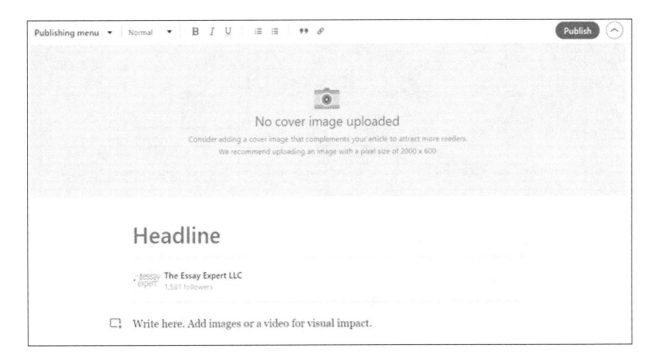

Over 130,000 articles are published every week. According to a study by OkDork and Search Wilderness,[112] the most successful posts followed these guidelines:

1. Keep your title short and sweet. Titles with more than 40-49 characters can get cut off.

2. Make it visual. Posts with at least 8 images perform 2.4 times better.

3. Don't use videos and other multimedia! This might be surprising, but fewer people view articles that include videos (as opposed to static images, which boost views).

4. Instruct. "How-to" and list-style Headlines performed better than Headlines posed as a question.

5. Keep it clear. Include subheadings—ideally 5 of them—so your article is easy to read.

6. Maintain a reasonable length. Articles between 1900 and 2000 words are read more often.

7. Go neutral. Posts that were neither positive or negative ranked higher.

8. Simplify. Articles that met the reading level of an 11-year-old ranked better.

9. Promote. Share your LinkedIn publisher post on other social networks!

10. Get Likes. The more Likes you have, the more views you will get.

Always proofread your article before publishing!

Here is what your post will look like on the homepage of your connections:

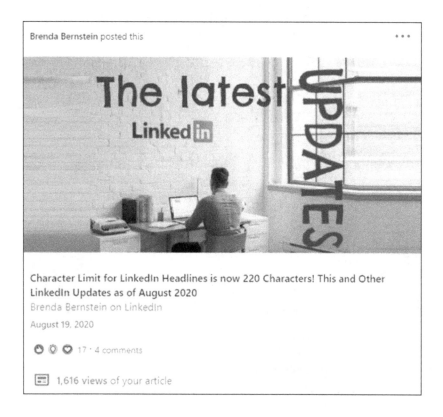

Each time someone likes or comments on your post, it is brought to the top of the page again.

Your posts will appear in your "Articles & activity" section of your profile. They can be searched via the search bar as well.

Interested readers will click through to see your articles and other posts, where they can then follow you and comment on your activity. Social media statistics and share buttons above your post allow readers to spread your work beyond LinkedIn!

A few tips:

a. Leverage SEO for Your Published Articles

Optimize the keywords in your posted articles. LinkedIn uses a special algorithm to tag long-form posts into categories called "channels" and to suggest posts for its members. If your article is tagged, it will appear to LinkedIn members with the most relevant profile content. So do some keyword research for your field, or hire someone to do it for you, and build your posts using SEO practices! This strategy will help you in Google search results too.

For LinkedIn's tips and best practices for publishing articles, visit LinkedIn's Help Center topic Publish Articles on LinkedIn.[113]

Have you utilized LinkedIn's article publishing feature? If so, what benefits have you enjoyed? And if not, what are you waiting for?

b. Post Your Articles on Social Media

Make sure to share your article with your social media networks, either by using a service like Hootsuite or by clicking the sharing upon publishing.

Posting Using Hootsuite

Hootsuite.com[114] allows you to send updates to Facebook and LinkedIn all with one click. Just create the update you want in Hootsuite and schedule it to post to the social media site you choose at the time you choose. Or if you have your own blog or a favorite blog by someone else, you can send an RSS feed (a stream that contains each of the articles as it is posted) to the social media account(s) of your choosing. That way your blog posts can automatically post to your LinkedIn Activity Update bar.

Here's how to share your blog:

After logging in to Hootsuite, hover over your profile photo on the right upper corner of your account. Click on Account & Settings:

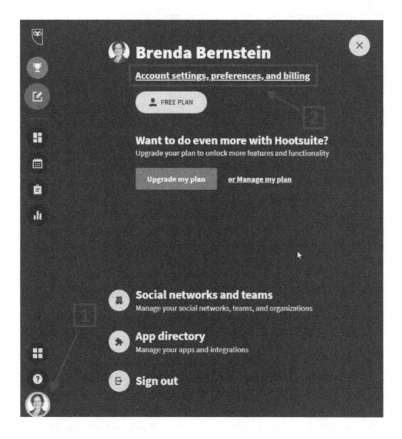

Select the RSS/Atom menu and click the "+" sign to add a new feed. You will need to upgrade to a paid account ($49/month) to use this feature.

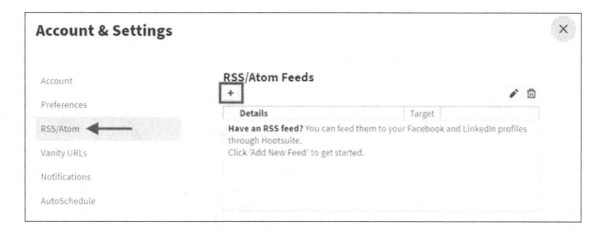

Paste your feed URL in the field provided. Then select the social sites you would like the feed to post to.

Edit any other preferred options and Save Feed.

For posting WordPress blogs to your LinkedIn profile or other social media accounts, you can also use the "Publicize" function from the JetPack Plugin.[115]

> ▶ **Publishing Hack:** One important tip, suggested by the Content Marketing Institute[116] and updated by Inc.,[117] is to send a tweet to "tip @LinkedInEditors" with your post to improve the odds a LinkedIn editor will see it and it be published on LinkedIn Pulse.

c. Increase Your Audience and Ranking

Publishing articles will generate a wide audience and could turn you into a "top influencer" on LinkedIn if your posts are popular enough. Some of mine have been viewed by thousands of people. Sharing original content will also result in Google rankings for your articles on LinkedIn.

When ranking articles in the LinkedIn feed, LinkedIn now measures "dwell time,"[118] not just click-throughs and comments, shares, and reactions. In other words, the algorithm now takes into account the amount of time someone spends "viewing" the content. This is good news and should improve the relevance of the content you receive in your feed.

According to LinkedIn's Official Blog,[119] "When a LinkedIn member shares six pieces of content, on average, they receive six profile views and make two new connections, which helps them strengthen their professional brands. At the same time, the company they work for receives six job views, three Company Page views, and one Company Page follower, which helps them better hire, market, and sell."

Every time you post original content, you establish yourself further as a thought leader in your field.

d. Check Out Who's Viewing Your Articles

To find out whose eyes are on your articles, scroll down to the "Your Dashboard" section of your profile and click on the "Article views" link.

Click on "Post Views" to get to your Activity screen. At the top, under "[Your] Activity," select "Articles" and you'll be brought to a feed of your articles:

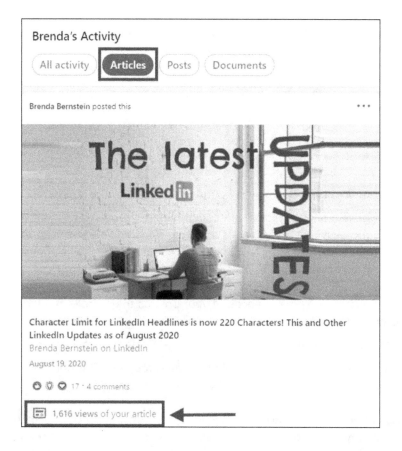

Click on the " . . . views" link at the bottom and you'll discover what portion of your readers are from certain areas, demographics and networks. If someone you want to connect with has viewed your article, it's a great foundation from which to reach out and send an invitation.

e. Write "Long-Form" Status Updates as a Complement to Publishing Articles

James Carbary suggests that "long-form" status updates get more views than published articles. This is your chance to get creative. Can you post a status update that conveys the same ideas as you would want to convey in your article? Here's what Carbary recommends[120]: "Status updates have a limit of 3000 characters (which is approximately 430-750 words). This means that you can spend much less time creating content that gets far greater reach. Make sure that the first sentence . . . is captivating. People [will] only see the first one or two sentences of your post as they scroll." Additionally, he recommends short 1-2-line paragraphs to keep the attention of readers on their mobile devices.

Still want to link to your article? Try doing this in a comment instead of in the main post.

Finally, whenever you get a comment on anything you post, respond! This helps get you to the top of news feeds, and it makes people feel good about engaging with your content.

> ▶ **Post original content!** According to an unofficial study by B2C, executives get up to 700% more engagement when sharing original content vs. sharing content from other people. It stands to reason that this would also hold true for non-executives. Make sure your content is always worth sharing and on brand.

Option #3: Create a Newsletter

With the advent of Creator Mode, LinkedIn has provided a way to share your very own newsletter. This is different from publishing an article, in that followers will only see your article if they come across it in their news feed, whereas subscribers are notified of each newsletter.

According to LinkedIn Help, "If a member follows a person or company, they'll receive some notifications about that person or company's content but they won't automatically be subscribed to that author's newsletter. If a member subscribes to a newsletter, they'll always be notified about each article that is published in that newsletter."

To set up a newsletter, go to your homepage and click "Write article."

Click Next (it doesn't matter which author you choose). If you have Creator Mode turned on, you'll see an option to set up your letter.

Give your newsletter a title and be sure to include keywords. You are limited to 30 characters. Enter how often you plan to publish and create a newsletter description. You have 120 characters to be clear on what kind of information you intend to share and what you have to offer your subscribers.

Finally, create a logo unique to your newsletter that stays true to your brand. Remember that when a reader sees your letter as a post, they will only see your logo. Image size should be 300x300.

Here's mine:

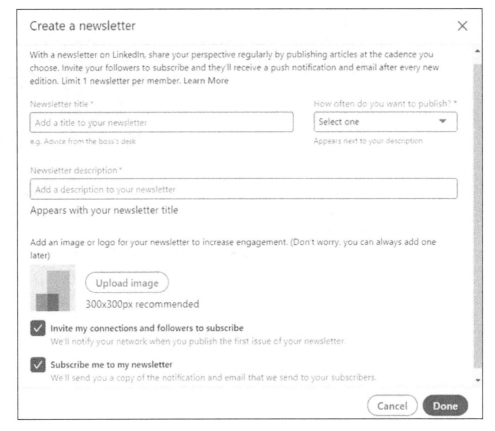

Now you'll see that when you go to your publisher page, you have the option to choose newsletter or article:

Publishing your newsletter is similar to publishing an article. Add your cover image and content, publish, and share!

Instead of using a new cover image each time, you can create a single, branded cover image for your newsletter to make it more recognizable.

Option #4: Share Others' Content from Your Homepage Feed

Sharing other people's updates and articles, while not as much of an engagement booster as sharing original content, is a great way to build your network and support your connections on LinkedIn. You will be not just well-connected but also well-liked!

LinkedIn has streamlined its search functionality to help you discover shareable people and content. Here's the search bar:

When you enter a connection's name in the search bar, you'll find content they shared, posts they commented on, and places they were mentioned, making it easier than ever to acknowledge those you want to engage with.

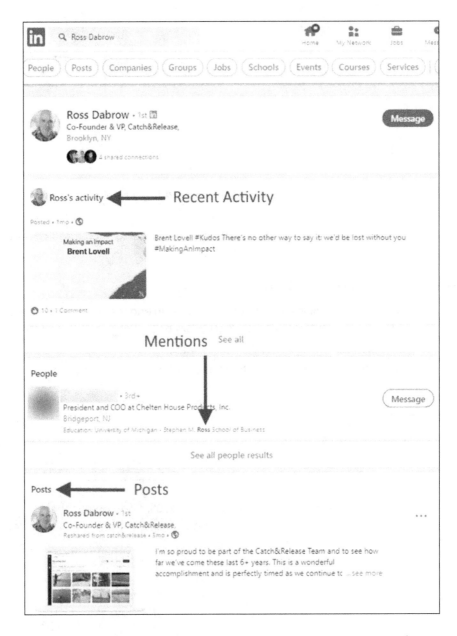

Or, search by topic to find news, posts, jobs, events, and conversations on topics that interest you.

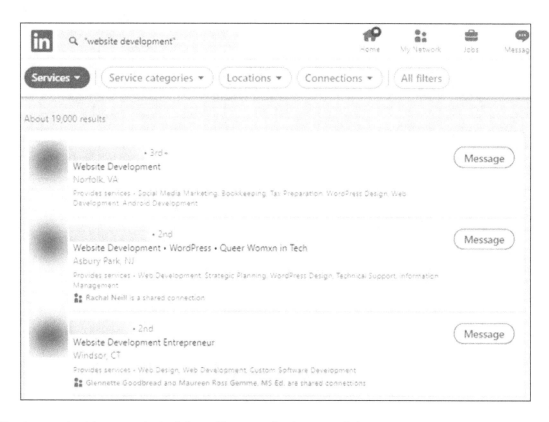

Sharing content is easy—just click on Share at the bottom of the content you want to spread to your connections:

You will have the option to share with anyone (Public), anyone on LinkedIn and Twitter, or just your network (Connections), or groups. Of course you can also share an article privately to one person you think would appreciate the content, which could be a great step in strengthening a connection.

To choose with whom you'd like to share the post, click on the drop-down button labeled "Anyone," which is the default setting.

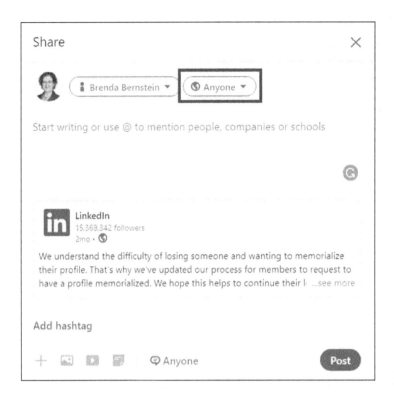

You'll be taken to a pop-up with options.

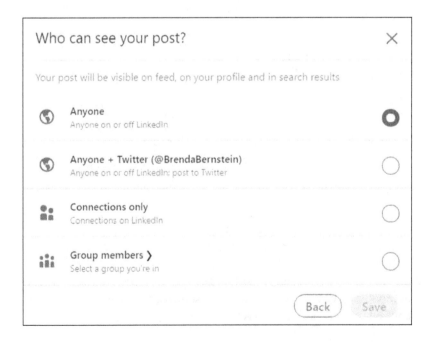

You can also decide who you want to post as: yourself (your main profile), your business page, or any showcase pages you have. Click the drop-down with your name to see your options.

Side benefit: Sharing other people's posts is a great way to encourage them to share yours. Helping each other out is a primary tenet of networking, and this is an easy way to do it!

Click the link, choose some hashtags to represent what you post about the most, and you're on your way. Your visitors will now see what topics you are an expert on and the number of followers you have. They'll also be prompted with the option to Follow you vs. connect. They'll still be able to connect by clicking the More button.

Curating Shareable Content

There are multiple ways to discover articles that you want to share with your LinkedIn connections. Here are a few:

a. Customize Your Homepage Feed

You can select what you want to see in your Homepage feed. This feature is designed to help you find content more easily and to control the type of information that comes through your LinkedIn feed, making it easier to read and share relevant news and articles.

Overwhelmed by articles in your feed that you really don't care about? LinkedIn expert William Arruda offers this tip: "To eliminate the content that isn't worth your while, you can unfollow certain connections. When you do this, you remain connected, but your feed won't be clogged with their posts. And don't worry, LinkedIn won't tell them that you unfollowed them." Brilliant!

To unfollow someone, just click the three dots in the upper right of the article and choose "Unfollow."

b. Search

Use LinkedIn's search tool to find the content that interests you most. Type your keyword into the search field, hit enter, and click on "Content" for a list of articles related to that keyword. Then follow (or share directly)!

c. Follow Hashtags

You can also use the search field to find hashtags for popular topics. Start by typing a # in the search bar, followed by a tentative keyword. You'll see a list of hashtags to choose from. Click one from the list (don't hit enter) and you'll be taken to a feed of relevant articles with that hashtag. If you like what you see, click on Follow. This will add articles that use this hashtag to your homepage feed.

When you come across an article you like with an interesting hashtag, follow it for more articles on the topic. Or click here to learn more about how to find hashtags to follow.[121] You can view the list of hashtags you're following here.[122] Follow topics that you can provide input on, ask questions and share!

See LinkedIn's Help article, "Using Hashtags on LinkedIn"[123] for more details on this useful feature.

d. "Subscribe" to Member Newsletters

Did you know you can subscribe to LinkedIn articles published by your favorite author? Well, you can if the author has been approved by LinkedIn as a newsletter author.

To subscribe to a newsletter, visit a recent article and click the "Subscribe" button:

When people you follow start a newsletter, LinkedIn will let you know.

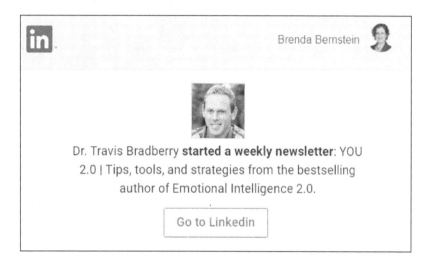

e. The Daily Rundown & Today's News and Views

On the mobile app, update your settings to receive a daily notification of the top professional news each day. Go to your settings, click on the Communications tab, and select "On LinkedIn," then "News."

Option #5: LinkedIn Live

LinkedIn is rolling out LinkedIn Live to many members. If you're a thought leader with good information to share, take advantage of this opportunity if it's given to you!

Live is similar to Facebook live in that you create an event and then stream live video via LinkedIn using one of the integrated streaming tools they recommend. To be eligible to use Live, you must meet the following criteria:

- Have at least 150 followers
- Recently shared original content
- Follow LinkedIn's Community Policy Guidelines

To find out if you qualify, you can try creating an event. If Live is an option, you can begin setting up and using it. To create an event, go to your homepage, scroll down to the bottom of the left sidebar, and click the plus sign to add an event:

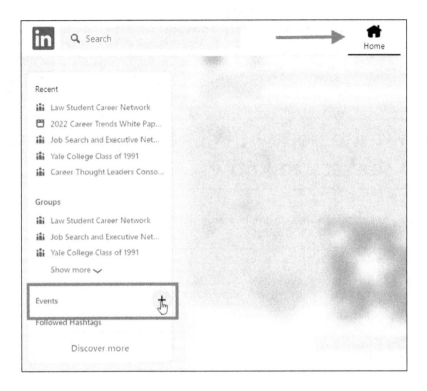

If you see LinkedIn Live:

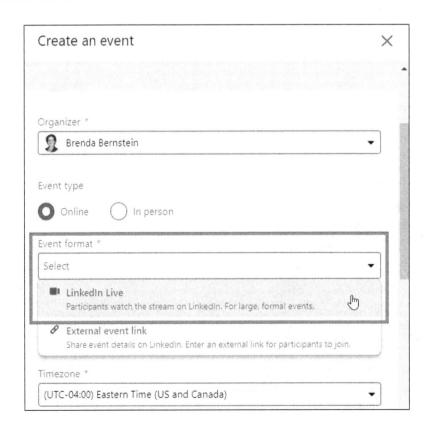

If you don't see LinkedIn Live as an option, you can also auto-apply by using certain third-party apps. Click here to learn more about auto-applying.

Once approved, you'll receive an email like this:

Linked in

Hi Brenda,

You're receiving this message because you or someone on your team recently requested LinkedIn Live access or started creating an event or live stream on behalf of How to Write a KILLER LinkedIn Profile.

LinkedIn Events that use LinkedIn Live see twice the engagement of Events that dont. To help you make the most of this benefit, we've granted your LinkedIn Page access to LinkedIn Live.

Now, all super and content admins on the Page can stream on behalf of this Page. Here's how to get started:

 Choose a streaming tool

Depending on your experience level with live streaming, you can choose from a few options. If you're new to streaming, we recommend our Preferred Partners.

 Follow our guidelines

Keep your live videos professional, respectful, and safe in accordance with terms and other streaming guidelines.

 Prepare to go live

You can choose to go live spontaneously or schedule a live event from LinkedIn or through your streaming tool.

Learn more about hosting successful LinkedIn Live Events.

We look forward to seeing you go live on LinkedIn!

The LinkedIn Live Team

LinkedIn Help also provides additional detailed information with links:

1. Choose a Streaming Tool: Depending on your level of expertise with streaming, you can choose to go live using a **third-party broadcast tool**[124] or a **custom stream (RTMP)**.[125] With either option, you can consider scheduling your **live stream in advance**[126] to promote it on or off LinkedIn.

2. **Leverage Broadcaster Features:** Once you have set up your live stream, explore **broadcaster features**[127] to optimize your live videos and achieve your goals.

3. **Stream Quality, Professional Content:** To produce professional content, be sure to follow these **guidelines**[128] and **best practices.**[129] For best streaming results, use these **encoder settings.**[130]

4. **Troubleshoot Issues:** If you're running into errors during the set up or streaming process, try these troubleshooting **recommendations.**[131]

You can also access LinkedIn Live's Getting Started checklist.[132]

If LinkedIn Live is not a good match for you, you can stick to posting short videos to your profile. See Mistake #15 for more on this topic.

Option #6: LinkedIn Polls

A poll typically consists of a single question with multiple choice answers on a topic relevant to your audience. Your poll may be related to your business or your industry, or you might choose to poll your audience on a light topic just for fun! Polls can generate conversation, keep your business top-of-mind, and provide important insight about your current and potential customers.

To create a poll, click to start a post:

Then click the bar graph icon to create your poll.

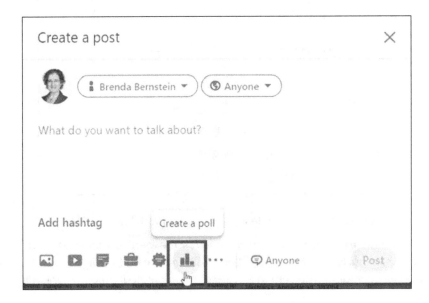

Add your question and up to four options, select the duration of your poll and click done.

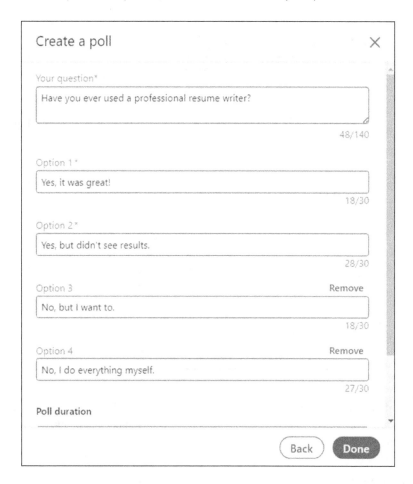

You'll see a preview of your poll and have the ability to introduce the reason for your question. Don't forget to select who you want to participate:

- Anyone (anyone on or off LinkedIn)
- Anyone + Twitter (anyone on or off LinkedIn, plus posts to Twitter if your account it connected)
- Connections only (includes 1st and 2nd-tier connections)
- Group members (select the group where you want to share your poll)

Stefanie Marrone, writing for JD Supra, suggests "providing a poll option encouraging people to add their answer in a comment if it's not a poll answer. That means you get additional comment engagement (which can help your post go viral)."

Option #7: Other Ways to Share & Interact

a. Interact with Company Pages

If you are a job seeker or if you are a vendor wanting to work with a particular company, it's more and more important to follow the company on LinkedIn and to interact with the company's talent brand. Recruiters are watching for this! So do your homework and show your interest by engaging with the company. You will make a big impact by showing up and participating in the company's conversations. Here's an example of what that might look like:

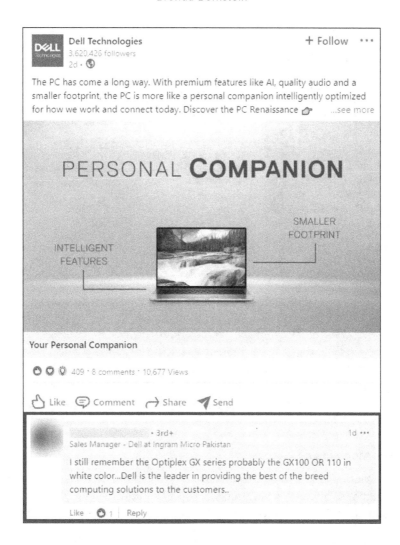

▶ **Note:** Only follow companies that are respectable and match up with your brand. Unfollow any others that could make you look unfocused. Following irrelevant companies could be a negative to recruiters checking you out.

b. Recommend Group Posts

Here's a tip on how to use LinkedIn effectively as a group owner: You can now recommend important posts to members. Recommended posts will appear in group members' home page feed so your group stays top of mind.

To recommend a post as a group owner, click the three dots in the upper right corner and select "Recommend this post":

If you're someone who writes articles and has been wondering whether it will ever be valuable to post them to groups, now you have an answer. Write good ones and perhaps the group owner will recommend your posts. As Josh Turner,[133] WSJ author and founder/CEO of LinkedIn Selling, points out, "Familiarity begets trust. The more group members see your name, the better. Now that your recommended posts show up in LinkedIn's main feed, members will be more aware of what's happening in the group, and hopefully will visit and participate more often."

c. Announce Team Moments and Kudos

The LinkedIn Team Moments and Kudos tool gives you the ability in a post to dole out a quick pat on the back to your connections. Doing this will keep you top of mind with your contacts and possibly help you in your LinkedIn search rankings, as the more active you are on LinkedIn, the better for you in LinkedIn's algorithm.

To use this feature on desktop, go to your home page and click to start a post. In the resulting pop-up window, click the plus sign and select "Celebrate an occasion."

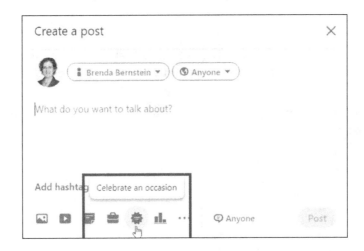

From mobile, click the plus/Post icon at the bottom of your home page to begin a post.

Then choose "Celebrate an Occasion" from the list.

Choose "Give Kudos." Then search for the person you want to give the kudos to, check the circle to the right of their name, and click Next.

LinkedIn will offer images to accompany your post, similar to a greeting card, and include accolades for being a team player, an inspirational leader, and more. You can even send a simple thank you.

Your post should mention the name of your connection (see how to use the @mention feature above) and why you are praising them. LinkedIn will provide a default message, complete with @mention of your connection with hashtags.

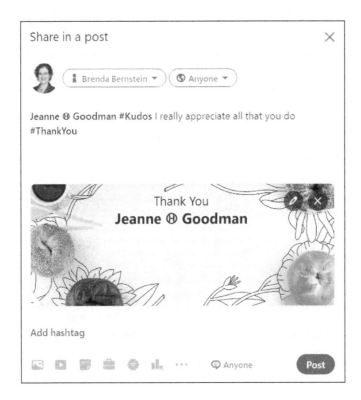

Your connection will see your post in their Mentions.

And your post will look like this:

Kudos can also be accessed from your connection's profile page by the "More" button below their Headline.

To welcome a teammate, click to start a post. In the pop-up window, click the plus sign and select "Celebrate an occasion." Then choose, "Welcome to the Team." You will have the option to include your teammate's photo, mention them along with a personalized message, and also tag them if you wish.

Your post will look like something like this:

Use kudos and welcomes to boast about your coworkers can show the world that you're a team player. If you own a business, this is also an excellent opportunity to acknowledge your employees or thank a colleague and build your social brand at the same time.

d. Comment and React

Commenting on content posted by other people and companies is another good way to gain attention as a job seeker. When you comment on a group conversation or podcast,[134] post a job, or even just like another Update, it will go into LinkedIn's news feed and show up on your connections' homepages.

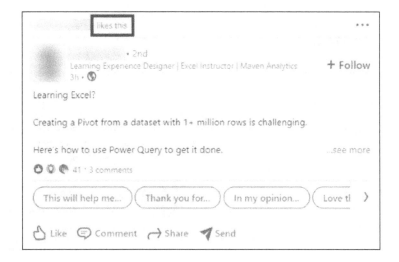

Your activity will show up in your Activity section:

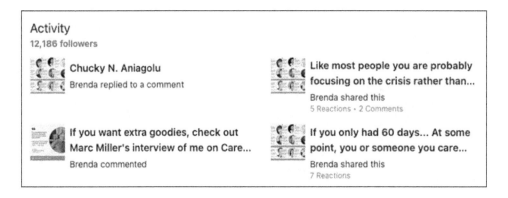

In addition, much like on Facebook, you can not only like a post, but also love it, celebrate it, tag it as insightful, or express your curiosity.

Plus, you can include your own images with your comments to really stand out. Options include sharing an event photo, a screenshot of an article with relevant content highlighted, infographics, and more.

An image can draw more attention to your comment, so go for it! Click on the image icon and attach any photo from your files. Note that you can't post an image only; you must also leave a written comment.

Here's what your image might look like in a conversation:

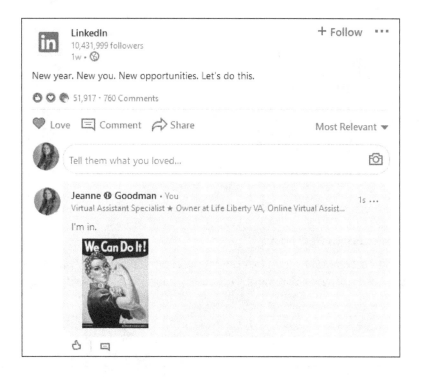

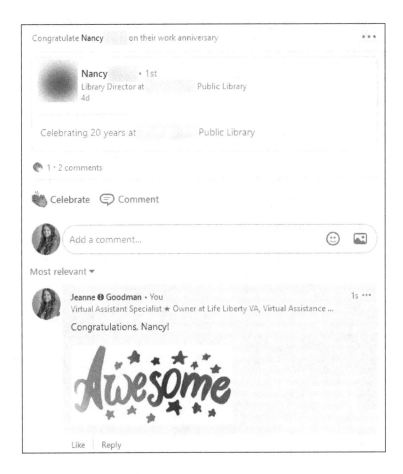

e. Turn Your Comments into New Posts

Whenever you leave a comment on a LinkedIn member's post, you now have the option to start your own conversation based off your comment. Note this option is not available when you are the original poster.

Click "Share this post":

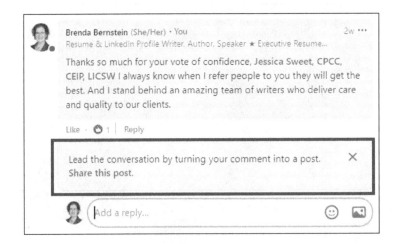

Much like sharing a Tweet, your new post will feature your comment at the top and include a snippet of and link to the original post:

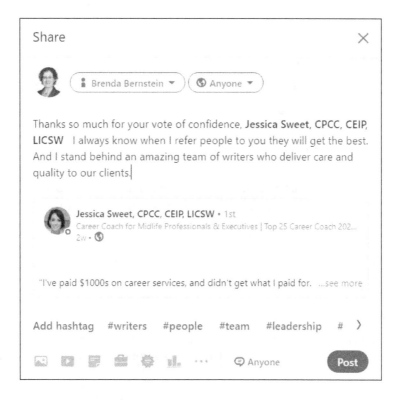

f. Embrace Your Fun Side with GIFs and Emojis

GIFs and Emojis in Conversations

Both GIFs and emojis are available in messaging, and emojis are available in comments. Use your professional judgment as to whether they are appropriate in your conversation. If you want to insert them, click the GIF or emoji option and type in a search term.

Here's what it looks like when posting a comment:

And here it is in messaging:

For more details on LinkedIn's available features in messaging, see LinkedIn's Help article, "Customizing Your LinkedIn Messages."[135]

You'll also find emoji options when you hover over any message, both on desktop and mobile. This is probably the easiest way to respond to a message on LinkedIn, and might be appropriate at the end of a conversation.

Emojis in Your Profile

You can now use colorful characters in your Headline, as well as in most sections and titles in your LinkedIn profile. If you want to add some visual appeal, an appropriate emoji can be a bold addition. You might try something like this:

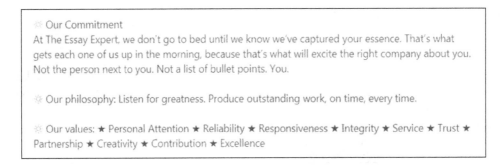

Note that not all symbols will render in color once you've updated, so you may need to experiment. Also, this function might not work on all computers or browsers, so some viewers may see an empty box instead of the symbol you chose. I would personally recommend sticking to Unicode characters to be safe. Have fun!

A Note on Privacy

Do you want your activity updates to be viewable to the public? You have a choice.

Go to your Settings & Privacy, click on the Visibility tab, and under "Visibility of your LinkedIn activity," click "Followers":

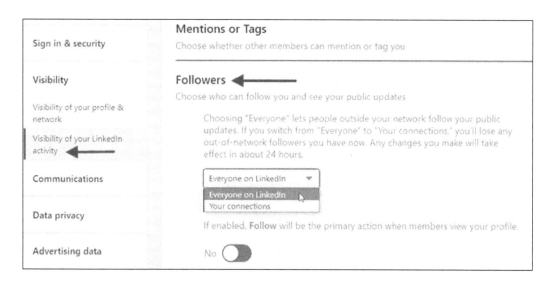

Everyone has different considerations when choosing how public to be with their profile, so choose the option that meets your needs and goals.

You also have control over whether you want your connections to be notified when you are @mentioned or tagged in a post:

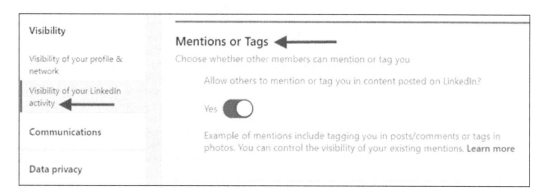

Results to Expect

According to the Influencer Marketing Hub,[136] LinkedIn reaches more followers per post (13%) than Facebook (5.2%) or Twitter (3.61%), and engagement increased by 38% from 2020 to 2021. So be sure to put this tool to good use.

The more you post updates and share them, and the more you interact with the content on LinkedIn, the more your activity will be publicized and the more you will stay top of mind with your connections and recruiters. If you play your cards right, you could very well start to be seen as an expert in your field.

If you've built your network to 1000+, you'll have more leverage when you post, as there will be more people who are likely to share your posts with their connections. This positive activity will attract the attention of recruiters and potential clients who want to know how you are participating and sharing on LinkedIn.

If my own experience is any indication, the more active you are in sharing information, the more you will be noticed by potential clients and employers; many of the people who read and engage with your offerings will remember you and tell their connections about you. In a business world where networking is king, you can't ask for better than that.

MISTAKE #14

Special Sections not Utilized

The Problem

Special Sections: LinkedIn frequently adds new sections appropriate for special groups like artists and students, for activities like volunteerism, and for skills like languages. You might fall into one of these categories and be at a disadvantage to the scientist who completed a Patents section; the student who completed the Courses section; or the civic-minded professional with a robust Volunteer Experience section. Furthermore, you might be at a loss when attempting to include all the aspects of who you are into your profile unless you utilize some of these special sections.

The Tune-Up

These sections allow you to present information in an organized fashion so you don't have to get everything across in your About or Experience sections. If you are an artist, use the Featured section. If you have taken courses you want to report, check out the Courses section. Speak languages? Try Languages. Volunteer? Complete the Volunteer section! And according to LinkedIn, 42% of hiring managers[137] said they consider volunteer experience equal to formal work experience. You don't have to fit it all into the Experience section! Other sections include Publications, Patents, Projects, Honors & Awards, Test Scores, Organizations, Causes, and Licenses & Certifications. You can even post your blog under your Publications section; just add a live URL that links directly to your blog for anyone who wants to take a look.

Many special sections will be listed in the "Additional" options. This is what they'll look like:

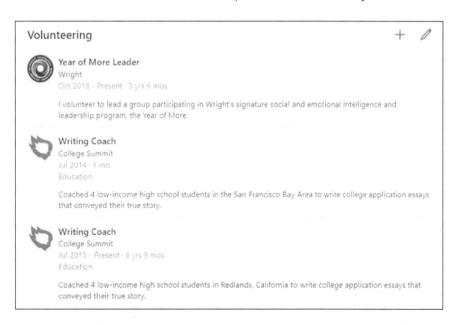

Publications

How to Write a STELLAR Executive Resume: 50 Tips to Reach Your Job Search Target
The Essay Expert · Sep 1, 2013

(Show publication)

As an executive conducting a job search, you might never have had to write a resume before, and you might be feeling unsure of where to start. This book provides an easy-to-read, practical and up-to-date guide on best practi ...see more

How to Write a WINNING Resume: 50 Tips to Reach Your Job Search Target
The Essay Expert · Sep 1, 2013

(Show publication)

If you're eager for a do-it-yourself resume guide that's easy-to-read, practical and up-to-date, this is the book you've been looking for! How to Write a WINNING Resume takes you through the resume writing process step by ...see more

How to Write a KILLER LinkedIn Profile - E-Book
Self-Published. #1 Top-Rated in Amazon's Business Writing Category · Feb 1, 2012

(Show publication)

Read this Best-Selling E-Book and Tune Up your LinkedIn Profile!

...see more

Show all 4 publications

Courses

Life Coach Training - Coaches Training Institute

Nourishment & Self-Care Lab

 Associated with The Wright Foundation for the Realization of Human Potential

Summer Leadership Training

 Associated with The Wright Foundation for the Realization of Human Potential

Show all 4 courses

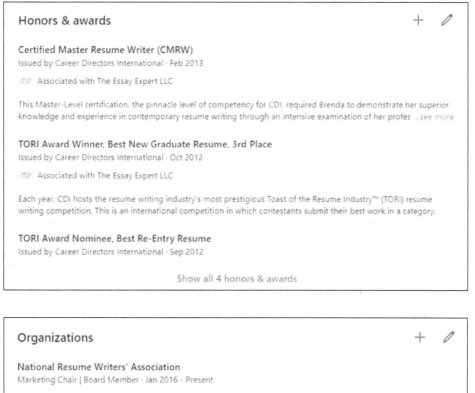

To add a section, click on the "Add profile section" button below your headline (if you scroll down past your Introduction Card, it will be in the upper right).

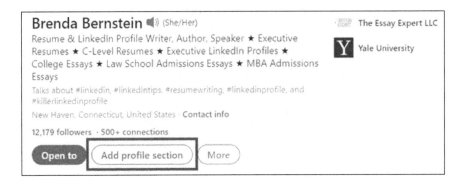

Then click the desired section to add it to your profile.

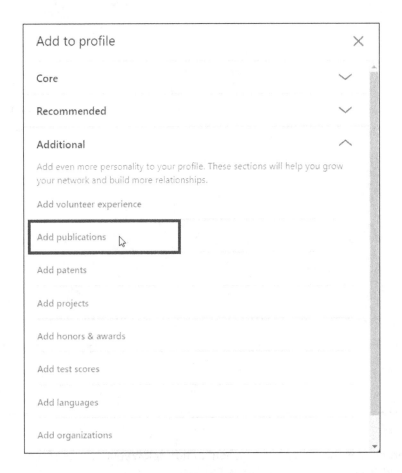

A pop-up window will appear and you can begin adding your information.

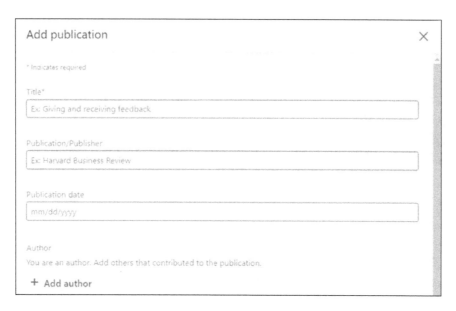

You can get creative with what you list where. As mentioned above, you can list your blog as a publication and include the link, allowing people to click directly to the blog. Or list details of projects in the Projects section that you don't have room to explain in your About or Experience sections.

Results to Expect

By adding special sections, you will be able to share much more information than would otherwise be possible; and you can organize it in a way that brings attention to important aspects of your career and education. No longer will you struggle with how to share about your volunteerism, impressive courses or accomplishments. It's all laid out neatly for you!

MISTAKE #15

No Media Items in Your Featured, Education, and Experience Sections

The Problem

LinkedIn's media attachment function allows users to include images, presentations, videos, and documents in their profiles.

If you don't use this function, your profile will be one-dimensional (*i.e.,* boring) and you will miss out on accessible, free marketing for yourself and your business.

The Tune-Up

In your Featured, Education, and Experience sections, you can add files or links to videos, images, documents, presentations, or even events.

Featured Section

Use the Featured section as your portfolio to display the work you are most proud of, and add to it regularly. You can create a multimedia experience by highlighting select activity updates or articles, web content, photos, and documents.

To add items to your Featured section, click the + sign to see a dropdown of media you can display, then click the + sign next to the item you want to appear.

Note that videos must be housed externally on the web. To add a video, use the "Links" option and plug in the video's URL.

File types allowed for upload under the Media option include:

- Documents: Adobe PDF (.pdf), Microsoft PowerPoint (.ppt/.pptx), and Microsoft Word (.doc/.docx)
- Images: .jpg/.jpeg, .png, and .gif (will not be animated)

Here's what my profile looks like with the Featured section:

The possibilities are endless of what you can link to or upload here. Get creative!

▶ **Resume Privacy:** If you choose to post your resume to LinkedIn, you may want to remove your address from the header. Assuming you have a public profile, your resume, along with the information on it, will be available to the public. Unfortunately, it will also be available to hackers if they break into LinkedIn.

What do you want to share with your LinkedIn audience? You can build your image by adding links to any important documents and web pages. Have fun!

Education & Experience

The same general procedures apply to your Education and Experience sections.

To add media, click the pencil icon next to the appropriate entry (or click the plus sign to add a new one).

Scroll down to the media area where you can upload or link your items.

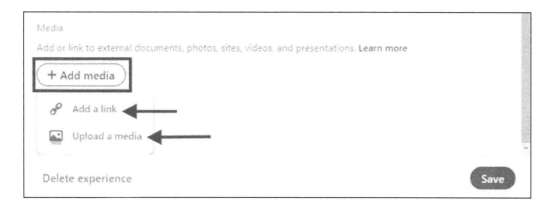

Results to Expect

Your profile will be a multi-media event! Readers will have an interactive, engaging experience scrolling through your profile.

By sharing your events, relevant reading, presentations, videos, documents, and resume in your Featured, Education, and Experience sections, you will remain a current and savvy LinkedIn user who attracts attention to your profile. Well-utilized media can lead to interest from both employers and customers who click on your links.

SECTION 3

Playing the LinkedIn® Game to Win

Having a KILLER LinkedIn Profile is just the beginning. You then need to use it.

You could sit there with a keyword-optimized profile hoping for recruiters to contact you, and someday they might do that . . .

You could fly solo, not joining or participating in groups . . .

You could laze around and hope your contacts are inspired to recommend you . . .

You could write your profile and let it idle there for years, thinking you've fulfilled your LinkedIn duty . . .

You could do all those things, and maybe someone would contact you. But it's unlikely.

Instead, be proactive in using LinkedIn's Jobs functions and reaching out to your networking contacts. Join groups and leverage opportunities to share, learn and connect. Risk asking your connections to endorse and recommend you.

Your LinkedIn profile is a living, breathing creation that requires attention and care. This section shows you how to treat it that way so you experience KILLER results from your LinkedIn presence.

MISTAKE #16

Not Utilizing LinkedIn's Jobs Functions

The Problem

Whether you are a job seeker or an employer, you need to know about LinkedIn® Jobs. Jobs are so important on LinkedIn, in fact, that they have their own tab right in the top menu. The LinkedIn mobile app allows job seekers to apply for jobs using LinkedIn right from their phones, which means you can apply quickly—hopefully before other applicants.

LinkedIn's partnerships with the data-driven matching technology company Bright,[138] leading online learning company Lynda, and job search site, Snagajob,[139] are making LinkedIn increasingly powerful as a center for connecting talent with opportunity. The potential to streamline the candidate training and locating process is immense. LinkedIn also offers "Learning,"[140] a service that helps candidates secure better jobs by connecting them with live training programs from Lynda.com.

With over 200 million job applications[141] submitted through LinkedIn each month and four people hired every minute through the site, LinkedIn is clearly becoming the #1 resource for jobs on the web. If you're not on this bandwagon it's time to jump on!

I have provided two Tune-Up sections below, one for job seekers and one for employers. Please read the one that applies to you!

> ▶ **Important Note:** LinkedIn takes the safety of its users very seriously. As a job seeker, you have the right to not be harassed while using any of LinkedIn's Jobs Functions. Please see LinkedIn's article on "Staying Safe During Your Job Search"[142] for information on spotting fake jobs and fake profiles, and on how to report them when you see them. LinkedIn's Safety Center also provides insightful tips on spotting spam and scams, and how to protect yourself. I recommend that people check company websites to confirm the job posting whenever possible. Check this Inc. article[143] for ways to confirm company identity.

The Tune-Up for Job Seekers

Start exploring by clicking on "Jobs" in the top menu.

Open to Work

Your first consideration when actively looking for a new position on LinkedIn is whether you would like to keep your job search confidential. LinkedIn's "Open to Work"[144] tool allows you to signal privately to hundreds of recruiters that you are open to new job opportunities.

▶ **Open to Work Status Caveat #1: A recruiter could potentially tip off your company that you are looking—so be careful**.

If you are an unemployed job seeker (as opposed to a job seeker with a current job), there's no significant downside to publicizing your job search status. Do what feels right to you.

If you decide it is beneficial for you to turn this feature on, go to your profile and click on "Show recruiters you're open to work" at the bottom of your Introduction Card.

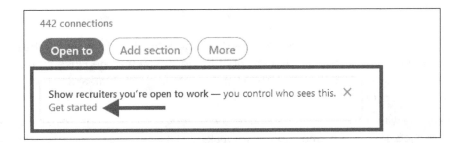

Once you click "Get started", you'll see options like title, base pay (private to you), preferred hours, and more.

LinkedIn will email you with helpful links to get you moving in the right direction.

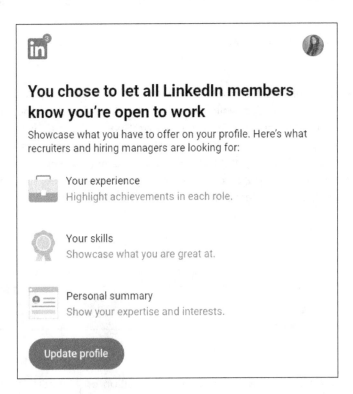

Of course, you don't want to be contacted for just any job. LinkedIn has thought of that! It's easy to customize the titles, salary and job types you're interested in.

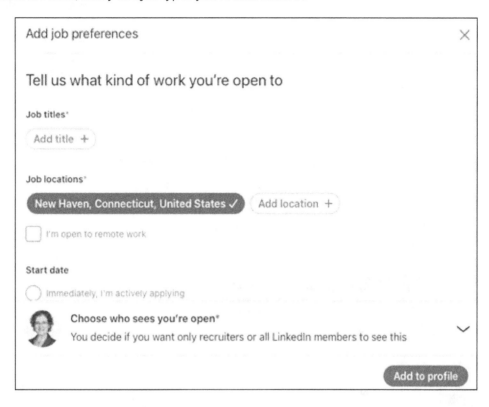

You'll also have the option to choose whether only recruiters can see that you're looking for a job, or everyone on LinkedIn, including recruiters.

▶ **Open to Work Status Caveat #2:** If you choose "All LinkedIn members," as LinkedIn is clear to point out, this includes "people at your current company"!

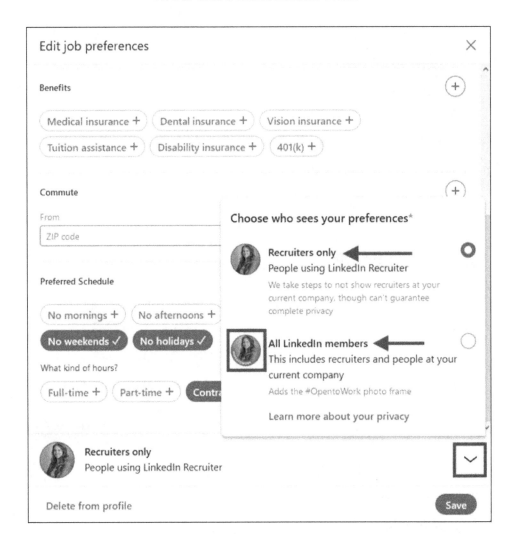

If you select the "All LinkedIn members" option, your profile photo will be adorned with a green frame that reads "OPEN TO WORK" and will look similar to this:

The Open to Work feature has some potential downsides:

1. It won't make you more visible to recruiters who are using LinkedIn's special software for recruiters. For those recruiters, you can use the Open Candidates feature and it will serve you fine.

2. You could turn off many recruiters who prefer to conduct a search for "passive" candidates.

3. There are some scammy, spammy "search firms" out there who might contact you. Beware.

4. You might think you can rely on having this marker on your profile, whereas in actuality, you still need to be active and accountable in your job search! Check out the Job Search Success System for support in your search.

Maybe you've already turned on this feature and have now decided to reverse your decision. Not a problem! You can turn it off. Go to the Open to Work section of your profile and click the pencil icon.

Then at the bottom of the "Edit job preferences" window, click "Delete from profile."

When you decide to remove "Open to Work" status, you'll receive the following confirmation, with an option to change your mind:

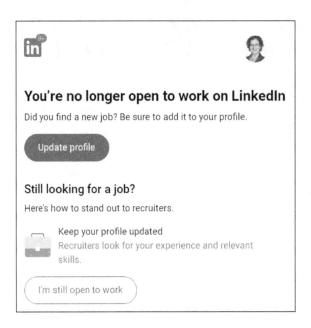

If you've used the "Open to Work" feature and have seen results, either positive or negative, please share those with me. I'd love to hear about your experience!

For more about the "Open to Work" feature, read LinkedIn's Help article, "Let Recruiters Know You're Open to Work."[145]

In addition to using the Open to Work feature, you can also go to the Job Seeking Preferences tab in your Settings & Privacy section, and turn on "Signal your interest to recruiters at companies you've created job alerts for."

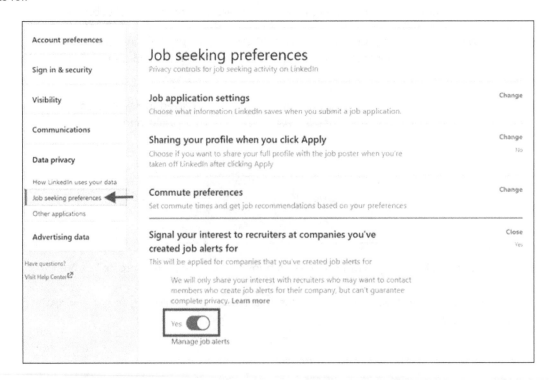

If you've optimized your LinkedIn profile by following the advice in this book, you should start hearing from more recruiters once you turn on this feature.

Conduct a Manual Job Search

You can also manually search for relevant positions on LinkedIn using the following three methods:

1. Jobs Tab

Under the Jobs tab, you will automatically see a list of jobs that might interest you, based on the keywords in your profile and recent searches you have conducted.

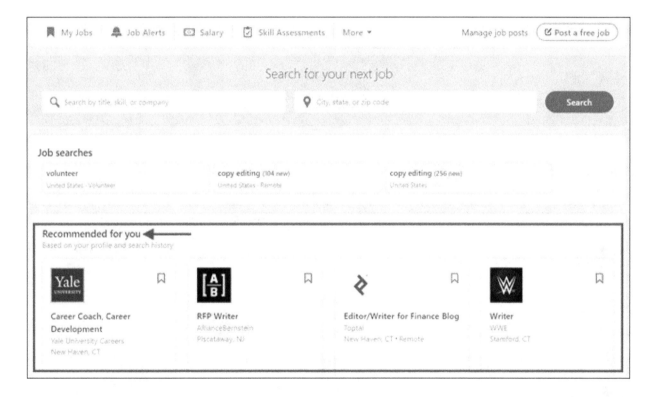

If you have a Premium account, you'll be greeted with a selection of jobs where you would be a top applicant. Other LinkedIn Premium features include company insights such as connections, teams you might work with, and growth and hiring trends. Examples of information you won't see with a free account:

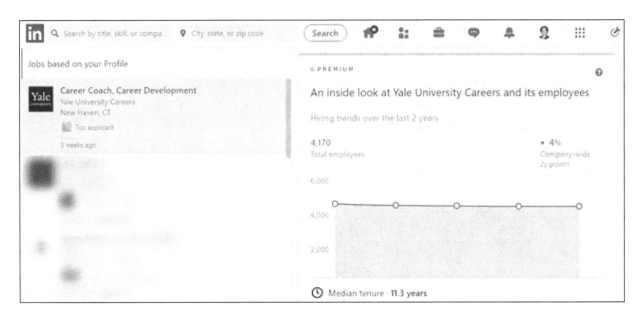

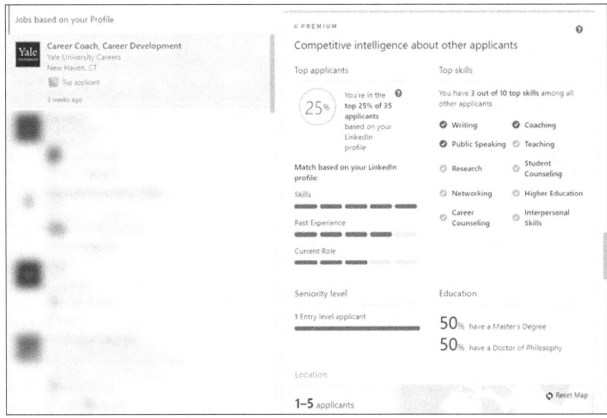

For more about job search features available with Premium, see LinkedIn's Premium Career[146] package options. I recommend that as a job seeker, you click on the Jobs tab daily. But don't stop there. Update your Preferences to search for the jobs you want in the geographic location that interests you.

2. Search Bar

The search bar is another option for finding relevant jobs. When searching for a specific job title, for example, "VP of Operations" (use quotes to hone your search), you'll find job postings and the number of applicants for those roles, related posts to browse, groups to join, and people who may be able to help. You can search Companies to find out whether a connection works there or if they're hiring.

When I searched for CIO in New York, NY, here are some of the related jobs I found:

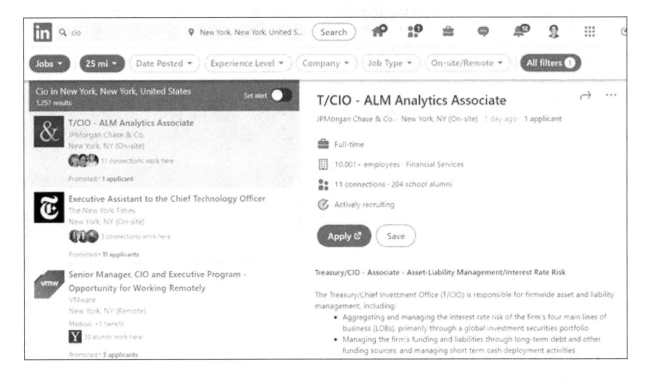

You can refine your search by date posted, company size, experience level, salary, benefits, whether it's remote, and more. Sort by most relevant and most recent. You can also use Boolean logic to aid your search. Words such as not, and, and or can be used to include and exclude search variables. For more details on how to use this method, read LinkedIn Help's article, Using Boolean Search on LinkedIn.[147]

Once you enter your search terms, LinkedIn will provide a list of current positions which you can fine-tune by location, company, date posted, job function, industry, experience level and title.

Conveniently, LinkedIn will automatically save your search to your jobs page for future searches.

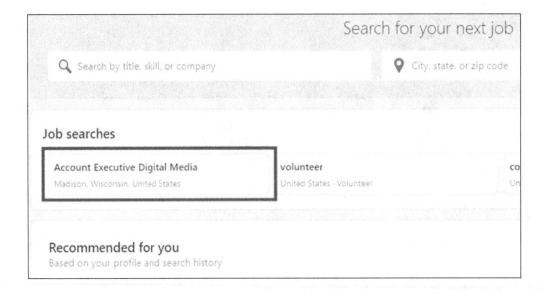

▶ **Job Search Tip:** You want your searches to be consistent with your skills, and consistent with each other. You will shoot yourself in the foot if you conduct searches for unrelated jobs because you will appear unfocused. So think through your job strategy on LinkedIn before starting your search!

3. Search Alerts

If you conduct a search and want to be notified when new jobs become available, create a Search Alert. First, toggle the "Job Alert" switch in the upper left-hand corner to "On."

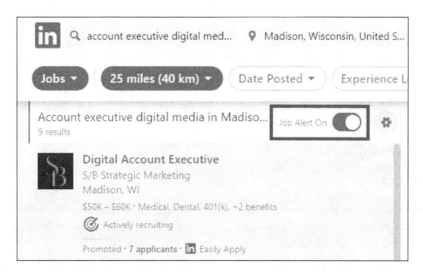

You will be given an option to receive an alert daily or weekly—via email, push notifications, or both—for jobs that match your criteria.

To receive push notifications about new job postings, make sure that option is on in your app's settings. To find it, click on your profile image in the upper left, then on Settings. Tap Communications, Push, and Jobs. You'll then be presented with a plethora of options to choose from.

Want to edit or delete your job alert? Click the gear icon to the right of the toggle switch.

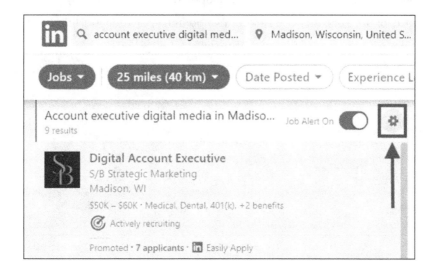

Once you create an alert, when you visit the Jobs tab, you will see your alert-enabled searches labeled with "Alert on."

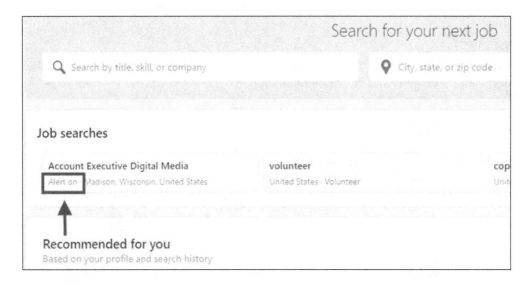

Your job recommendations can also be tailored by how far you're willing to commute. From the Jobs tab, click on the "Career interests" tab (above) and then on "Commute preferences" to enter your preferred method of transportation, start time and desired travel duration.

Wondering what happened to the LinkedIn Job Search app on your iOS or Android device? The app was discontinued as of May 2019. But never fear! All the functionality of the app is now available in your main LinkedIn app.

LinkedIn's Statistical Treasure Chest

Once you click on a position that interests you (not in search view), you will see all kinds of super useful information: a job description, a count of the number of people who have applied through LinkedIn, any of your connections that work there, and even other jobs openings at that company.

If you are a good fit for a job according to LinkedIn's algorithms, LinkedIn will tell you "Your profile matches this job":

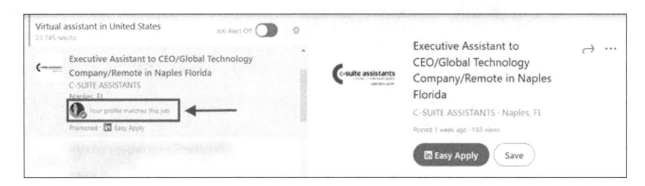

If you have a Premium account, LinkedIn will also tell you what skills you have that match the ones sought for the position. Scroll down to the "Competitive intelligence about other applicants" section:

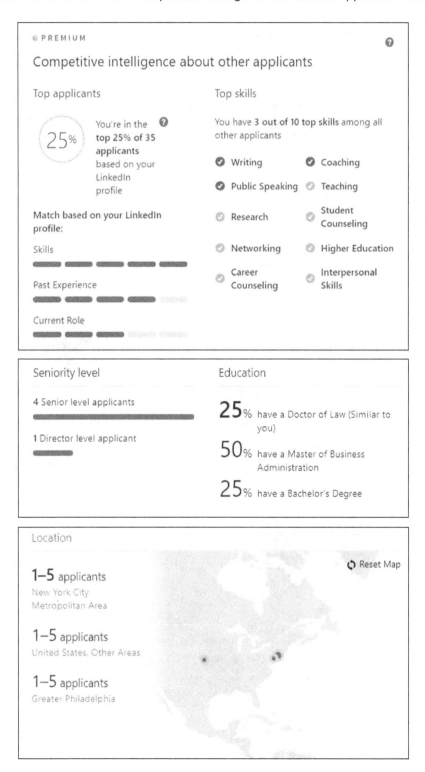

As you can see, LinkedIn pulls the skills indicated as required by the job poster and tells you how well you meet those requirements based on your profile (the exact way they determine this match percentage is not divulged by LinkedIn). If you match 80% of the skills, you're probably a good candidate for the position—you are qualified and also have some room to grow.

▶ **Add Matching Skills.** If you have the skills required but they're not listed in your Skills section, add them before submitting your application!

When applying for a position, you also get an insider view on what types of people are applying to the job, how many people have applied, and even how many have applied in the last day, so you know how competitive it is and whether applications are still coming in.

LinkedIn Premium also allows you to see valuable insights about the company, its employees and its hiring trends. Plus you'll be able to view similar jobs that might interest you.

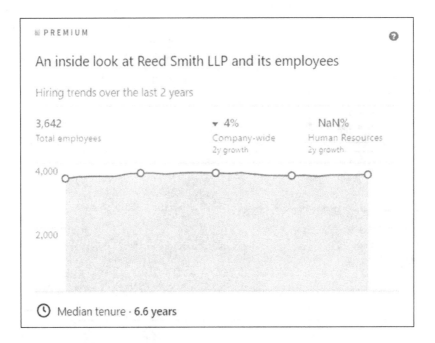

All these statistics are what make LinkedIn Jobs stand out from other job application sites. Use the information you're given to get the best ROI from your job search!

Ask for a Referral

Perhaps the most valuable information LinkedIn provides is the names of people you know who work at a company. If you have a true connection with the person, reach out and see if they can refer you. They could get a referral bonus and you could get a job!

Here's an example of what you'll see when you look at a job on LinkedIn:

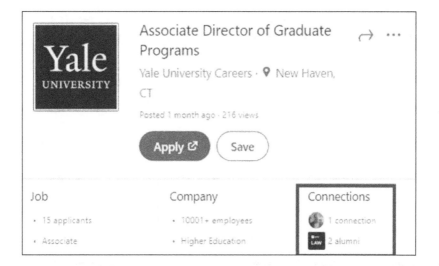

If the company is accepting referrals, you will also see "Ask for referral" next to your connections:

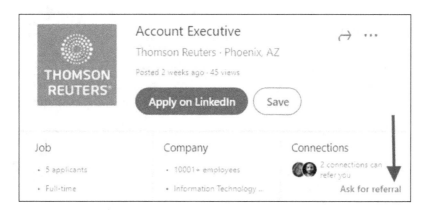

If you don't see this option, you can still request a referral the old-fashioned way!

Click on the connections and then select a member to message.

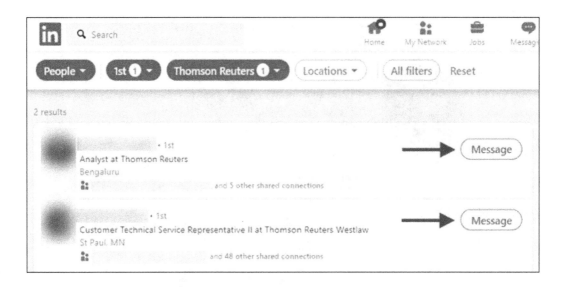

The more personal your message, the better. Here's the standard referral request message provided by LinkedIn:

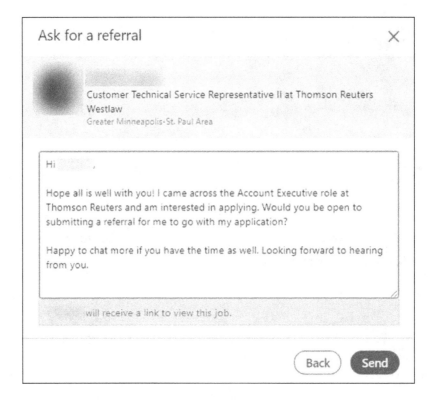

I highly recommend that you use this feature, since 85% of jobs are found through networking![148] What a goldmine!

Career Path Research

LinkedIn uses your search history to determine your career interests and intermittently will send an email like this:

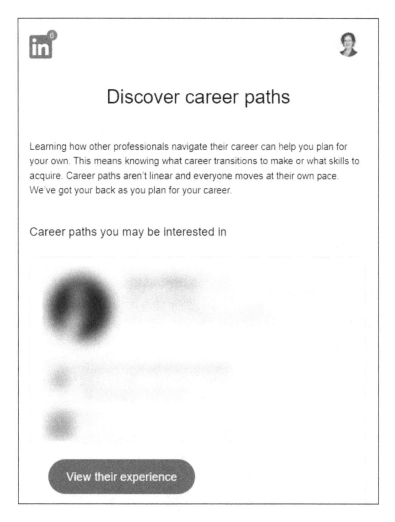

What a great opportunity to see how other people got to where you want to go! You can use career path information to research a position and what you can do to progress to that role. You can also add these folks to your network and even arrange face-to-face (in person or Zoom) information meetings with them.

Applying for Jobs Through LinkedIn

If you are serious about applying to a particular job, use the "Apply/Easy Apply/Apply on LinkedIn" or "Save" feature:

Once you save a job, you can find it from your jobs page, by clicking on "My jobs":

You can view a list of all the jobs you've applied for from this same page, under the Applied tab. For more on how to work with Applied Jobs, see the LinkedIn Help article, Viewing Jobs You've Applied for on LinkedIn.[149]

"Easy Apply/Apply Now" is offered by businesses that use an applicant tracking system (ATS) to filter applications. LinkedIn hosts the application, "enabling you to pre-fill information from your profile to make it easier and faster to apply."

Here's what the application looks like:

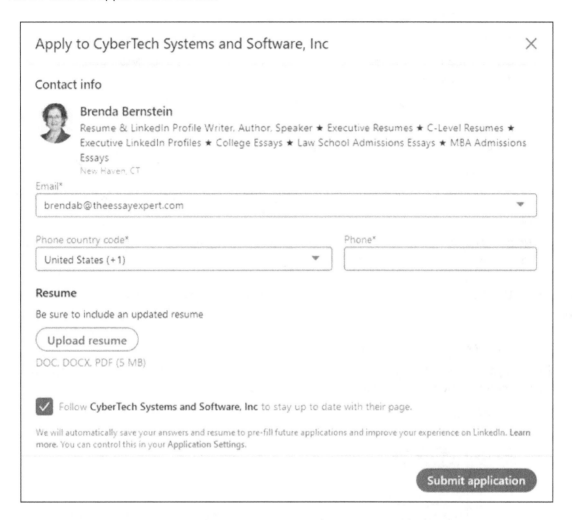

For more about the Easy Apply/Apply Now feature, see LinkedIn Help's article, "Apply to Jobs Directly on LinkedIn."[150]

What Recruiters See

When you apply with Easy Apply/Apply Now, recruiters and hiring reps will see the following information:

- Your name, Headline, About section, current & past job titles, education, and recommendations
- Your connections, including mutual connections at the company
- Your contact information
- Your resume (if attached).
- Who you are following, what you're commenting on, and what you've shared.

I probably don't have to tell you that you want all this information to be available and complete. Make it easy for potential employers to find you and learn about you by having a complete profile, including your contact information in those fields, and staying active on LinkedIn.

What will turn recruiters and hiring managers off?

- Selfies or missing photos
- Dormant profiles (not responding to InMails, outdated info, minimal connections)
- Asking for free help, such as extensive resume/profile reviews, jobs (without establishing a connection and rapport first), etc.
- Bashing recruiters or your current company (always stay positive!)
- Liking, sharing, or commenting on inappropriate content
- Inconsistencies in your profile and resume
- Invalid contact info
- Not reading job postings or hiring reps' profiles and therefore communicating inappropriately
- Applying for every job posting (qualified or not)
- Responding negatively to rejection (posting, tagging, or sending InMails complaining about a rejection or sounding like a victim)

Enough said. Don't do the 10 things listed above! You'll just get the recruiter to click on "Not a fit" when they have a chance.

Should I Upload My Resume to LinkedIn?

LinkedIn gives you the option of uploading a resume to attach to your profile. You have the option, which I do **not** recommend, of clicking the "More" button and selecting "Build a resume."

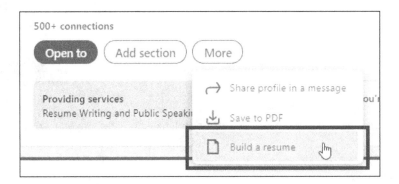

If you do this, your resume will go out automatically with any job applications through LinkedIn. Why do I recommend **against** doing this?

If you apply through LinkedIn, a recruiter or hiring manager will always ask you for your resume—so you can tailor the document you send them to the position, as opposed to sending a "one-size-fits-all" resume. Also, for safety reasons, never attach a resume with your home address to your profile.

Again, I can't emphasize enough how important it is to be consistent with your job search. If you apply for every job in a company, from a mail clerk to a CEO, recruiters will see this and disregard your application. In contrast, if you are focused with the position you want, you will be seen as more attractive.

Even more attractive is applying to similar positions at the same company when you weren't selected the first time. Past applications may be seen as a positive indication of your true interest in working at the company and of your persistence and organization.

Share the Wealth!

Is a job not quite right for you but perfect for someone else in your network? Use LinkedIn's social media sharing buttons to spread the word.

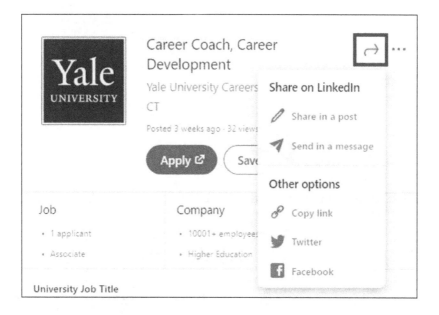

Do Your Research

To find out more about a job or company, reach out to the person who posted it. Or, if one job isn't the right fit, take a look at similar postings with the "People also viewed" or "Similar jobs" features. To view similar jobs, click on the job title:

Then scroll down to the last section to view a list of similar jobs:

At the bottom of this list, you can click to "See more jobs like this" or scroll back up to set an alert for similar jobs.

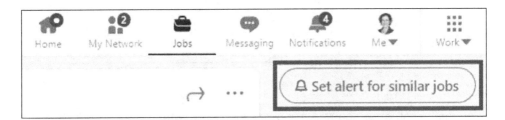

You can also search connections with similar titles. To see LinkedIn's Job Title Highlights, go to your Homepage and enter your desired title in the search bar.

Now you'll see a list of LinkedIn members with the title you're searching for, top companies hiring for the position, and similar job titles.

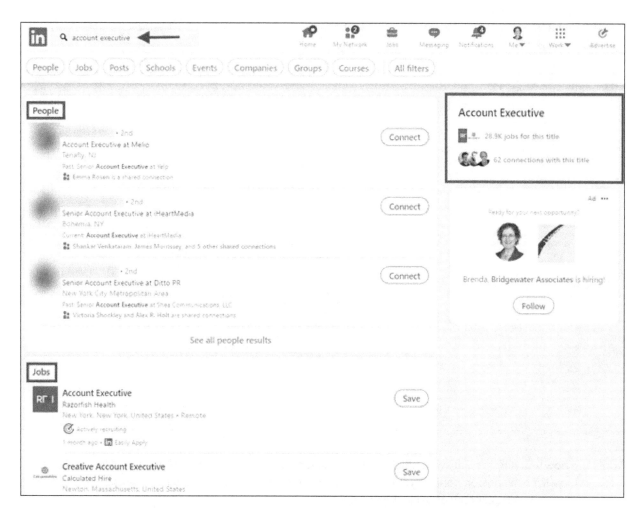

Interested in jobs similar to yours that pay more? Go to the Jobs tab and click on "Salary."[151]

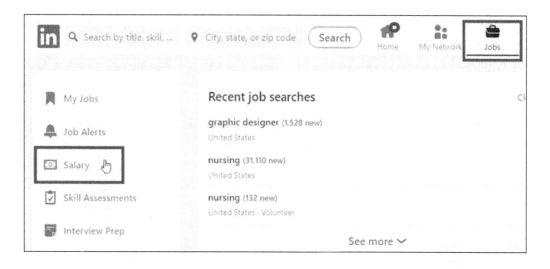

Enter your desired title/skill/company and location to see salary ranges for similar jobs. Then click on "See more insights."

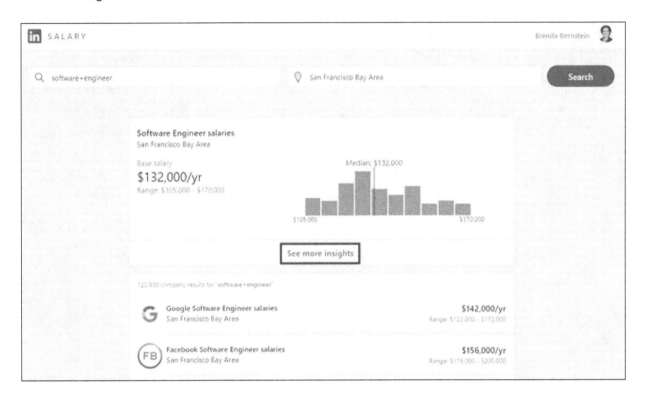

You'll see how you rank in salary with others in your position, as well as top-paying locations. Clicking on these will provide a list of hiring companies in that area. Take advantage of this free tool while it lasts. Read this article about the privacy and accuracy of Salary Insights.[152]

Tip Your Hand

You can let a company know you are interested in working for them by following the company on LinkedIn. Here are several reasons to follow a company, courtesy of WiserUTips[153]:

- **More visibility**. Representatives at your target companies can see who their followers are. By being on their followers list, you're telling companies that you are interested in them and you're also getting your skills and/or services in front of them.

- **Staying up to date**. View all recent updates about your target companies, including company news, job openings, new hires, and recent employee departures.

- **Making an impression.** Like and comment on posts about your target companies.

- **Making connections.** Review "How You're Connected." Click the "See all" link to view first-, second- and third-degree connections at the organization, as well as former employees. Use this knowledge to ask key people to help you land a job or make the sale.

- **Showing your support**. Providing recommendations for a company's products and services makes the company look good on LinkedIn and shows them that you care about their success.

Hiring entities that use LinkedIn Recruiter can view those who follow their company. They will then consider you a "warm lead" and most likely check out your profile. Plus, you can follow up to 1,000 companies! The downside is that all your connections will also be able to see what companies you follow; so if you have an ummm, "overprotective" boss, be careful about how you use this feature.

LinkedIn Learning

Are you just a training or two short of being qualified for the positions you want? LinkedIn Learning might be a valuable resource for you. An online learning platform, LinkedIn Learning "enable[s] individuals and organizations to achieve their objectives and aspirations. [LinkedIn's] goal is to help people discover and develop the skills they need through a personalized, data-driven learning experience."

LinkedIn has added a new "Courses" filter just for their Learning courses.

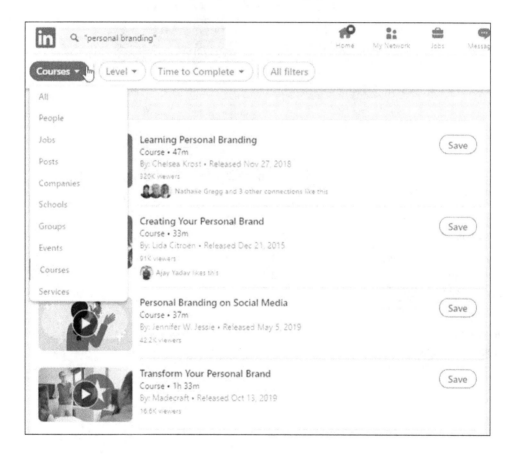

LinkedIn will even send suggested courses.

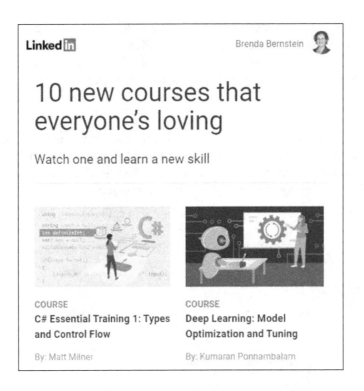

Both individual and organizational memberships are available for LinkedIn Learning. To find out more, go to https://www.linkedin.com/learning/.

Interview Prep Help

The interview can be the most intimidating aspect of job search—and if it's true that 122 million LinkedIn users have been invited to an interview through the platform, it's important for LinkedIn to help with this aspect of the job search. Even if you know everything about how to use LinkedIn to get a job, once you get to the interview, what kind of help will you get?

LinkedIn has created a way for you to familiarize yourself with the most common interview questions and get tips and sample answers from career experts around the globe. To access it, go to the Jobs tab and under More resources, select "Interview prep."

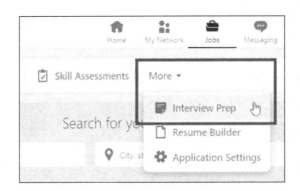

For more about using this tool, read LinkedIn's Blog articles, Introducing New Tools to Help You Prep for Your Next Interview,[154]and Interview Preparation on LinkedIn.[155]

Talent Solutions

On the Company side, LinkedIn has created the "Next Generation of Career Pages."[156] If you are a job seeker, the new career pages could mean that you are getting a much better customer experience when a company is interested in your candidacy. You will be able to learn more about a company's culture and have better access to people in similar roles to the ones that interest you. I'd love to hear your stories of how this feature works for you.

A Note on Contacting Recruiters

One way to find jobs on LinkedIn is through recruiters. Most of the time, contacting recruiters requires the use of InMail, which means you probably need to invest in a paid subscription. Job Search Premium gives you InMail privileges, plus it allows you to access metrics on why your application is not being selected; there is also evidence that you'll come up higher in recruiter searches.

Even without a Job Search Premium subscription, you might be able to send an attention-getting connection request and communicate via regular messaging after that, but you'll have a more difficult time without InMail. As you can imagine, recruiters get bombarded by InMails and connection requests every day, and it truly takes something to grab their attention.

When you're not reaching out to friends who have an automatic personal connection with you, you need to establish one. Breaking through that barrier might be as simple as mentioning a mutual connection (someone you really know). Or you could refer to an article written by the person you want to connect with, or that mentions the person. All these points of connection can be found with simple LinkedIn searches.

If your LinkedIn investigations come up blank, try Googling the person and their company. Look at their blog if they have one, or their company website. You're likely to find some interesting information that you can use as a conversation starter. One LinkedIn user discovered a mutual interest in SCUBA diving with her intended connection and was able to get creative with that, going so far as to mention seahorses in her subject line! She got a response within 10 minutes.

If you're not so fortunate as to discover an eclectic mutual interest, you can always try the direct approach. Former recruiter Catherine Byers Breet suggests something like this: "I'm a healthcare data analyst. Do you ever need folks like me?"

Another pointer: The shorter the better. Start with your main point and don't go much beyond that. You'll need to catch their attention in the first line (or 86 characters), which is all that will appear in the notification about your message.

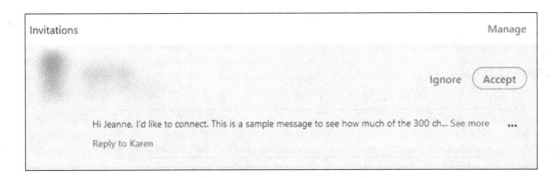

I highly recommend Byers Breet's article[157] for sample emails to recruiters that include humor and sizzle. Model after those, whether you're writing to a recruiter or someone else!

When Recruiters Contact You

If a recruiter contacts you via InMail, your well-worded response could be the difference between an interview and radio silence. According to Glassdoor, "Seasoned recruiters have a keen eye and can spot red flags like dishonesty, misrepresentation and job seekers who are 'wishy-washy' on whether they'd consider the opportunity." Here are some great templates for How to Respond to a Recruiter's InMail on LinkedIn.[158]

Tricks for Finding Hiring Reps—courtesy of Ashley Watkins of WriteStepResumes.com

If you want to contact a hiring rep outside of LinkedIn, try this tool for finding their company email address: Anymailfinder.com.[159] This site shows the formula for company emails, e.g. First.Last@company.com. Often you'll get the correct formula and be able to reach a hiring rep directly.

Other sites and links that can help you find or verify someone's contact information:

- TruePeopleSearch.com[160]
- Zabasearch.com[161]
- Radaris.com[162]
- VerifyEmailAddress.org[163]
- search string: (contact OR email OR phone OR cell OR mobile) "john doe" "company name"

Here's a super-cool way to find hiring reps on LinkedIn who might be outside your third-degree connections. It's called the "X-ray technique." To work some serious LinkedIn magic, type into Google:

site:linkedin.com (inurl:pub) "executive recruiter" "new york"

Here are my results:

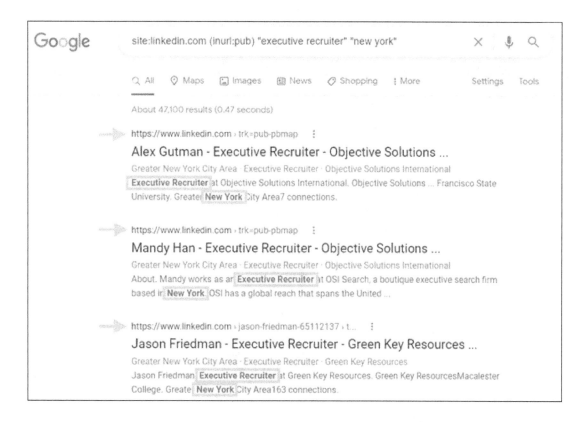

I'd love to hear what results you get by using this trick!

Volunteer Marketplace

Looking for volunteer opportunities while you search for a full-time position, or to add more fulfillment to your life? LinkedIn Jobs has a search option just for volunteer positions. To access it, go to the Jobs tab, then type the word "volunteer" in the search field.[164]

> For a more specific search, you can click on the Jobs tab, leave the search fields blank, and hit enter. Then click on All filters and select your Experience Level, Job Type: Volunteer, Location (or Remote), job function, etc. Here is a sample search for volunteer marketing roles for non-profit organizations in Washington, D.C. The search returned 241 results:

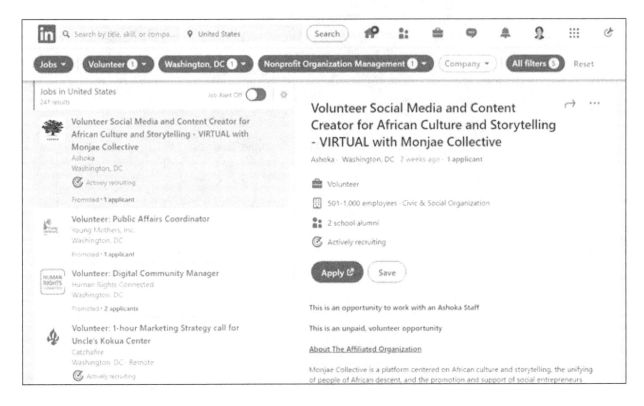

The Tune-Up for Employers/Recruiters

If you have a company page on LinkedIn, after clicking on the Jobs tab, you will see a "Manage job posts" section in the top right corner. Click on the "Post a free job" button:

You will be brought to another screen where you be asked to supply information about the company and position.

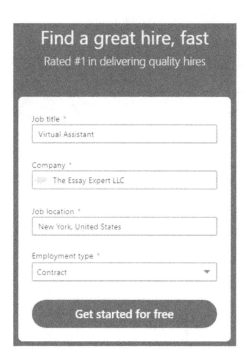

LinkedIn allows you to post one job at a time at no cost. For more details, see the LinkedIn Help article, Posting a Free Job on LinkedIn.[165]

Posting a job on LinkedIn provides credibility to your company that will attract top candidates. Simply put, in my opinion, LinkedIn is one of the best job boards currently in existence. Where else do you get such complete information on both candidates and companies? If I were looking for an employee, I would not hesitate to post the opening on LinkedIn. Even if referrals are your best source of job candidates, LinkedIn is a central place to get the word out.

The advantages of posting jobs on LinkedIn:

1. You can share the posting easily with your LinkedIn groups, LinkedIn Network, Facebook and Twitter.

2. You can link a job posting to your profile so that everyone who views your profile sees the job posting.

3. The Recommended matches feature provides the best candidates matched to your position.

4. There's a 10-applicant guarantee for members who have not previously posted a job on LinkedIn.

5. When you post a job, your network will get notified in their feed. Or if you share a job as a Page super admin, your Page followers will see the post in their feed.

6. Candidates are automatically asked to upload their resume and cover letter. Once someone applies, you get an email with a summary of the applicant's LinkedIn profile and all the documents they submitted; you can then review their full profile if you'd like.

7. When a new applicant applies, you get a link to view all the candidates who have applied for the job to date. You will find this feature very useful!

8. LinkedIn is probably the best database of professionals worldwide in just about any industry. If your candidate is not leveraging LinkedIn, they might not be the right candidate.

Once you've created a posting, share it. For complete details on sharing job posts, see Share That You're Hiring on LinkedIn.[166] I've provided some of the main points below.

You can share a job from your homepage by using the "Share that you're hiring" option:

You can also use the "Open to" feature on your profile page.

Note that when you create a job via this route, a #Hiring frame will be added to your profile photo.

You can also invite coworkers to share. See LinkedIn Help's "Share That You're on LinkedIn"[167] article for more on how get your job postings out there.

Note that if you have upgraded your Company page with Career Pages,[168] featured jobs will be displayed on that page and will be targeted to viewers based on how relevant their profile is to the job posted. This function provides tremendous screening value to you as an employer or recruiter.

LinkedIn has also made "limited listings"[169] available to its job-seeking members. Not to be confused with Job Slots or Job Posts which are visible to all job seekers, limited listings are job listings aggregated from sources outside of LinkedIn that are displayed only to members who are the most relevant candidates for the position, based on their profile content and the employer's criteria.

Group Job Postings

You can post jobs in your groups. After logging into one of your group pages, click on the field to "Start a conversation in this group," and then the "Share that you're hiring" button. Select which company or showcase page the position is for, then post your job opening. Click Post and the job will appear in the group's feed. You can also opt to add a frame to your photo that you're hiring.

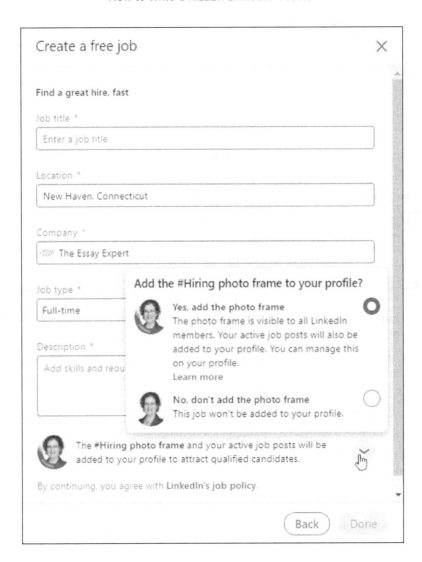

Results to Expect

The evidence, based on my own client base, is that more and more qualified job seekers are finding employment by diligently applying for jobs on LinkedIn. This is good news for both applicants and employers. Whether you are looking for a position or looking to fill one, LinkedIn is a powerful tool to achieve your intended result.

The better use you make of the Jobs function, and the more quickly you respond to job postings, the better chance you have at landing your next job. According to Ada Yu, Director of Product Management at LinkedIn, "Applying within the first 10 minutes of receiving a relevant job notification can increase your chances of hearing back by up to four times."

If you are a job seeker, and if you look in LinkedIn® Jobs daily and apply for positions appropriate to your background, you will likely see results! Just one example is one of my clients who got 12 interviews that way, and a job!

MISTAKE #17

No Recommendations, Very Few Recommendations, and/or Boring or Error-Filled Recommendations

The Problem

Profiles with recommendations rank more highly in searches than those with the exact same keywords but without recommendations. Members with recommendations are also three times more likely to be contacted. If you are short on recommendations from your connections, people might wonder whether they can truly trust you.

There is some evidence that search results are ranked partly by how many recommendations you have. If this rumor is true, then fewer recommendations can mean a lower ranking.

As Laurie Phillips,[170] business consultant and CEO at Sundance Research, offers: "Even if candidates don't give me their LinkedIn profile link, I check them out here [because] LinkedIn gives me descriptive personal references that corporations typically prohibit. Even though I know those references are biased toward the positive, they give me some idea of your personality."

With the advent of Endorsements (for more about Endorsements, see Mistake #12), it might be tempting to rely on those easily checked boxes and become complacent about requesting more personal recommendations. Don't be lulled! Endorsements take no energy on the part of the person making the endorsement, and sometimes people who cannot actually vouch for your skills endorse you for those skills.

Also note: Errors and poor writing, or simply a lack of spark in your recommendations, reflect poorly on both you and the recommender—and the recommendation can backfire. So demand excellence in your recommendations!

The Tune-Up

Whether you own a business or are looking for work, recommendations are an opportunity to have people sell you—so you don't have to do all the selling yourself.

You have the opportunity on LinkedIn to request recommendations from people you know: your colleagues, clients, supervisors, or even staff. Don't be shy! Write to your connections and ask them to recommend you.

I recommend displaying at least 5 recommendations, with 5-10 being ideal for most professionals. Many hiring professionals agree, "The more the merrier!"

Requesting Recommendations

You will find the option to request or offer recommendations when you are viewing anyone's profile. Just click on the "More" button in the person's Introduction Card:

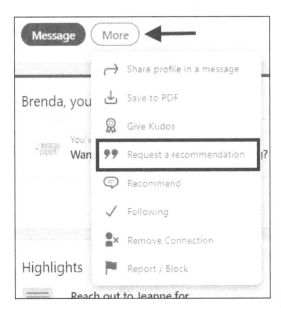

If you want the person (in this case "Jeanne") to recommend you, choose "Request a recommendation" and you'll be brought to this screen:

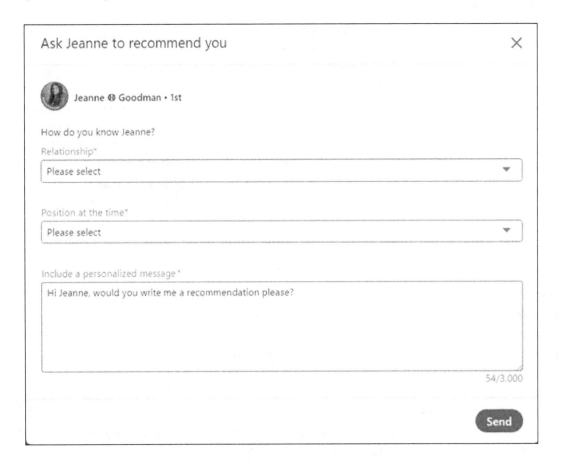

Another way to request a recommendation is to scroll down to the Recommendations section of your own profile and click on "Ask for a recommendation," then type in the person's name:

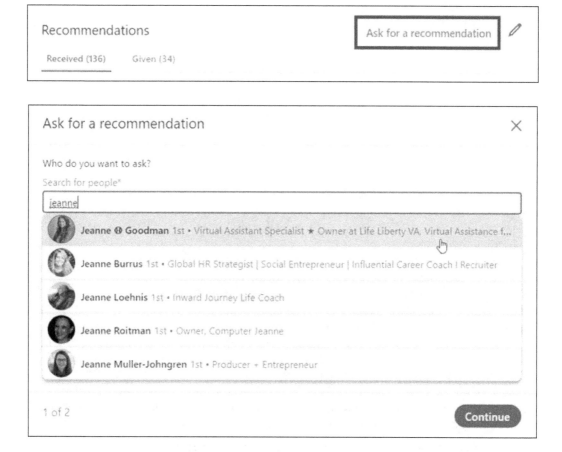

Don't simply use the default message here ("Hi [Name], can you write me a recommendation?"). Instead, say hello to the person and ask how he or she is doing (or, ideally, do this by phone before asking for the recommendation at all). If you haven't been in contact for some time, remind this colleague, boss, or other connection of a project you worked on together, a deal you made, or something else that will refresh their recollection of your professional skills. Then ask your recommender to tell a clear, specific story or two about you (positive ones of course). Examples of how you handled a situation, what you accomplished, or how you helped someone are always more informative and interesting than generalizations!

Consider, if you have more than 10 recommendations, whether you are displaying too many (the answer to this question will depend on your situation). If I applied at your company and gave you 150 letters of recommendation, how much attention would you pay to each one?

You can save all recommendations and display the ones you choose at any given time. You may choose to display certain recommendations when job seeking, others when starting a new business.

To show or hide your recommendations, click on the pencil icon:

Then use the toggle switch provided:

The default is to show the recommendation. If you do not want to display it, click the "Show" slider to change it to "Hide" and the recommendation will be hidden (see above example).

If you prefer to display recommendations other than the ones that appear by default on your profile, you can hide them; but then no one will be able to view the hidden recommendations and they will NOT be counted in the number of recommendations displayed on your profile.

Accepting or Revising Recommendations

Once you receive a recommendation, you should be notified in your inbox.

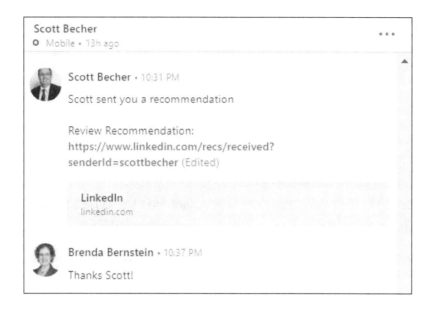

You can also check your pending recommendations by clicking the link in your Recommendation section:

Or visit this direct link: https://www.linkedin.com/recs/received.

You'll have the opportunity to accept or dismiss the recommendation. If there is an error or something you'd rather that someone say differently, you can ask your recommender to correct it, which I encourage you to do if what they wrote is not exactly the way you want it! Just click the "Ask for revision" button.

Also, make sure each recommendation says something compelling about you—that it tells a story of some sort and could not have been written about anyone else. Most people are very cooperative when you make a request for a replacement. Remember, the recommendations say as much about the recommender as they do about you! If you're afraid to request a replacement, just tell them I sent you.

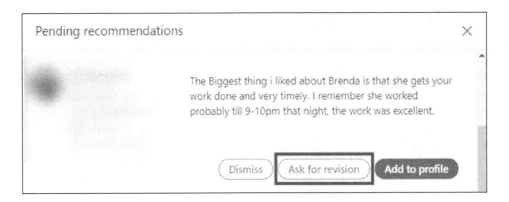

Accompany your request with a copy of the original recommendation and your suggested changes so your recommender does not have to start from scratch.

In one instance, I received a recommendation from a law school admissions client. He wrote great things about me, but didn't include some key information. I wrote him the following message:

> Hi M, could you please revise your recommendation for me? Specifically, could you add that you were accepted into USC which was your top choice? Thank you!

The resulting recommendation was exactly what I wanted:

> Working with Brenda was one of the best decisions I made while applying to law schools. I was accepted into my top choice, USC, and I do not think this would have been possible without Brenda's help. Her talent for crafting a compelling and authentic narrative was invaluable throughout the application process. I am confident the paper we worked on together helped me tremendously when it came time for the admission committee to review my file. I look forward to working with Brenda in the future and would not hesitate to recommend her to anyone I know.

> ▶ **Note for Recommenders:** If you're the one writing a recommendation, craft it well, as it reflects on you as much as on the person you're recommending. Only recommend people whose work you truly know!

Reordering Recommendations

LinkedIn used to allow reordering of Recommendations and have hinted that this feature may return, but for now, Recommendations are ordered by the date they are accepted. The ones attached to your current experience will also get priority. Some workarounds:

1. Hide the recommendations you don't like as much, so your favorites rise to the top of the list.

2. Use the "Request a Revision" feature to ask your connection if they would submit their recommendation again. Once you have accepted it anew, it will appear at the top.

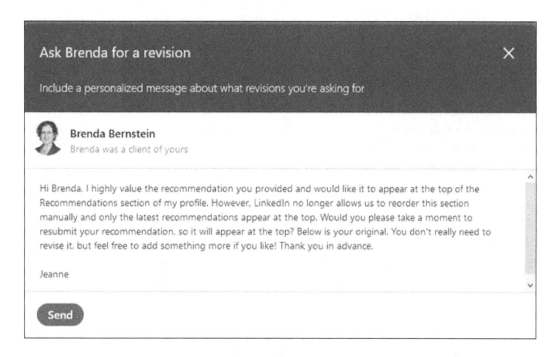

3. Delete an old position with an important recommendation attached to it. The recommendation will become free to reassign to other positions. It would be a rare instance, however, where an old recommendation is also applicable to a new one.

Tracking Your LinkedIn Recommendations

Want a quick run-down of all your received and given recommendations? Scroll down in your profile and here's what you'll see:

Or, want to see all the recommendation requests people have sent you? Go to https://www.linkedin.com/recs/received.

Recommendation Challenges

Here are some issues that commonly come up with people on my LinkedIn webinars:

1. "I haven't talked to my recommender in 10 years . . . I would be so embarrassed to ask!"

In this situation, think about how you would respond if the tables were turned. Wouldn't you be happy to hear from someone who did good work for you or who was a great boss or colleague 10 years ago? If you thought highly of the person, wouldn't you be happy to provide a recommendation? And seriously, what's the worst that can happen? They don't respond or they say no? In that case, you won't be any worse off than you are without their recommendation now!

2. "My recommenders aren't on LinkedIn."

In this situation, there are at least three options that can address the issue:

- Invite the person onto LinkedIn. It might be just the nudge your recommender needs to join the millions of LinkedIn users!

- Attach your recommendation under the relevant job as a link or file, using the instructions in Mistake #15. If you do this, you may want to write a line in that section directing readers to view your attached recommendations.

- Include the recommendation in the About or experience section of your profile. Most people will trust that it's real, though some might be more trusting of a recommendation that comes through LinkedIn's official Recommendations system. If the comment is persuasive and flows in the context of the section, I say go ahead and type it in! Here's an example of what it might look like:

CAREER HALLMARKS:

▲ Drove integration of $2.8B acquired company, a process involving data, systems, staffing, and client management.

▲ Orchestrated $6M urgent relocation of 2,000 government-agency employees displaced by Hurricane Katrina.

▲ Managed the first fully outsourced government relocation of >1,200 employees with revenue of $3.1M.

▲ Saved $1M by consolidating six international locations into one U.S.-based processing center.

🏆 Awarded **Support Department of the Year** and received **Global President's Award**.

"Your work has been critical in positioning us for future success. I can't thank you enough." – Cartus CEO

▶ Note: There are three downsides to these last two options: 1) Theoretically, you could make the recommendation up; 2) It is harder for viewers to find the recommendation; and 3) The recommendation will not be counted by LinkedIn so will not show up in your number of recommendations received.

3. "My previous company has a policy against recommendations."

If your past supervisors are precluded from recommending you due to company policy, you might have hit a dead end—but your coworkers might still be able to write a recommendation; and keep track of those supervisors, as they might move to a new company and be freed up to write a recommendation for you. Pay attention to the daily emails you receive with updates and look for news about potential recommenders!

Note that some supervisors, even if they are not officially permitted to recommend you, might sign a letter of recommendation that you draft for them. Or if you present such a letter to them, they might decide to write one themselves. This type of thing happens more often than you think! So even if you can't extract a public LinkedIn recommendation from someone, see if you can get an old-fashioned letter!

4. "My best recommendations are getting pushed to the bottom."

For tips on how to handle this issue, see Reordering Recommendations, above. Note that one of these options requires reaching out to your recommender for an update. I would approach this issue by telling your recommender how much you value what they wrote, and that you want their recommendation to appear at the top of your profile. Compliments will get you everywhere!

Giving Recommendations

I encourage you to recommend people as well as to request recommendations. It feels great to help someone out, and if you have your Privacy settings set to share your profile edits, your connections will get notified that you recommended someone. Plus, recruiters like to see that you've recommended people in addition to having received recommendations.

Word to the wise: Make sure to have some "one-way" recommendations, as "mutual" or "reciprocal" recommendations are often not as highly trusted.

Here's how to give a recommendation:

If you want to recommend Chris, go to his profile and click "Recommend."

You'll be brought to a page with this start box:

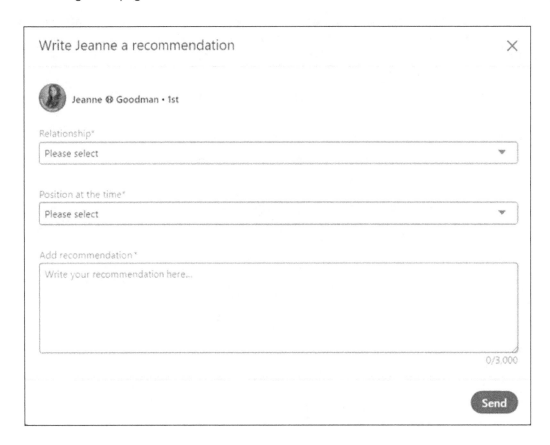

You can also view Recommendation requests by adding /detail/recommendations/requests/ to the end of your LinkedIn profile URL.

Write something that will support the person you're recommending with some concrete examples of their strengths, written in a way that also reflects favorably upon you. You might want to get your recommendation edited by someone you trust. You don't inadvertently post anything with a typo!

I've always liked the saying, "Give until it feels good." Giving recommendations on LinkedIn is a great way to create positive feelings for both yourself and others!

Results to Expect

By giving and accumulating recommendations, you will build positive relationships with people in your network while also gaining the trust of potential employers, clients, and whomever else you want to impress on LinkedIn—trust that can translate into business or into a job. I have had many people choose to work with The Essay Expert based on the strength of the recommendations posted on my LinkedIn profile. Imagine, if you are a business or sales person, having clients come to you already having decided you're the person they want to work with!

Recommending people can also get you attention from recruiters. Read Are LinkedIn Recommendations Important? Here's What 10 Hiring Managers Say[171] for some insightful views from recruiters on how much weight recommendations hold when choosing the right candidate. Also, it's a little-known fact that recruiters search on the recommendations you've *given*, not just on the ones you receive! You will be seen and recognized as a team player if you give great recommendations to people you know.

If your recommendations are compelling and error-free, both you and your recommenders will make a great impression. The strength of your recommendations can get you your next client or your next job.

MISTAKE #18

A Static (Unchanging, Outdated) Profile—and Thinking all You Need is a KILLER LinkedIn Profile

The Problem

Your LinkedIn profile is not a static, unchanging document. Members expect to find up-to-date information there! You wouldn't send out a resume without your most current position listed, or with past positions listed as if they are current. Why would you have a LinkedIn profile with outdated information?

If you earned a degree in 2018 and haven't worked since 2015, it would be a shame to forget to list those three years you were in school! You could appear to be unemployed when you really were a hard-working student that whole time.

Sometimes you want your networks to know you've completed a degree, gotten a promotion, or landed a new job. If "Share job changes, education changes, and work anniversaries from profile" in your Settings & Privacy is set to "Yes," every time you update your Experience or Education sections, a message goes out to all your connections. Newsflash: If you don't update your profile, this feature won't help you and your connections won't be updated on your career milestones.

Let's face it: Even if you have the most amazing LinkedIn profile in the world, you won't get results by sitting there doing nothing.

The Tune-Up

Regularly update your Headline, About, Experience (Job Titles) and Education sections. Add accomplishments when you achieve new ones. Join new groups. Make and request new recommendations. Post links and Activity Updates relevant to who you are and what you're up to. Stay active.

If you don't want your changes shared, turn off your notifications before you make your edits. You can access this feature at the bottom of the pop-up window any time you update or add a new entry to your Experience or Education sections:

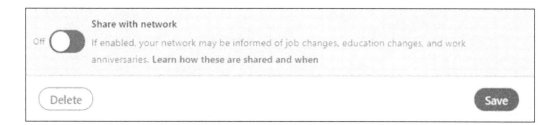

Or, see Appendix H for instructions on how to control this setting.

Announcement of your profile changes will only be viewable via the Notifications tab of your connections. LinkedIn does not send out a notification of profile changes immediately, nor for every change. It can take up to 48 hours after your last change before a notification is generated. This is LinkedIn's way of ensuring that announcements are not sent each time you save. Here's what the notification will look like:

Remember to Update!

If you tend to forget that your LinkedIn profile exists, you might want to put a tickler in your calendar reminding you to update your profile at least every month. Also, read articles about new features on LinkedIn and about how to write a great profile. Update your profile according to what you learn. Reading this book—and future editions—is a great first step.

Finally, unless you stay active in groups, conversations, and . . . most important . . . OFFLINE, you will not get the greatest possible results out of your LinkedIn profile.

LinkedIn provides a wealth of information about every one of your contacts. Be an explorer!

Read through someone's entire profile before starting a conversation. You may discover videos and other documents in addition to basic education and employment information. If they have recommended people, you can get insight into their values system. If they have received multiple recommendations, you'll get a sense of their greatest strengths. Do they volunteer somewhere? If so, talking about their volunteer experience can be a great icebreaker.

Get Personal

Pay attention to your Notifications page where you get notifications of people's birthdays and job changes/anniversaries. Respond to them! Don't forget to write comments, post questions, give and receive recommendations and endorsements—and ask people you want to truly connect with to talk with you on the phone or even meet you for coffee or lunch.

Ready to meet with someone? Sync your calendar to LinkedIn. LinkedIn will provide your contact's details and also remind you to follow up after the meeting. To use this feature, go to your profile by clicking on your picture, then Settings, and Account Preferences. Scroll to Syncing Options and select "Sync your calendar."

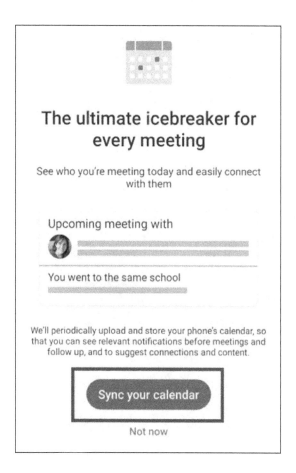

To learn more about this feature, visit LinkedIn's Help article, "Syncing Your Calendar in the LinkedIn Mobile App."[172]

Results to Expect

By staying updated and active, you will likely get emails from your connections congratulating you on your new position, your new accomplishment, or the new look of your profile. You will be seen as someone who is active in your profession and serious about your online presentation. Not only that, but if you comment on people's news, they will **like** you (and I don't mean click on the "like" button. I mean actually like you)! Who doesn't appreciate getting congratulated or being wished a happy birthday?

See how you're doing at making business connections by checking your Social Selling Index.[173] According to LinkedIn, "Salespeople who excel at social selling are creating more opportunities and are 51% more likely to hit quota."[174]

Here's what your score will look like:

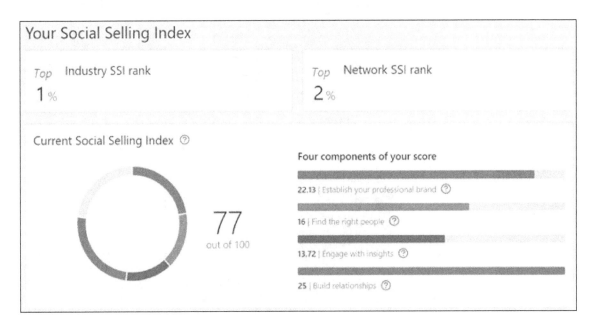

To find read more about this feature, go to LinkedIn's Social Selling Index[175] page.

The Power of Connections

The more activity you generate, the more people will view your profile and the more likely you are to make connections.

I'll tell you a secret: A huge proportion of my business was built because I was active in a group and the manager of the group connected me with one of its other members who lives in Austin, Texas. I happened to be visiting Austin and met with that member, and he was so impressed with our meeting that he began referring multiple clients to me and giving me opportunities to present webinars with his company. That connection led to webinars and a huge expansion of brand awareness for me and my company.

More recently, on a trip to New York and New Haven, I met in person with three connections I had initially met via LinkedIn. All three meetings led to results I never would have imagined—results that probably would not have manifested if we had kept our communications to LinkedIn and telephone.

Please take my story to heart. Don't stop at online LinkedIn connections! Bring them to the next level with a phone call or in-person meeting, and the possibilities are endless.

BONUS TIP #1

Save Your Work . . . and Your Connections!

The Problem

LinkedIn is not a perfect system, and there have been stories of disappearing profiles. If you haven't saved the results of all your hard work, you can lose it. I'm guessing that would be aggravating for you. Furthermore, if your profile gets axed for any reason, you could easily lose your hundreds or thousands of LinkedIn connections.

The Tune-Up

To retain the results of your labors, back up your profile! I recommend doing this at least 2x/year minimum, once/month if you're regularly updating, or every time something significant changes in your profile (new position, new headline, new recommendation, new education, etc.).
LinkedIn has created a way for you to save all your information in one fell swoop by requesting an archive of your data.

To request your archive, go to your Settings & Privacy and under "Data Privacy", click "How LinkedIn uses your data." Select "Download larger data archive, including connections, contacts, account history . . ." Then click the "Request archive" button:

You will need to enter your password, then wait! If you have a lot of connections, your archive might be split into two parts.

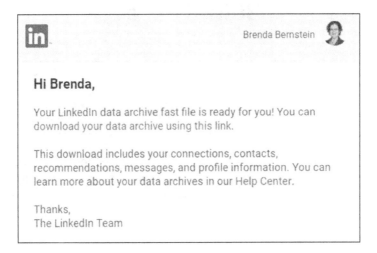

You should receive your download file within 24 hours—and you might be excited to see all the information it contains— including a complete history of your account activity, a list of your connections, your endorsements and recommendations, and more! For a list of everything that's exported, visit LinkedIn's help center article regarding downloading your account data.[176] I personally discovered the following:

1. My LinkedIn account was created 5/21/08 and I was invited by an old acquaintance, to whom I wrote a quick thank you as soon as I got my archive!

2. This is a great way to export a connections list (see Exporting Connections Only below)!

3. You'll have a fully preserved html version of all of the articles you've published on LinkedIn, including images.

4. Recommendations and Inbox messages are viewable in .csv format for easy sorting by date or connection.

Exporting Profile Only

On your View Profile page (in the Profile drop-down), click on the "More" button below a connection's Headline to open a drop-down with an option "Save to PDF."

Save the document that gets generated and you will instantly have a record of all the fruits of your labors. You'll have something that looks like this:

Repeat this export process every time you make a change to your profile.

Exporting Connections Only

Note that as of December 2018, your connections export will contain a limited number of email addresses. This is due to LinkedIn's change to member privacy settings, which makes email addresses not downloadable by default. I'm happy about this change since it will prevent a lot of the spamming that occurs on LinkedIn;

but it also makes it more of a challenge for me to communicate with my LinkedIn connections outside of LinkedIn.

If you want others to be able to download your email, go to Settings & Privacy under "Who can see your email address" and switch it to Yes. And if you want to send a blast to your LinkedIn connections, well, you'll have to populate most of the list by hand now.

To save your LinkedIn connections, click on My Network:

Then click on your number of connections in the left sidebar:

In the upper right of the following page, find "Manage synced and imported contacts."

In the right sidebar, click on "Export contacts."

Choose "Connections" then click "Request Archive."

![Get a copy of your data interface showing Data privacy settings with Connections checkbox selected and Request archive button]

Your file will be emailed to you, usually within the day. You will then have the first name, last name and email address of every person in your LinkedIn contact list. Do NOT use this list to send out spam emails! Be courteous please.

> ▶ **Note:** If you are exporting your connections to a Mac and you use Mac mail, connections will export directly to your address book (not an Excel spreadsheet). When prompted to import them into your contacts, you may think you are duplicating them, however, they will be saved as a "Smart Group." For more instructions on exporting connections to your Mac, read, How to Import Excel Contacts to Apple Address Book Efficiently.[177]

Results to Expect

A recoverable profile and a secure contacts list. Peace of mind.

BONUS TIP #2

Create a Profile Badge

The Problem

If an employer or client receives any online document from you and wants to look at your LinkedIn profile, you want to make it easy for them to do so.

The Tune-Up

To create an email signature that links to your LinkedIn profile page, click "Edit public profile & URL" in the upper right of your profile page:

Then scroll down to the bottom of the right sidebar and click "Create a badge."

To create a button that links to your LinkedIn profile, read LinkedIn's instructions for adding a profile badge to your blog, online resume or website. If you like the badge image(s) LinkedIn provides but don't know how to use the code, you can take a screenshot of the image instead, then paste it into a document, and insert a hyperlink. It will look like this:

If you choose to put a hyperlink into your resume, be aware that some recruiters' programs will strip out hyperlinks due to the possibility of viruses. So unless you're sending the resume to someone personally, include your full LinkedIn URL.

Results to Expect

Recruiters, employers and clients will have everything they need at their fingertips to get a full picture of who you are and what you offer. They will be ready, if they like what they see, to invite you to take the next step, whether that is submitting a resume or scheduling an interview or a meeting.

BONUS TIP #3

Don't Violate LinkedIn's Terms of Service

LinkedIn's User Agreement is located at https://www.linkedin.com/legal/user-agreement.

The Problem

This document contains many rules and regulations that you might not be aware of, and that, if violated, could cause your account to be suspended or terminated. The section entitled "LinkedIn Dos and Don'ts" is especially important to read. You might discover that you are violating one or more of the items on this list. You might also discover that another member is violating the User Agreement.

The Tune-Up

First of all, read LinkedIn's User Agreement! It's essential to be aware of all the terms of service that apply to you.

You will want to read LinkedIn's "Professional community policies"[178] for more on how to generally be a better LinkedIn community member.

Results to Expect

By understanding and abiding by LinkedIn's User Agreement, you'll retain your LinkedIn membership status so you can create relationships and produce results through LinkedIn for many years to come. And by protecting your account, as well as taking action if someone else violates the User Agreement, you will feel more secure and in control of your LinkedIn experience.

BONUS TIP #4

Protecting Yourself from Phishing

The Problem

LinkedIn is an amazing online tool. Unfortunately, in this age of technology, there are unsavory characters looking to create havoc on the web and in your email boxes. While LinkedIn works hard to protect your privacy, there are measures you must take to safeguard your account and your identity.

The Tune-Up

First of all, create a strong password and change it often. Don't share your login information. You can see all of the places you're currently logged in by going to Settings & Privacy and from the Account access tab, clicking on "Where you're signed in."

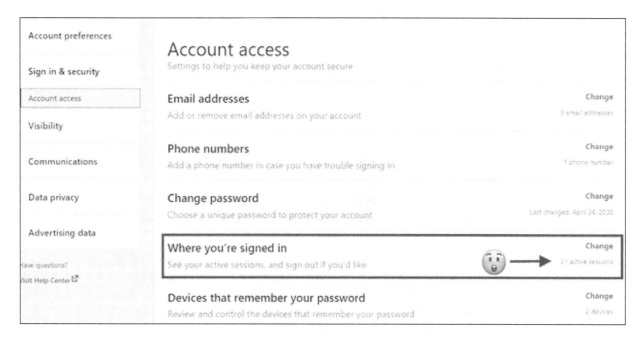

If you receive a notice that an unknown person attempted to log in or logged into your profile, change your password immediately!

LinkedIn provides a few tips here[179] for protecting your email address from spammers, such as never connecting with anonymous profiles using group or company names.

As with any emails, do NOT click on any suspicious links in LinkedIn messages, inside or outside of your account. They could be hackers. Here's an example of a spam message one of my connections received on LinkedIn:

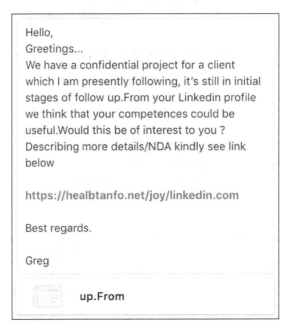

Hello,
Greetings...
We have a confidential project for a client which I am presently following, it's still in initial stages of follow up.From your Linkedin profile we think that your competences could be useful.Would this be of interest to you ? Describing more details/NDA kindly see link below

https://healbtanfo.net/joy/linkedin.com

Best regards.

Greg

up.From

Unfortunately, my contact clicked on the link and the same message went out to all his connections. Two-step verification might have prevented this fiasco. Read this LinkedIn Help article[180] to learn how to turn on two-step verification.

Phishing

In February 2022, email phishing incidents were up 232%. If you're not identifying phishing emails properly, you are at high risk of become a victim.

Phishing email messages can arrive in your regular email inbox and look very similar to the emails sent by LinkedIn. They can say things like "You appeared in XX searches this week," "Your profile matches this job," or "You have 1 new message."

Don't be fooled!! Clicking the links within these emails can infect your computer or mobile device with viruses, malware, and/or spyware, or expose your login credentials. Often after clicking, you'll be taken to a blank page and wonder what happened. Or you may be taken to a fake login page where once you "sign in" you're simply bounced to the real login page. In both instances, the damage has been done: either your device has been infected or the attackers have harvested your credentials to gain access to your LinkedIn profile and spam your connections.

How do you spot the fakes?

- Whenever you receive an email with a link or button, always check the address it's coming from. Official LinkedIn messages will almost always come from an email address ending with @linkedin.com. The only exception I've seen is the LinkedIn Official Blog digest, which comes from @mail.feedblitz.com.

- Hold your cursor over the main link or button they're asking you to click and look at the link's preview. It should be a URL beginning with https://www.linkedin.com/.

- Genuine LinkedIn emails will also include a "security footer"[181] that displays your LinkedIn profile Headline as proof the message came from within LinkedIn.

Like they say in the banking industry, the best way to spot fake is to know what the real thing looks like. Here are some elements of the real thing:

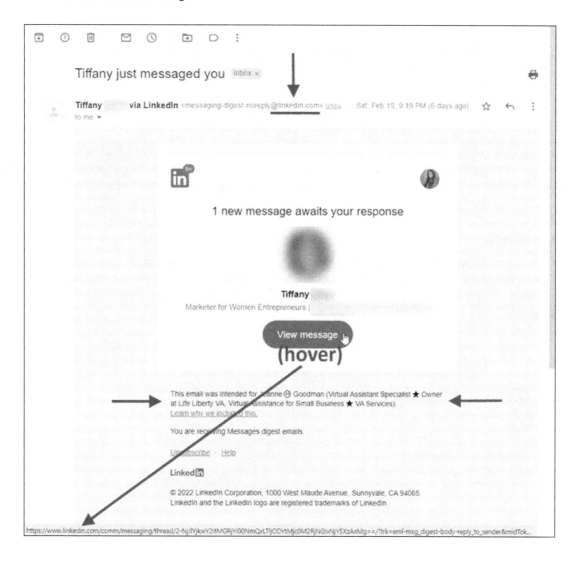

Please be sure to use the tips above and do not fall victim to a phishing email!

What To Do If You Experience Hacking

If you experience any violations of LinkedIn's User Agreement or have questions about its terms, contact LinkedIn. Here's how:

Contact them online[182] or by physical mail.

For Members in the United States:
    LinkedIn Corporation
    Attn: Legal Dept. (Privacy Policy and User Agreement)
    1000 W. Maude Avenue
    Sunnyvale, CA 94085
    USA

For Members outside the United States:
    LinkedIn Ireland Unlimited Company
    Attn: Legal Dept. (Privacy Policy and User Agreement)
    Wilton Plaza
    Wilton Place, Dublin 2
    Ireland

There are, unfortunately, some inappropriate activities that LinkedIn will not address. If someone obtains your email address through your LinkedIn account and then sends you email outside of LinkedIn, there is nothing that LinkedIn will do about it—even if the person explicitly says they got your contact information from LinkedIn. So be careful about whom you connect with on LinkedIn!

Results to Expect

Safeguarding your LinkedIn login information, keeping an eye out for who might be accessing your account, and not sharing your email address with suspicious members will go a long way toward maintaining your safe and secure experience on LinkedIn. The extra steps you take to identify spam will save you many hours of hassle in the future.

BONUS TIP #5

Creating a Secondary Language Profile

The Problem

LinkedIn reports that 70% of its members are located outside of the US. Because such a large portion of users are multilingual and interested in connecting with people both inside and outside of English-speaking countries, I am including this special section on how to set up additional LinkedIn profiles that cater to secondary languages.

If you are multilingual, you probably have people searching for you in multiple languages. If you post your profile only in one of them, you could be losing the opportunity to connect with at least half your audience.

The Tune-Up

If you speak two languages and want people to find your profile in a second language, you can create a secondary language profile. To do this, go to your Profile page and click on "Add profile in another language" in the right sidebar:

Choose your language from the drop-down menu. LinkedIn supports the following languages as of January 2020:

English, Arabic, Bahasa Indonesia, Chinese (Simplified), Chinese (Traditional), Czech, Danish, Dutch, French, German, Italian, Japanese, Korean, Malay, Norwegian, Polish, Portuguese, Romanian, Russian, Spanish, Swedish, Tagalog, Thai, Turkish

> ▶ **NOTE:** You cannot change the default language of your profile once you've set it up in a particular language. It's recommended that you set up a secondary language profile instead.

Be sure to update your name and Headline before clicking "Create Profile."

LinkedIn does not translate your content for you, so now you'll need to edit your secondary language profile. To do so, go to your new language profile by selecting it from the upper right corner:

While viewing your secondary language profile, you can edit the About, Experience, and Education sections as you normally would. When you click the pencil icon to edit one of these sections, you'll see that LinkedIn provides a snapshot of your primary profile to help you:

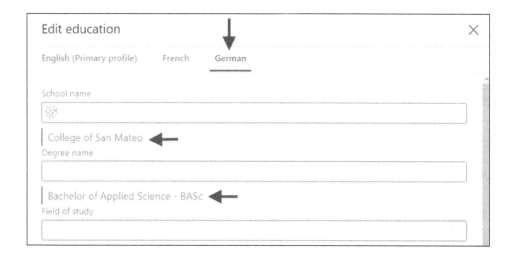

▶ **Note:** Your Skills can't be edited and will only appear in the language of your primary profile. Recommendations will also only show in the language in which they were written.

When a member signs in to LinkedIn and views your profile, they will see it in the language of your primary account; or, if you have multiple profiles in several languages, viewers will see the one most relevant to them. The viewer can choose from your language profiles by selecting one from the upper right corner of your profile.

All of your language profiles will show up in search engines and have their own URL that includes "/?locale=" and the code for that language. For instance, a profile in French would appear as https://www.linkedin.com/in/yourname/?local=fr_FR.

If you no longer want your secondary language profile, you can delete it by clicking the globe icon, then on the "x" next to the language you no longer want to list:

Note that when you make a post on your page or publish an article, regardless of the language, it will be connected with both your language profiles but will only be shown in the language in which it was written. So you might want to post things in multiple languages to reach multiple audiences and to appear in both newsfeeds and searches in multiple languages.

Results to Expect

Here's the good news: All of your language profiles will show up in search engines and have their own URL, searchable in Google. Plus, having multiple language profiles will make the user experience for your viewers a more fluid and positive one, since they will be able to explore who you are in their own language. You'll also be found for your skills in multiple languages when people search for someone like you on LinkedIn. So if you do business in more than one language, a secondary language profile is a must-have!

BONUS TIP #6

Insufficient or Ineffective Group Membership

LinkedIn groups are communities of individuals with similar interests or a professional common ground. There are groups for people who are job seekers (which also contain recruiters and employers); groups for people with particular technical knowledge; and groups for lawyers, project managers, graduates from various schools, and even cooks.

Once you join a group, you have access to conversations and job postings relevant to that group, so you can post discussions and answer questions asked.

There are reportedly over 2 million groups on LinkedIn and on average, each user is a member of 7 groups. You can choose to join up to 100 LinkedIn groups.

While LinkedIn groups are not as active as they once were, they can still be an effective tool to make connections and establish thought leadership.

The Problem

LinkedIn groups can provide you with access to thousands of potential readers. If you're not a member of groups relevant to you, you won't be reaching the targeted people you want to reach, and your networking opportunities will be limited.

As business consultant Laurie Phillips states, "Group memberships and activity gives me a clue about whether the candidate is building a broad business network, as well as what topics/organizations they associate with closely. It's a great source for insight on someone before I meet with them."

The Tune-Up

Search for and join groups where you will connect with your target audience. For instance, if you are seeking a job in the IT industry, join IT-related groups and job-seeking groups such as Linked:HR that contain recruiters. If you provide services to small businesses, join groups such as the Entrepreneur & Small Business Forum. If you provide services to children, join groups that contain parents. You will then have access to the people you want to reach.

There are several ways to find groups to join:

1. Conduct a search

To find groups that might interest you on LinkedIn, In the search box, type the search terms that are relevant to you, and a link for groups with that topic will come up. If you type "Project Manager" into the search bar, then select "Groups" from the drop-down menu, or scroll down to the Groups section . . .

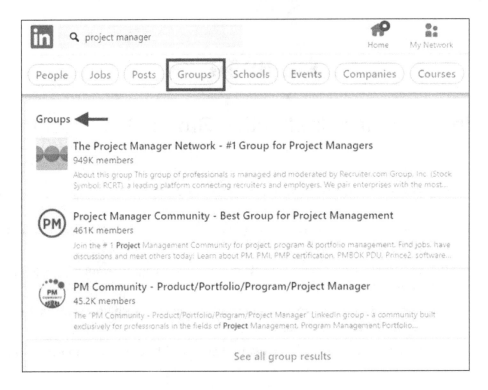

. . . you'll be taken to a list of groups that you can join.

You can also select "People" and find out what groups they belong to. See my next point below!

2. Join groups based on who is in them

Are there people you particularly respect on LinkedIn? Perhaps they are members of groups you would want to belong to. When you view someone's profile, you can view their group membership, unless they have hidden this information.

To find out what groups someone belongs to, scroll down to the bottom of their profile, where you'll see a block of people, companies, groups and schools they are following. To view just the groups, click on the "See all" link:

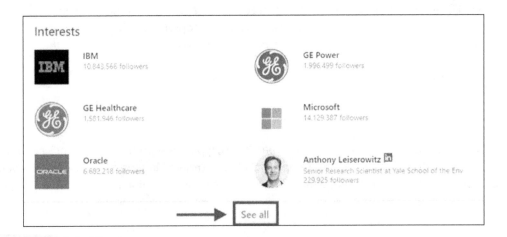

Then select the Groups tab and click on the name of the group(s) you are interested in joining.

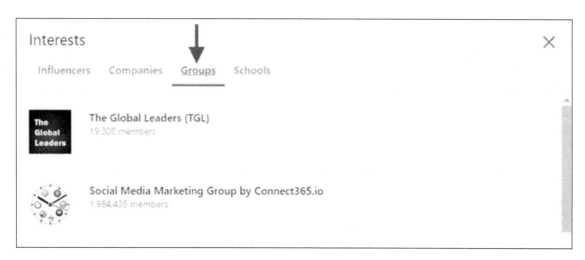

Post to groups

To start a conversation, go to your Groups page and click on the group you'd like to engage with.

Click on "Start a conversation in this group," add a captivating introduction, and then enter any details you'd like.

Best practice is to enter a true conversation starter that will engage your audience. If you put spammy marketing material into the details section, you will likely be chastised with a warning from the group moderator. Make sure you're following group rules ("About this group" in the right sidebar) before posting anything to any group!

Posting Videos

LinkedIn has improved the sharing experience in groups and article posts by allowing videos.

To post a video in a group, "Start a conversation in this group" by clicking in the details field and pasting in the URL of the video. You may need to add a space after pasting in the URL to see the video populate the preview field below. Once the preview is in place, you can delete the ugly URL and give your post a title and further details if you like.

Or, click on the video icon to attach a video file up to 10 minutes long from your computer.

Once you hit post and the video is fully uploaded, it will look something like this:

According to Entrepreneur.com,[183] you're more likely to get viewers who don't know you to watch by keeping your videos short and sweet (around 90 seconds), not introducing yourself in the video, and providing an accompanying post explaining what your video is about, including relevant hashtags.

General advice on joining and participating in groups:

Before joining a group, check the number of members. Ideally, you will join a mix of groups, some with membership in the thousands and some smaller ones. Groups with only a few hundred members might get you more attention if you post something, since there are not as many people posting. I have personally found that members of local groups tend to respond more often to my posts than people in bigger groups with wider membership.

There are hundreds of thousands of members in many groups! If you're looking to greatly expand your network, you might want to join one of these mammoth connector groups (LION is one of them) and start making invitations.

To join a group, just click "Request to join." Your request will go to a moderator who will approve or deny your request. Most of the time you will be approved.

Once you join a group, don't just sit there . . . do something!

Use conversations to share articles relevant to your groups. Start discussions that the group will find interesting. Share images. Respond to other people's comments. Post news articles. Put yourself out there. Then let the group take your conversations and run with them.

You can hover over a person's name within a group discussion to find out more about them. If you like what they said and see value in having them in your network, send them a customized invitation! After you have connected, you can mention them in a group conversation using the @ symbol. This is an effective way to make long-lasting connections and maybe even get some help with an issue you're facing. I recommend setting up a phone call or coffee date to really get to know the people in your group who could be valuable connections.

▶ **Messaging Hack:** When you share group membership with someone, you can send them a message without being connected. To message a group member, click on the "See all" link.

Click the message button to the right of your fellow group member to reach out.

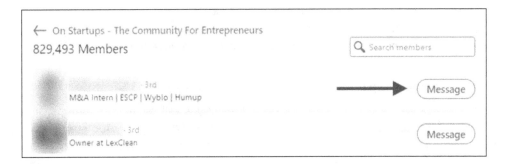

If a member has caught your attention with an interesting post, you can message them by clicking on their name and messaging them directly.

▶ **Commenting Hack:** If you're looking to stand out and be noticed on LinkedIn, prioritize participating in conversations where there are already a LOT of comments—over 100 at least. Most of those people will be following the discussion and will therefore get an email when a new comment is posted. That means they will read your comment—and if you impress them, they might soon be asking you for help!

Participation gets you noticed. If your goal is effective networking, your participation, more than how many groups you've joined, is what's important.

▶ **Hiding Group Membership:** If you are a member of a group but don't want the public to know for any reason, you can hide the groups in your list. To do this, click on the three dots in the upper right of the group's feed and select "Update your settings."

To hide the group, switch the "Display group on profile" option to No.

As of January 2019, LinkedIn does not provide any email notifications for group discussion/ activity. However, the group notification is visible on the "Notifications" tab on the Homepage. When and if LinkedIn reinstates group email notifications, I recommend opting for weekly digests, since the email traffic can be heavy! Or you can choose not to receive updates from certain groups if you are feeling overwhelmed by the volume of email you are receiving.

Results to Expect

According to LinkedIn Business,[184] "You are 70 percent more likely to get an appointment with someone on an "unexpected sales call" if you are in a common group than if you aren't. Some other results might not have specific statistics attached to them, but you can bet that if you participate in active discussions, you will gain visibility and potentially attract employers or clients. By using groups to find valuable connections and build your network, you will get the value they offer.

BONUS TIP #7

Finding the Services You Need

How it works

Step 1	Step 2	Step 3
Discover	**Review**	**Hire**
Browse nearby providers or answer a few questions to receive up to 5 proposals from trusted providers	Choose the right provider by reviewing their experience, recommendations, and connections	Start working together by sending a free message to providers that best fit your needs

If you're looking for professional services, you can find them by clicking the Work tab and selecting "Services Marketplace."

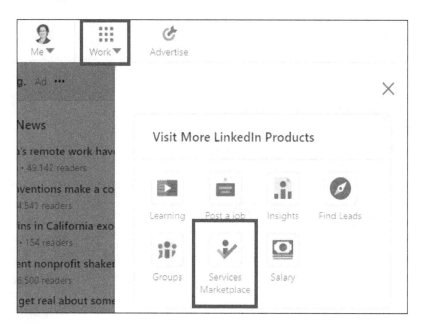

There are currently more than 5.5M providers in 17 categories including Accounting, Coaching & Mentoring, Consulting, Design, Events, Finance, Home Improvement, Information Technology, Insurance, Law, Marketing, Operations, Photography, Real Estate, Software Development, Writing.

To find a provider, begin typing in the service you're interested in, or manually choose from the "Popular Services" options.

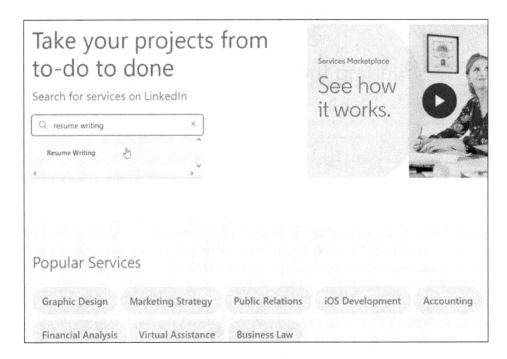

You can then browse the service providers listed or search by location. Click "See all" to view the list, which is currently limited to just 30 cities.

Note that if the provider has received reviews for their services, LinkedIn will show one here as a teaser (see previous image).

Click on the provider's name to be taken to a special page where you can learn more about them and their services, read all of their reviews, and directly request a proposal.

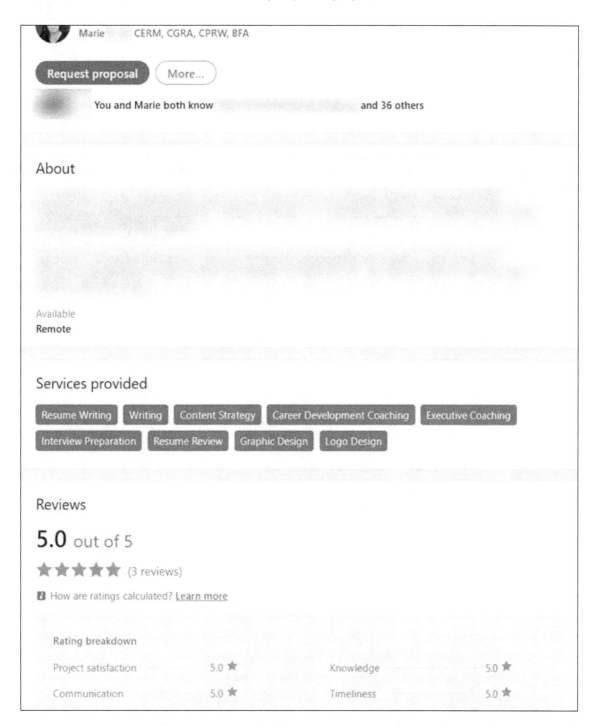

If you'd prefer LinkedIn match you with a service provider, click "Get proposals."

LinkedIn will take you through a series of questions to help clarify your needs and match you with their top five providers. You can manage your proposals by clicking the Work tab and choosing Services Marketplace, then clicking on "My projects."

Your request for proposal will look something like this:

Resume Writing

Bergen, New York

Open · Created less than one minute ago

Project details

What type of resume?

LinkedIn profile

What stage of resume writing are you in?

I need revisions to an existing resume

Where are you in your career?

Late career

Which industries are you focused on?

Other

How would you like to work with the resume writer?

I am comfortable working virtually

What are your goals in seeking a resume writer? Anything else the resume writer should know? (Optional)

I would like my LinkedIn profile optimized for my current industry.

They will receive a message like this in their inbox:

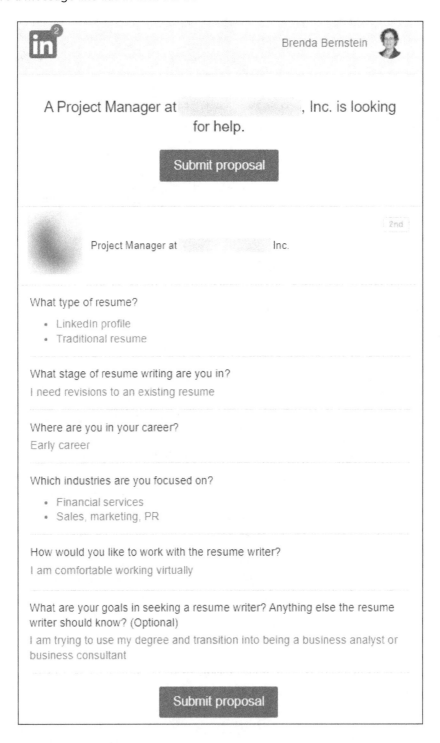

I recommend letting any providers that don't make the final cut know that you appreciate their time but have decided to go with someone else.

SPECIAL SECTION FOR BUSINESSES

Ensure Brand Consistency—and Create a Company Page

The Problem

Reportedly, 80% of B2B leads come through LinkedIn. According to LinkedIn internal data, "LinkedIn members interact with Pages more than 1 billion[185] times per month. And in a study conducted by HubSpot,[186] LinkedIn was discovered to be 277% more effective at generating leads than Facebook or Twitter."

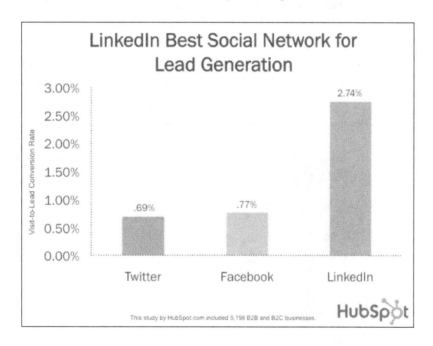

Despite this data, many companies often don't consider how they want to be perceived by the LinkedIn community. Employee profiles are inconsistent, sometimes company names are spelled wrong, and there is rarely an effort to use LinkedIn methodically for SEO purposes. Furthermore, many companies don't have a company page, which means no image will appear next to the company name in employees' profiles.

If you own a company, you want your employees' profiles to build your brand. If employees are misspelling your company name or creating job descriptions willy-nilly, you lose out on brand consistency—and on attracting business and new employees.

The LinkedIn user base is a sophisticated group. Forty-nine percent of people in the $75,000+ earnings bracket, and 51% of those with a college degree, use LinkedIn. This savvy demographic will notice when you haven't done a good job as a company in presenting a consistent image.

If all you have on LinkedIn is a personal profile, how will people find your company? They certainly won't find you when searching the company pages.

There are more than 57 million companies listed on this important B2B site. If you're not one of them, you are missing out not just on LinkedIn searchability and engagement, but also on Google search results, where your rankings will suffer.

The Tune-Up

While I certainly don't advocate becoming "Big Brother" and keeping close watch at all times over the profiles or people working at your company, I do believe it's important to create consistency across your employees' profiles.

LinkedIn is indeed a job search tool and employees will use it for that purpose. My philosophy: Focus on keeping your employees happy rather than preventing them from exploring other opportunities! I recommend that you create a culture of trust by working with your teams to create a consistent brand and to form community on LinkedIn. Build optimized profiles for company leadership, for all existing employees, and for all new employees, and continue to train your staff on LinkedIn best practices. I believe the benefits to your company will outweigh any risks.

In addition to building consistent management and staff profiles, you must have a company page.[187] To create one, click on your "Work" icon in the upper right navigation bar and select "Create a Company Page" from the drop-down menu.

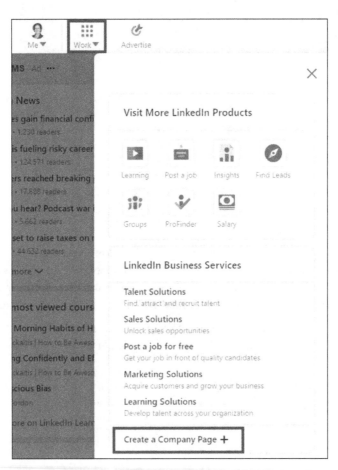

You will be brought to a screen that looks like this:

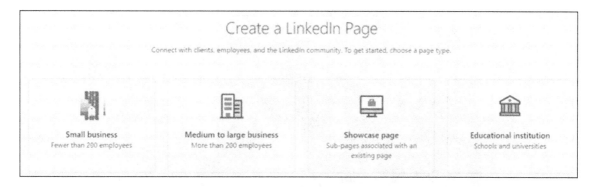

Add your company name, select your custom company profile URL, verify that you are the official rep for the company, and click "Create page." (You no longer need to have an email address at the company, but you do need to have a verified email address associated with a LinkedIn account.) LinkedIn provides some helpful tips to get you started:

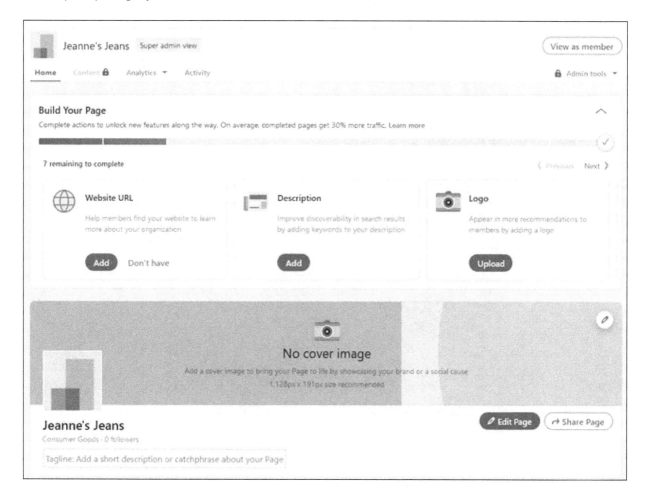

You'll also receive an email with tips to improve your page:

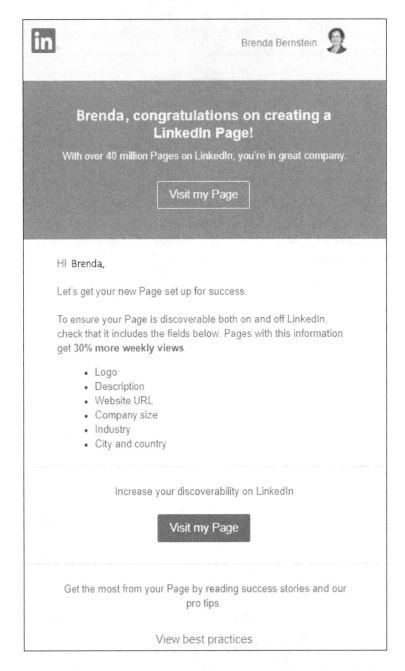

LinkedIn has made it possible to create a very attractive company profile, whether or not you purchase their premium service.

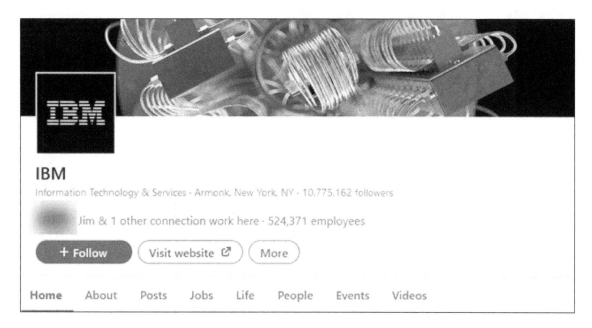

[You may notice that some company pages boast an animated logo. Sadly, this feature is no longer available, as LinkedIn has discontinued the ability to upload GIFs as company logos.]

Showcase Pages

You can promote specialized products or services with Showcase Pages (or Affiliated pages). For example:

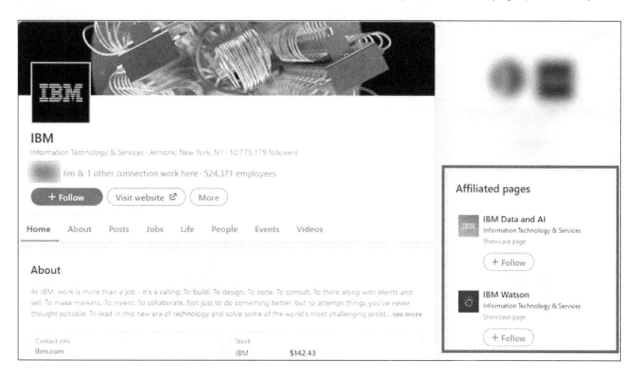

To create a Showcase page, first go to your Company Profile page by clicking on "Me" in the upper right of your menu bar and selecting your company:

From your Company page, click on the "Admin tools" drop-down and select "Create a Showcase Page."

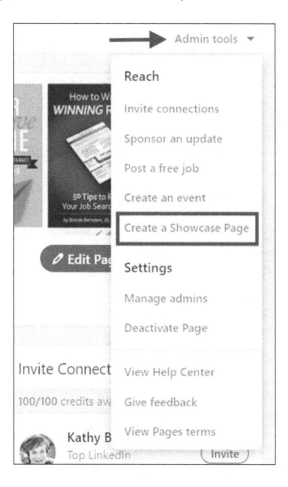

Optimize your page by including keywords in your product/service description. You have 200 characters to do so.

You can have up to 10 Company Showcase pages. Here's what you can do on those pages:

- **Post videos** and important updates regarding your featured product/service. Videos are a very effective marketing tool, and LinkedIn users will watch longer videos at 30 or 50 seconds and up!
- Identify a specific audience to whom you want to promote your product or service based on company size, job function, industry, seniority, and geography.
- Create specific videos tailored to your chosen audience.
- Pin an introductory post at the top of each page.

Interested viewers can follow your page and receive updates in their homepage feed. If you succeed in creating buzz around your offerings, you will be well on your way to being a LinkedIn company superstar! For more on Showcase Pages, see LinkedIn Help's, "LinkedIn Page Showcase Pages - Overview."[188]

Product Pages

If you're a business that sells B2B software, you're one of the lucky few who gets to test out LinkedIn's latest rollout: Product Pages. An extension of Business Pages, you'll be able to break out and feature 35 of your top products.

Products will be categorized for searchability. LinkedIn has already started creating a list of categories here.[189] Also, URLs will be customized with a hashtag based on the product's name. For instance, if your product is "B2B Software," your URL will end with #b2bsoftware.

Note that product pages are subject to review and must be approved by LinkedIn admins, which can take up to two weeks. Once approved and then officially published by you, it will then be accessible from the Products tab on your LinkedIn company page.

Once your company page is ready, invite your connections to follow!

Hashtags

There's an option to follow hashtags on your business page. Posts that include those hashtags will appear in your page's feed. To add hashtags, scroll down the right sidebar of your page and click the plus sign:

▶ **Be careful which hashtags you choose**, as you may end up curating a feed full of posts and solicitations from your competitors!

Weekly Invitation Limit to Crack Down on Spammers

LinkedIn, like any other social media platform, is vulnerable to spammers, especially when it comes to business solicitations. In an effort to cut down on spam sent from LinkedIn company pages, LinkedIn has set a limit of 100 invitations per week.

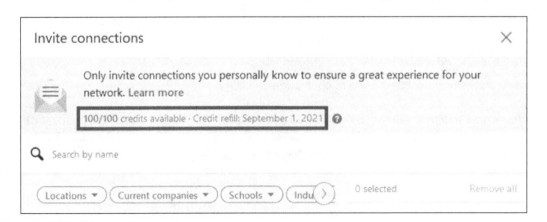

If you are a business, choose your invitations wisely. And if you are an individual member, this limit applies to you as well—so build your network slowly and consistently.

Staying Active with Your Company Page

You can post status updates for your company, just as you would for yourself, to keep your followers informed of all your latest news. Some things you might want to share include news/press about your company, job openings, and new products/services offered. Keep your posts short and include videos whenever possible. Use LinkedIn's tools to target different audiences and track metrics on your posts.

"Content Suggestions," available for Company pages with a following of 300 or more, is a curated list of trending content LinkedIn thinks you might like to comment on and/or share with your company page followers. For more about how to make the most of this feature, read LinkedIn Help's article, Use Content Suggestions on Your LinkedIn Page.[190]

Engaging in conversation with your company's followers is an essential part of a customer service strategy. Use the time and resources you have dedicated to LinkedIn activities to respond to comments or any interaction people have with your Company page.

> ▶ **Get employees involved!** The My Company page is a great place to invite employee activity on LinkedIn and to build workplace community. According to LinkedIn, "when an admin posts on their Page, 30% of the engagement comes from their employees, who are 14x more likely to share that content vs. other content types." It's free advertising!
>
> Want to learn more? Take a look at this resource from LinkedIn Talent Solutions[191] for turning employees into brand advocates.

Utilizing LinkedIn Polls

You can use LinkedIn polls to generate interest in your business, spur conversation, and garner feedback on topics that interest your followers. Consisting of one question and up to four answer choices, they can also serve as an important tool to gather intel on your customer base.

To learn more about polls and how to create one, see Mistake #13, Option #6.

LinkedIn Ads

As stated earlier, LinkedIn generates almost 3x the number of leads as other social media platforms—including Google Ads. To create an ad, first create a Campaign Manager account. LinkedIn will then walk you through the steps of setting up your first campaign.

To get started, click the Work tab and select "Advertise":

Associate your campaign with your LinkedIn page and start creating.

▶ **Post on your personal page**. Your followers will generally be more interested in what you have to say as an individual than as a company. Sharing business content via your personal account is more, well, personal, and creates a strong brand. Link back to your company page.

Tell Everyone You're Open for Business

Once you have a working Company page, be sure to connect it to your current position in your profile. Then create a Service page to tell everyone what services you offer right from your Introduction Card.

The "Providing services" module (formerly the "Open for Business" feature) was released to U.S. small business owners with Premium memberships in July of 2019 and then rolled out to all users as of early 2022. Once you're "open for business," members who search for connections with your area of expertise will see that you provide those services.

If the Providing services module has been activated for your account, you'll see a box under the top portion of your profile page asking you to showcase your services.

Click on "Get started":

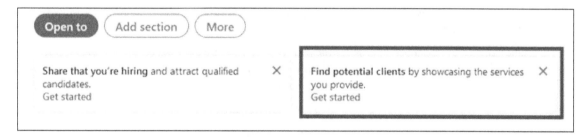

You'll then see this:

Click Continue to start selecting the services you offer. If you don't see the service you want right away, you can find it by typing it into the search field. If you choose a service that falls within the Accounting, Coaching and Mentoring, Design, or Marketing categories, members who use the "Find an Expert" feature on their mobile app will be able to find you.

After you've selected your services, add details about what you offer in the About section. Keywords likely play a role here, so make them count!

You can also specify your location and whether you'd like to receive business inquiries. Note that potential clients can contact you even if they're outside your network.

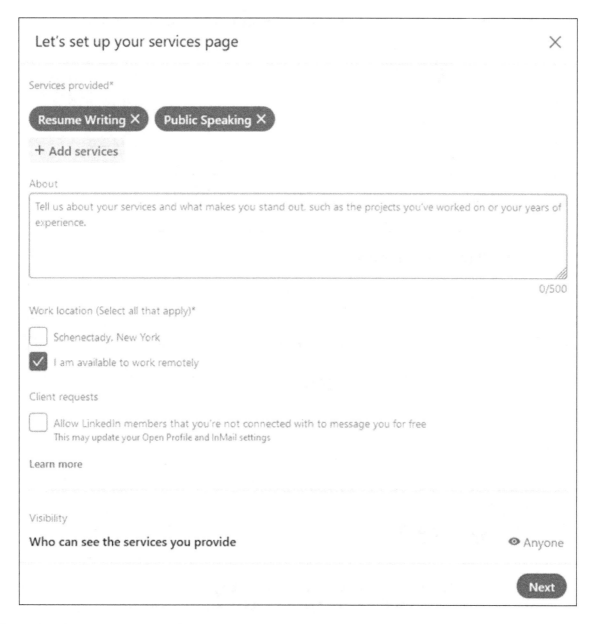

Currently, who can see your available services is set with the same limits as your profile visibility. As of March 2022, there is no way to change that.

When someone visits your profile, they see your services listed at the bottom of your Introduction Card.

Clicking on "See all details" reveals a message button.

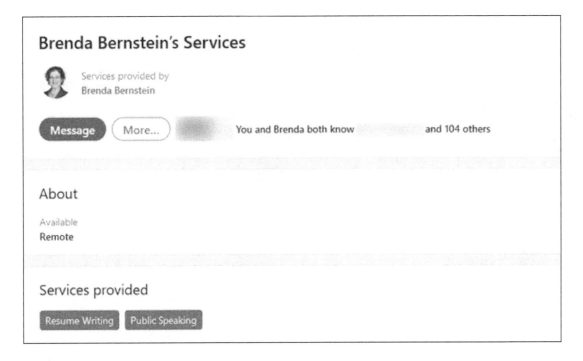

Clicking this message button will provide a suggested script to begin the conversation, though as always, I recommend personalizing this message if you're the one who's looking for services.

▶ The services feature replaces LinkedIn Profinder. As of February 2021, LinkedIn is no longer accepting new Profinder applications, although businesses who currently use Profinder can still work with clients via this feature.

You might see the message below if you try to join LinkedIn Profinder:

Applying to be a Professional on LinkedIn ProFinder
Important: We're temporarily not accepting new applications for ProFinder professionals. In the meantime, we recommend interested professionals to use Open for Business to showcase and provide services on LinkedIn as a great alternative.

LinkedIn members looking for professional services can find them by clicking the Work tab and selecting "Services Marketplace."

Services Reviews

If you use LinkedIn's "Providing services" feature, you can invite up to twenty clients to review your services. Click the "See all details" link to access this tool:

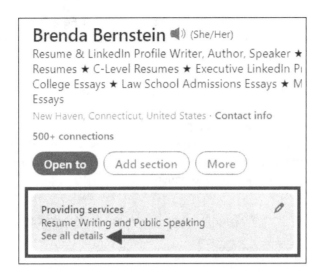

Click the "Invite to review" button to ask a happy client to complete a brief, 3-question survey. Note that your client will need to be a first-tier connection before you can invite them.

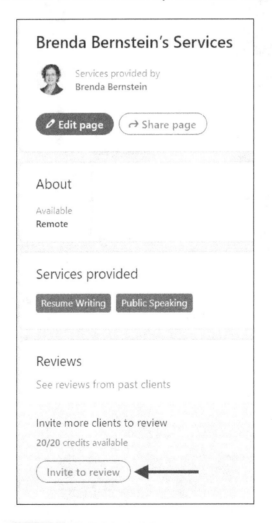

Decide for which of your services you'd like to receive the review(s), then select your connections.

► **You only have 20 invitations, so make them count!**

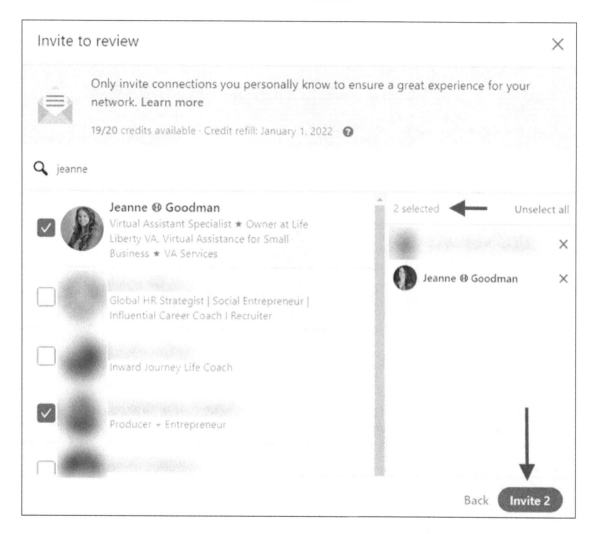

Questions your client will receive include:

1. Would you recommend [your name] as a service provider? (yes, no, I haven't worked with [your name])

2. How would you rate your project with [your name]? (1-5 stars on project satisfaction, knowledge, communication, and timeliness)

3. How was your project with [your name]? (clients are required to leave a response of at least 50 characters)

Your invite will then show up in your contact's Notifications.

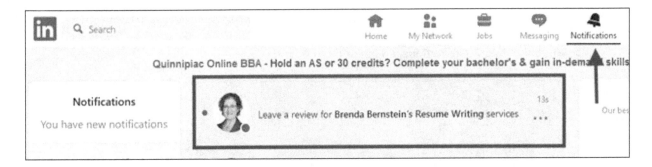

They will also receive an external email like this:

Your connection will not receive a message in their LinkedIn inbox. Since the message above is rather generic and can be easily overlooked, I recommend following up with a short message on LinkedIn and by email letting your client know you've sent them an invite.

Once your invitations are sent, view them from your services page by clicking on "Reviews status" in the left sidebar.

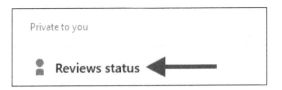

From here you can withdraw or message your invitees.

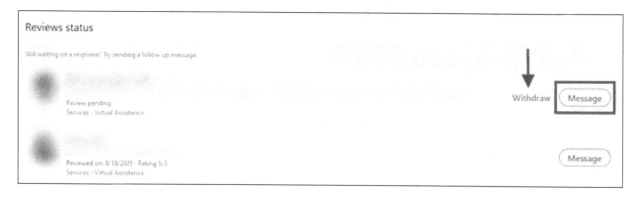

When you click the "Message" button, LinkedIn will provide you with some canned text. Take the time to personalize this message. Make sure to include the link provided—this will take your invitee directly to the survey and eliminate the need to dig through their sea of notifications to find your review request. This link looks like this:

https://www.linkedin.com/services/page/7684513078b314b008/review/create/ (your services page URL with "/review/create/" tacked on the end).

> ▶ **Services reviews differ from personal recommendations in that they are by invitation only.** And although the same link is provided to all reviewers, you can't just send it to anyone and everyone. It will only work for those you have officially invited.

If you haven't gotten a response from your reviewer and want to invite another person instead, you can withdraw the invitation[192] and use it for someone else. Note that once you have withdrawn an invite, you cannot send to that contact again for 30 days, so withdraw wisely.

You can also withdraw an invitation by visiting the member's profile and clicking the greyed-out button that says "pending."

This is what your review will look like when someone clicks the link to learn more about your services:

Services provided

Resume Writing   Public Speaking   Writing

Reviews

5.0 out of 5

★★★★★ (5 reviews)

ℹ How are ratings calculated? Learn more

Rating breakdown

Project satisfaction	5.0 ★	Knowledge	5.0 ★
Communication	5.0 ★	Timeliness	5.0 ★

Essye Miller · 2nd   · · ·
Former DoD Principal Deputy CIO; Fortune 100 Advisory Board Member; Cybersecurity;
Strategic Governance; Technology; Advanced Technology

Resume Writing

★★★★★ 5.0 · January 23, 2022

Brenda and team are great! She was attentive to my needs; made the process comfortable and delivered a
high quality product!

Dharti Arvind Desai · 2nd   · · ·
Global Business Architect, Marketing Strategist, Investor & Advisor | Senior Non-Profit Leader
| Multi-Hundred-Million-Dollar Revenue Generator | D&I Change Agent Enabling Daring
Women to Develop Transformative Companies

Resume Writing

★★★★★ 5.0 · January 23, 2022

Brenda has the pulse of this space. She is brilliant. I also had the pleasure of working with her colleague,
Julio Mesa, who is amazing too! Thank you.

Ted Izydor, MS, MBA, LPC, CSAC, ICS · 2nd   · · ·
Health Care Trainer / Mental Health & Addiction Counselor & Supervisor / Podcast Host

Resume Writing

★★★★★ 5.0 · January 22, 2022

It was great working with Brenda. She was prompt and took my resume to the next level!

This feature began rolling out in October 2021, so it might be a while before an overall rating is displayed.

If you prefer not to get reviews, you can also turn them off[193] entirely. But you risk being overlooked for another similar company with reviews.

Company Page Resources

You can change your company page settings from your main company page, share from the Content tab, see how your page is doing with Analytics, or review your latest activity from the Activity tab. For more information on setting up and leveraging company pages, see the LinkedIn Help article, LinkedIn Pages - FAQ.[194]

Marketing Insights

The LinkedIn Insights and Research[195] page, introduced in August 2019, is a feature within the Success Hub for Marketers.[196] With the data available through this tool, you can research your ideal audience and their behaviors to create a comprehensive marketing strategy. Read here[197] for more information on how you can use People, Industry, and Advertising Insights to ramp up your business.

Results to Expect

By optimizing your company's profile and the profiles of your employees, you will present a professional and savvy image on LinkedIn. The company will be searchable on LinkedIn not only in multiple ways: through your profile and the profiles of your employees, and also through Company Pages. This multiple exposure will boost your company in LinkedIn's search rankings *as well as on Google*.

Leveraging LinkedIn for company communications reaps great benefits. LinkedIn states that simply using InMail features for sales lead generation can "help senders achieve a 300% higher response rate than emails sent with the same content."

▶ **Good news:** LinkedIn currently has the 2nd highest lead conversion rate for B2B of any social media platform.[198]

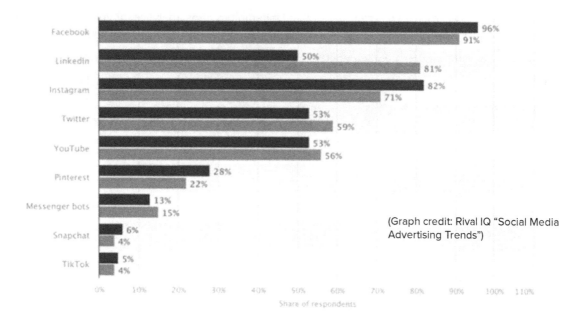

(Graph credit: Rival IQ "Social Media Advertising Trends")

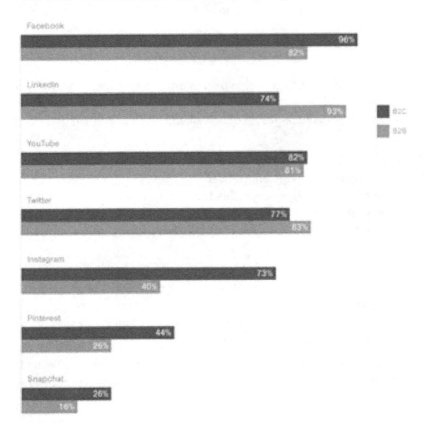

The Value of Social Media Platforms: B2C vs. B2B

Graph credit: MonsterInsights "40+ Conversion Rate Optimization Stats Show What You've Been Missing"[199]

For the metrics-minded, you'll be happy to know that LinkedIn provides analytics for your page's activities. To view them, go to your Analytics page as described above. You'll be able to review these metrics:

- Statistics on all the updates you've posted, including impressions (or reach) and percent engagement.

- Demographics and trends of your followers, including how you compare with similar companies.

- Visitor statistics and demographics.

Here's a sample:

Use these statistics to identify your target audience and measure what activity has generated the most views of your page. Then do more of what's working to build your audience and client base.

Learn more about LinkedIn Company page best practices here.[200]

APPENDIX A

LinkedIn Profile Completion Checklist

Use this checklist to assess and update your LinkedIn profile based on the tips in this book. You can also download and print this checklist here.[201]

_____ My profile uses highly searched keywords and an informative Headline.

_____ My photo is a professional, closely cropped headshot.

_____ I have a background image that reflects my brand/profession/industry/company.

_____ My contact information is complete, including my website URLs.

_____ I have a custom URL for my public profile (possibly with keywords included).

_____ I have at least 500 (preferably 1000) connections.

_____ My profile contains a compelling About section.

_____ My job duties and accomplishments are described in clear, concrete language.

_____ My profile is free of spelling, grammar, and punctuation errors.

_____ My profile is formatted consistently and attractively.

_____ I have completed the Skills section and chosen my top three.

_____ I have endorsements for my most essential skills.

_____ I have taken advantage of Special Sections to provide additional detail about my accomplishments.

_____ I have attached media items in my Featured and Experience Sections.

_____ I have optimized the Jobs function on LinkedIn (if you are a job seeker or employer).

_____ I have at least three (and preferably 10), well-written, current recommendations.

_____ I have given at least three well-written, current recommendations.

_____ I review my LinkedIn profile at least monthly and update it when needed.

_____ I have exported and saved a backup copy of my profile in .pdf format.

_____ If I own a business, I have created a Company page.

_____ I use my LinkedIn profile URL in my email signature and on my resume.

_____ If I am unemployed, my Headline and Experience sections contain appropriate information.

_____ If I am bilingual, I have created a Secondary Language Profile.

_____ I am in full compliance with LinkedIn's Terms of Service & Professional Community Policies.

Total Completed: _____

Notes:

_____

_____

APPENDIX B

Character Limits for your LinkedIn Profile Sections

When writing your LinkedIn profile sections, it is helpful to know the character limits you are working with! Here are some of the most important character limits to know that will help you plan your work and work your plan on LinkedIn:

The Basics

First name: 20 characters
Last name: 40 characters
Former/Maiden name: 50 characters
URL: 3-100 characters following "linkedin.com/in/"

Main Profile Sections

Professional Headline: 220 characters (entered on desktop or iOS; 120 on Android)
About: 2,600 characters
Company Name: 100 characters
Activities and Societies (in Education): 500 characters
Education Description: 1,000 characters
Education/Degree: 100 characters

Background Title (Work Experience, Education, Licenses & Certifications (255), Volunteer Experience): 100 characters
Background Description (Work Experience, Licenses & Certifications, Volunteer Experience): 2,000 characters
Skills: 80 characters each (up to 50 skills)
Accomplishments Title (Publications, Patents, Courses, Projects, Honors & Awards, Test Scores, Languages, Organizations): 255 characters
Accomplishments Description (Publications, Patents, Courses, Projects, Honors & Awards, Test Scores, Languages, Organizations): 2,000 characters
Recommendations: 3,000 characters

Contact & Personal Information

Website Anchor Text: 30 characters
Website URL: 256 characters
Address: 1,000 characters (visible only 1st degree connections)
Phone: 25 characters
Personal Info-Instant messenger: 25 characters

Activity and Publishing

Activity update: 3000 characters (only 140 will transfer to Twitter)
Publisher Post Headline: 150 characters
Publisher Post Content: 120,000 characters

Connections & Invitations

Number of direct, first-level connections: 30,000

Company Pages

Section	Field	Character Limit
Page Tab	Company Update Text	3000
Page Tab	Company Name	100
Page Tab	About Us	2000
Career Pages - Life Tab	Page Name	50
Career Pages - Life Tab	Company Leaders Headline	150
Career Pages - Life Tab	Company Leaders Description	150
Career Pages - Life Tab	Employee Testimonials	400
Career Pages - Life Tab	Custom Module Title	150
Career Pages - Life Tab	Custom Module Body	500
Career Pages - Life Tab	Custom Module URL Label	70

Groups

Group Discussion Title: 200 characters
Group Discussion Body: 1,300 characters
Group Discussion Comments: 1,250 characters
Profile 'Publication' Title: 255 characters
Profile 'Publication' Description: 2,000 characters
Maximum number of groups: 100
Maximum number of pending groups: 20
Maximum groups managed by one individual: 30
Number of mentions you can use in one group conversation: 20
Number of owners a group can have: 1
Number of managers a group can have: 20
Maximum number of members in each group: 2,000,000

For more group-related limits, read General Limits for LinkedIn Groups.[202]

APPENDIX C

LinkedIn Image Dimensions

All LinkedIn images can be uploaded in PNG, JPEG/JPG or GIF formats.

Profile Photo

The maximum size of a LinkedIn profile photo is 8MB.

Background Photo

Maximum size is 8MB. Recommended pixel dimensions are 1584 x 396px.

Company & Career Pages

The following chart is borrowed from LinkedIn Help:

Tab	Module	Minimum Image Size	Recommended Image Size
Page Tab	Logo Image	300 (w) x 300 (h) pixels	300 (w) x 300 (h) pixels
Page Tab	Overview Tab Image	360 (w) x 120 (h) pixels	360 (w) x 120 (h) pixels
Page Tab	Cover Image	1192 (w) x 220 (h) pixels	1536 (w) x 768 (h) pixels
Life Tab	Hero Image	1128 (w) x 376 (h) pixels	1128 (w) x 376 (h) pixels
Life Tab	Custom Modules	502 (w) x 282 (h) pixels	502 (w) x 282 (h) pixels
Life Tab	Company Photos	264 (w) x 176 (h) pixels	900 (w) x 600 (h) pixels

Note that Career Pages are a paid feature.

APPENDIX D

Overused Buzzwords

LinkedIn's Overused Buzzwords

LinkedIn used to create an annual list of the top 10 buzzwords found in LinkedIn. While the lists are no longer being published, you still might want to avoid some of these overused terms. Read my articles on LinkedIn's buzzwords from 2010 through 2018.[203]

In all the years LinkedIn listed these buzzwords, only 30 total words have ever shown up. Indeed, less than three dozen words have dominated LinkedIn profiles for almost a decade.

Want to see all of the lists side-by-side? I did!

LinkedIn Buzzwords from 2010 to 2018

	2010	2011	2012	2013	2014
1	Extensive experience	Creative	Creative	Responsible	Motivated
2	Innovative	Organizational	Organizational	Strategic	Passionate
3	Motivated	Effective	Effective	Creative	Creative
4	Results-oriented	Extensive experience	Motivated	Effective	Driven
5	Dynamic	Track Record	Extensive experience	Patient	Extensive experience
6	Proven track record	Motivated	Track Record	Expert	Responsible
7	Team player	Innovative	Innovative	Organizational	Strategic
8	Fast-paced	Problem solving	Responsible	Driven	Track Record
9	Problem solver	Communication skills	Analytical	Innovative	Organizational
10	Entrepreneurial	Dynamic	Problem solving	Analytical	Expert

	2015	2016	2017	2018
1	Strategic	Specialized	Specialize	Specialized
2	Organizational	Leadership	Experienced	Experienced
3	Motivated	Passionate	Skilled	Leadership
4	Driven	Strategic	Leadership	Skilled
5	Passionate	Experienced	Passionate	Passionate
6	Track Record	Focused	Expert	Expert
7	Responsible	Expert	Motivated	Motivated
8	Extensive experience	Certified	Creative	Creative
9	Dynamic	Creative	Strategic	Strategic
10	Creative	Excellent	Focused	Successful

The Only 30 LinkedIn Buzzwords Ever Published

Here are the 30 words that have appeared in LinkedIn's Buzzwords article over the years, ranked by the number of times they've appeared.

Rank	All Buzzwords Since 2010	How Many Times They Appeared in the Top 10
1	Creative	8
2	Motivated	7
3	Strategic	6
4	Expert	5
5	Extensive experience	5
6	Organizational	5
7	Passionate	5
8	Innovative	4
9	Responsible	4
10	Track Record	4
11	Driven	3
12	Dynamic	3
13	Effective	3
14	Experienced	3
15	Leadership	3
16	Problem solver/Solving	3
17	Specialize/Specialized	3
18	Analytical	2
19	Focused	2
20	Skilled	2
21	Certified	1
22	Communication skills	1
23	Entrepreneurial	1
24	Excellent	1
25	Fast-paced	1
26	Patient	1
27	Proven track record	1
28	Results-oriented	1
29	Successful	1
30	Team player	1

Seven of the same words have been on the list for the last three years consecutively.

These 7 have been on the lists the last 3 years in a row.	Specialized
	Experienced
	Leadership
	Passionate
	Expert
	Creative
	Strategic

What Should You Make of the Top 10 LinkedIn Buzzwords?

While there's an idea out there that we should avoid these "overused" words, at some point we need to accept that some of the Top 10 LinkedIn Buzzwords have longevity for good reason. They are important and might not be going away.

Stop and think before you publish a profile full of buzzwords—but don't avoid using them completely either! For more guidance, see my past articles.

APPENDIX E

LinkedIn For Students

Calling all 46 million student members: Did you know that LinkedIn has resources tailored just for you?

LinkedIn Higher Education[204] is filled with videos and tips on the most effective ways to use LinkedIn, from building your personal brand to getting an internship.

- Available videos cover a variety of topics to get you started with networking, discovering your career passion, and prepping for interviews.[205] You'll also find checklists and tip sheets for building your student profile and utilizing LinkedIn's Alumni tools.

- The Student Job Hunting Handbook Series[206] provides tips for optimizing your LinkedIn® profile, approaching the college job hunt, and applying for internships and entry-level positions.

- LinkedIn Student Careers[207] is LinkedIn's search engine for internship positions and jobs for recent graduates. Search by industry for a list of positions that may interest you.

- LinkedIn for Students Articles[208] contains a collection of articles written by LinkedIn's top writers related to college and career. While they stop at 2019, the content is still completely relevant!

Add to Profile

LinkedIn's Add to Profile[209] feature will make adding your degrees and certification to your LinkedIn Profile a breeze. Released to colleges and universities in March 2015, "educational institutions can embed a simple link on their websites and in emails sent directly to graduates. When graduates click the "Add to Profile" button, they'll have the option to add that achievement directly to the "Education" section of their LinkedIn profile by previewing it and hitting Save."

For more information on this feature read the LinkedIn Blog article, LinkedIn Opens Up Profiles to Higher Education Partners with One-Click Program.[210]

APPENDIX F

Information on Paid Accounts

A survey by Statista[211] found that 79% of LinkedIn users use the free account; only 39% of those surveyed paid to use LinkedIn.

While a large proportion of paid subscribers are recruiters, many others who value the paid features of LinkedIn are signing up for premium accounts. If you want to promote your services on LinkedIn, you'll need a premium account. Or, if the ability to send InMail, view more information about who viewed your profile, and organize your contacts is worth a bit extra, you might want to upgrade.

LinkedIn frequently offers free month-long trials, which you can take advantage of before paying for features you're not sure you'll need.

For more information, go to these links:

LinkedIn® Free[212]

LinkedIn® Premium[213]

LinkedIn® Marketing Solutions[214]

LinkedIn® Talent Solutions[215]

LinkedIn® Sales Navigator[216]

LinkedIn® Recruiter Lite[217]

APPENDIX G

Get Free E-Book Updates

Kindle Version

Amazon provides published updates as follows:

1. Major Updates

If Amazon considers an e-book update to be "critical," they will send a notification email to all customers who purchased the e-book. You will be able to opt in to receive the update through the Manage Your Content and Devices[218] page on Amazon.com.

Whenever there is a "major" change to a book, Amazon will update it for free. Just make sure your "Automatic Book Update" is turned on. Here's how:

- Log in to your Amazon account and go to Your Content and Devices page. You can also access this by selecting it from the "Accounts & Lists" drop-down menu and clicking on "Your devices and content" then on "Manage digital content."

- Go to the Preferences tab, scroll down to "Automatic Book Updates" and make sure the switch is set to ON.

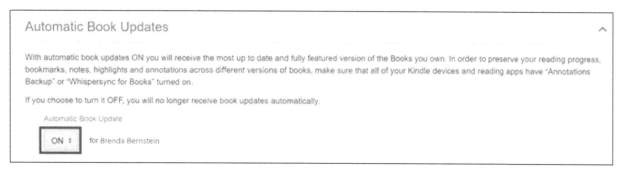

- You should then receive a notification whenever an updated version of the book is available, which you will be able to access via your Manage Your Content and Devices page.

If you do not receive a notice, it's possible you missed it; simply log in to your Manage Your Content and Devices page and check to see if the new version is there. If it isn't, you may want to contact Amazon directly to find out why.

When a new edition of *How to Write a KILLER LinkedIn Profile* is available, you'll see "Update Available" next to the title.

Click on "Manage digital content" and scroll down to your copy of *How to Write a KILLER LinkedIn Profile*.

You should see the following:

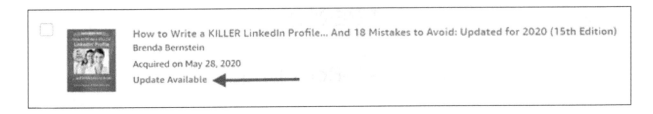

Click the link and read the notice, then hit Update. The new version will be delivered to your device.

2. Minor Updates

If changes to the content are considered minor by Amazon, customers will not be notified by email; however, Amazon will still activate your ability to update the content through the Manage Your Content and Devices on Amazon.com.

If you would like to be alerted by The Essay Expert when there are future revisions to the Kindle edition, you can **sign up at https://theessayexpert.com/amazon-e-book-update-notifications/**

APPENDIX H

Settings & Privacy

ACCESSING YOUR SETTINGS AND PRIVACY

I've referred to many privacy settings throughout this book, and since many people are not aware of many of the settings, or have questions about where to find them, it's worth devoting a section to this important topic. You have control over many aspects of your LinkedIn profile you might not even know about! It's all in the Settings & Privacy portal.

To access Settings & Privacy, click on your profile image thumbnail in the upper right of your account and select "Settings & Privacy" from the drop-down menu. Once there, a whole world of options will open up to you! Here's a breakdown of the most important things you can do to take control over what's visible and accessible in your LinkedIn profile. It's not a complete list—because that would be a **very** long list—but I think you'll find a lot of goodies here.

ACCOUNT PREFERENCES

Profile information

- **Name, location, and industry:** Choose how your name and profile fields appear to other members

Site preferences

- **Language:** Select the language you use on LinkedIn
- **Content language:** Select a language for translation
- **Autoplay videos:** Choose to autoplay videos on LinkedIn
- **Showing profile photos:** Choose to show or hide profile photos of other members
- **Feed preferences:** Customize your feed
- **People also viewed:** Choose if this feature appears on your profile
- **People you unfollowed:** See who you have unfollowed or muted and resume following if you'd like

Syncing options

- **Sync calendar:** Manage or sync calendar to get timely updates about who you'll be meeting with
- **Sync contacts:** Manage or sync contacts to connect with people you know directly from your address book

Subscriptions & payments

- **Premium Subscription:** See your billing information and cancel Premium
- **View purchase history:** See your previous purchases and transactions on LinkedIn

Partners & services

- **Microsoft:** View Microsoft accounts you've connected to your LinkedIn account
- **Twitter:** Manage your Twitter info on your LinkedIn account

Account management

- **Merge accounts:** Transfer connections from a duplicate account, then close it
- **Hibernate account:** Temporarily deactivate your account
- **Close account:** Learn about your options, and close your account if you wish

SIGN IN & SECURITY

Account access

- **Email addresses:** Add or remove email addresses on your account
- **Phone numbers:** Add a phone number in case you have trouble signing in
- **Change password:** Choose a unique password to protect your account
- **Where you're signed in:** See your active sessions, and sign out if you'd like
- **Devices that remember your password:** Review and control the devices that remember your password
- **Two-step verification:** Activate this feature for enhanced account security

VISIBILITY

Visibility of your profile & network

- **Profile viewing options:** Choose whether you're visible or viewing in private mode
- **Story viewing options:** Choose whether you're visible or viewing in private mode
- **Edit your public profile:** Choose how your profile appears to non-logged-in members via search
- **Who can see or download your email address:** Choose who can see your email address on your profile or in approved apps or download it in their data export
- **Who can see your connections:** Choose who can see your list of connections
- **Who can see your last name:** Choose how you want your name to appear
- **Representing your organization and interests:** Show your name and/or profile information with other content shown on LinkedIn
- **Profile visibility off LinkedIn:** Choose how your profile appears via partners' and other permitted services
- **Profile discovery using email address:** Choose who can discover your profile if they haven't connected with you, but have your email address
- **Profile discovery using phone number:** Choose who can discover your profile if they haven't connected with you, but have your phone number
- **Blocking:** See your list and make changes if you'd like

Visibility of your LinkedIn activity

- **Manage active status:** Choose who can see when you are on LinkedIn
- **Share profile updates with your network:** Choose if your network is notified about key updates from your profile

- **Notify connections when you're in the news:** Choose if your network is notified when you've been mentioned in an article or blog post
- **Mentions or Tags:** Choose whether other members can mention or tag you
- **Followers:** Choose who can follow you and see your public updates

COMMUNICATIONS

How you get your notifications

- **On LinkedIn:** Received via LinkedIn web and app
- **Email:** Received via your primary email
- **Push:** Pops up on your device

Who can reach you

- **Invitations to connect:** Choose who can connect with you
- **Invitations from your network:** Choose what invitations you'd like to receive from your network
- **Messages:** Allow select people to message you
- **Research invites:** Choose if you want to get invites from LinkedIn to participate in research

Messaging experience

- **Read receipts and typing indicators:** Turn on read receipts and typing indicators
- **Reply suggestions:** Turn on recommended replies when messaging

DATA PRIVACY

How LinkedIn uses your data

- **Manage your data and activity:** Review the data that you've provided, and make changes if you'd like
- **Get a copy of your data:** See your options for accessing a copy of your account data, connections, and more
- **Salary data on LinkedIn:** See and delete your salary data
- **Search history:** Clear all previous searches performed on LinkedIn
- **Personal demographic information:** Choose what details you provide about your personal demographics
- **Social, economic, and workplace research:** Choose whether we can make some of your data available for policy and academic research

Job seeking preferences

- **Job application settings:** Choose what information LinkedIn saves when you submit a job application
- **Sharing your profile when you click Apply:** Choose if you want to share your full profile with the job poster when you're taken off LinkedIn after clicking Apply
- **Commute preferences:** Set commute times and get job recommendations based on your preferences
- **Signal your interest to recruiters at companies you've created job alerts for:** This will be applied for companies that you've created job alerts for
- **Stored job applicant accounts:** Match which third-party job applicant accounts are stored on LinkedIn

Other applications

- **Permitted services:** View services you've authorized and manage data sharingChange7 connected apps
- **Microsoft Word:** Choose whether work experience from your profile can be shown in Resume Assistant within Microsoft Word

ADVERTISING DATA

Advertising preferences

- **Profile data for personalizing ads:** Choose how ads appear to you
- **Interest categories:** See more relevant ads, such as job ads, based on your and similar members' activities on LinkedIn and Bing

Data collected on LinkedIn

- **Connections:** Choose whether your connections can be used to show you relevant ads
- **Location:** Choose whether your location can be used to show you relevant ads
- **Demographics:** Choose whether your age or gender can be used to show you relevant ads
- **Companies you follow:** See more relevant ads, such as job ads, based on companies you follow
- **Groups:** Choose whether the groups you've joined can be used to show you relevant ads
- **Education:** See more relevant ads, such as job ads, based on your education
- **Job information:** See more relevant ads, such as job ads, based on your job information
- **Employer:** See more relevant ads, such as job ads, based on your company information

Third-party data

- **Audience insights for websites you visit:** Choose if your data can be used anonymously by third party websites you visit to help them better understand their audiences
- **Ads outside of LinkedIn:** Choose if you want to see relevant ads on websites and apps outside of LinkedIn
- **Interactions with businesses:** Choose how your information given to businesses is used to show you relevant ads
- **Ad-related actions:** Choose if your actions on ads can be used to understand and report aggregate ad performance

I hope at least a few of the above items were good news for you and that you feel more confident in the control you have over your LinkedIn profile.

APPENDIX I

Recommended Resources

Need LinkedIn Technical Help?

From time to time, you might encounter technical questions about how LinkedIn works, or LinkedIn might change something unexpectedly. For those sticky situations, I recommend contacting LinkedIn Help[219] or submitting a support ticket.[220]

There is also a public forum for LinkedIn-related help topics.[221] Although it's not currently active, you can still search for discussions to find answers to your questions.

Are You a Job Seeker?

LinkedIn has still not eliminated the need for a static resume! To that end, I've written 2 resume do-it-yourself books. These easy-to-read, practical and up-to-date guides will take you through the resume writing process step by step, from thinking through your approach to creating a great format, crafting effective branding statements and bullets, and handling specific challenges.

Available on Amazon:

How to Write a WINNING Resume . . . 50 Tips to Reach Your Job Search Target[222]

Kindle: $6.97 US

"Brenda's book provides the serious kick a jobseeker needs to get motivated and keep moving. The book includes lots of resources - so many, in fact, that I stopped reading on my Kindle and moved to my PC reader so that I could get a better look at all the material provided."
– JoAnne Goldberg, Stanford MBA

"Bernstein's guide was incredibly useful in helping me to understand how I could deviate from the white-bread chronological resume to best highlight and illustrate the skills I had developed in that time that would be of interest to an employer. The end result is that I actually got the first job for which I applied, one that many people may have considered a bit of a reach for an individual returning to a career path from which he deviated nearly a decade ago."
– Ryan G., Madison, WI

"I was struggling to update my resume after letting it go stale for a few years before I contacted Brenda. Within a few weeks of updating it as well as my LinkedIn profile, I was contacted for an interview."
– J. Jung, Senior Systems Analyst, Irvine, CA

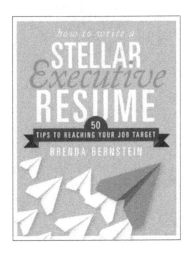

How to Write a STELLAR Executive Resume . . . 50 Tips to Reach Your Job Search Target[223]

Kindle: $8.01 US
Print: $12.23 US

"If you put Brenda's easy-to-follow tips and guidelines into action, you will, without a doubt, set your resume apart from the competition. Brenda's 'can do' suggestions are sure to kick both the substance and format of your résumé up a notch, or two, or ten!"

– Posey Salem, Professional Resume Writer and Certified Instructional Systems Designer, Jacksonville, NC

"Brenda offers tips galore, covers new technology, and includes links to more resources! I will be strongly suggesting that my own Executive level clients consider adding this amazing resource to their library. Well done!"

– Stephanie Clark, Master Resume Writer and Master Certified Resume Strategist, Canada

Go to my website to get free excerpts[224] of both of these books!

Just having a great resume and LinkedIn profile is not enough. You need to know how to use them! To that end, I've partnered with Mary Elizabeth Bradford to offer a trusted and award-winning resource, The Job Search Success System.[225]

Save yourself the cost of a job search coach with this proven 10-step system!

Free Webinar and Podcast Recordings

I've hosted multiple webinars and made guest appearances on several radio shows on the topic of LinkedIn, job search, resume writing and more. See The Essay Expert's Webinars & Podcasts page[226] for recordings and here for upcoming events.[227]

APPENDIX J

Important Opportunities to Give and Receive

Get Free Updates Until the Next Big Release

LinkedIn is constantly changing, and I will be issuing small revisions to this book throughout the year until the release of my new product.

- **For PDF version owners:** You will automatically receive the latest revisions to *How to Write a KILLER LinkedIn Profile* when they become available.

- **For Kindle version owners:** Amazon only notifies book owners that an updated version is available when they consider the changes to be "significant." Sign up at http://theessayexpert.com/amazon-e-book-update-notifications/ and we'll be happy to give you a heads up if a new Kindle edition becomes available.

Here's the easiest way to get PDF updates hassle-free: Just email us at TEESupport@TheEssayExpert.com with a copy of your receipt and we'll be happy to add you to our list to get all future KILLER updates automatically!

Want to see the answer to your LinkedIn question featured in the next edition of this book?

If you have a question regarding LinkedIn that you would like to see covered in the next edition, please email TEESupport@TheEssayExpert.com with your suggestion. The answer to your question might be featured in the next edition of *How to Write a KILLER LinkedIn Profile*.

We Want Your Feedback!

We hope you've enjoyed *How to Write a KILLER LinkedIn Profile*! Did you find this book helpful? Please share a review on Amazon and let others know about the value you received.

Post a Review[228]

Check Out Our Services

If you are still stuck on how to write your LinkedIn profile or your resume, consider The Essay Expert's LinkedIn or Resume Writing services. Contact us at TEESupport@TheEssayExpert.com or through our web form at https://theessayexpert.com/contact/, or call/text us at 718-390-6696. We look forward to working with you.

Book purchasers receive special discounts on LinkedIn services from The Essay Expert. **See Appendix K for coupon codes** you can use right now.

Contact Us at theessayexpert.com/contact

Get on My Lists

Want news and updates from The Essay Expert? Sign up for my Blog. You will receive a free e-book preview that you can give to a friend!

Subscribe to our **Blog** at theessayexpert.com/subscribe-2-the-weekly-blog

Connect with The Essay Expert on Facebook

"Like" our Facebook Fan page now to connect with other readers and additional resources . . ..

KILLER LinkedIn Profile Facebook Fan Page
facebook.com/linkedinprofiletips

And of course, please connect with me on LinkedIn!

Linked**in**

Brenda Bernstein

Resume & LinkedIn Profile Writer, Author, Speaker ★ Executive Resumes ★ C-Level Resumes ★ Executive LinkedIn Profiles ★ College Essays ★ Law School Admissions Essays ★ MBA Admissions Essays
The Essay Expert LLC

View LinkedIn profile

APPENDIX K

Discounted LinkedIn Services from The Essay Expert

If you're still struggling with what to write about yourself, it's time to stop!

You might wish to work with The Essay Expert directly. If so, we have discounts available for you on our LinkedIn packages. To take advantage of these offers, go to our LinkedIn Profile Services page,[229] order one of the following packages, and enter the coupon code.

Feel free to start with this amazing offer:

$100 LinkedIn Profile Review Special[230]

We'll begin with a questionnaire to help us get a better idea of your goals, target audience and professional background. Then Brenda will personally read through your profile to get a sense of what could be improved. She will follow up with a 15-minute phone conversation to answer your questions and advise you on the best direction for your LinkedIn profile! And if you decide to purchase a full package after that, you'll get $100 toward your purchase. It's a WIN-WIN!

Or, save yourself time and hassle with our full-service LinkedIn packages, using these codes (note: these discounts may not be combined with other offers):

KILLER300 ($300 Discount)
- Senior Executive Resume + LinkedIn Profile Success Package[231]

KILLER250 ($250 Discount)
- Senior Executive Resume + LinkedIn Headline & Summary/About[232]
- Executive Resume + LinkedIn Profile Success Package[233]

KILLER200 ($200 Discount)
- Executive Resume + LinkedIn Headline & Summary/About[234]

KILLER175 ($175 Discount)
- Senior Executive LinkedIn Profile Complete[235]
- Mid-Level Resume + LinkedIn Profile Success Package[236]

KILLER150 ($150 Discount)
- Executive LinkedIn Profile Complete[237]
- Senior Executive LinkedIn Headline & Summary/About[238]
- Mid-Level Resume + LinkedIn Headline & Summary/About[239]

KILLER100 ($100 Discount)
- Mid-Level LinkedIn Profile Complete[240]

KILLER75 ($75 Discount)
- Mid-Level LinkedIn Headline & Summary/About[241]

Here's what people are saying about The Essay Expert's LinkedIn Services:

"Good news! I was offered a job with better pay and benefits using the resume I created with the suggestions you gave me. I start my new job in two weeks!"

— **Yuna Kim**, Operations Coordinator, Rhenus Logistics, New York, NY

"I saw an immediate and dramatic improvement in the quantity and the quality of inquiries and invitations to interview after re-launching my LI profile, and I accepted an offer as VP of Global Marketing after just 2 months. Worth every dime."

— **S.I.**, Chief Marketing Officer, Chicago, IL

"The proof is in the pudding, and I am thrilled that my keyword search hits on LinkedIn have sky rocketed. I have also sent my resume to several contacts and have had a positive response thus far. If you want an executive resume service who does what they say they will do, and does it well, The Essay Expert is your clear choice."

— **Jim M.**, C-Level Technology Executive, Sioux Falls, SD

"I was able to switch from an agency leadership to a brand-side leadership role. Not an easy task. I credit much of it to the guidance I received in her books."

— **Teresa Caro**

"My goals, my values, and my revamped resume and LinkedIn profile were all in sync for the first time in my 20-year career. This led directly to an interview (and offer) for a position as Accessibility Services Team Lead at a highly respected consulting company. The Essay Expert was there with me, doing what they do best, so I was free to concentrate on what I do best."

— **Mitchell Evan**, Digital Accessibility Strategist, Berlin, Germany

"I can honestly say that it was the best career investment I ever made! Since that time, I am consistently being contacted by talent recruiters who have found me from my LinkedIn profile."

— **Bill Cooley**, Global Sourcing & Supply Chain Executive, Weston, MA

"As a result of my LinkedIn profile changes, I have had 17 requests made of me to meet with various potential clients and partners!"

— **Aaron W.**, Business Consultant, Madison, WI

"[Brenda] provided thorough feedback on my LinkedIn profile, immediately increasing exposure, and leading to one new interview offer per week since that time. Amazing . . . truly amazing!!"

— **Brian Hobbs**, Asia/Middle East Security Specialist, Washington, DC

Thank you! Here's to your success as you craft a KILLER LinkedIn Profile!

NOTES

There are 200+ hyperlinks (URLs) contained within this book. Because links continually change, we've created a web page with a current list of links. You can also go here to report any broken links and sign up to receive updates. Simply point your favorite web browser to this URL:

https://theessayexpert.com/killer-linkedin-resource-links/

Or scan this QR Code:

1   https://www.linkedin.com/in/jeannehgoodman/

2   https://www.linkedin.com/in/scottbecher/

3   https://www.linkedin.com/in/50interviews/

4   https://www.amazon.com/Write-KILLER-LinkedIn-Profile-Mistakes-ebook/dp/B019ELXR8W

5   https://theessayexpert.com/how-to-write-a-winning-resume/

6   https://theessayexpert.com/write-stellar-executive-resume/

7   http://www.theessayexpert.com/

8   http://www.theexecutiveexpert.com/

9   http://www.killerlinkedinprofile.com/

10   http://www.linkedin.com/in/brendabernstein

11   http://www.facebook.com/TheEssayExpert

12   https://www.linkedin.com/company/linkedin/about/

13   https://business.linkedin.com/talent-solutions

14   https://blog.hootsuite.com/linkedin-statistics-business/

15   https://money.usnews.com/money/blogs/outside-voices-careers/articles/2017-05-05/how-headhunters-use-linkedin-to-find-talented-candidates

16   https://www.statista.com/chart/17535/linkedin-profile-boosts-job-chances/

17   https://www.linkedin.com/legal/user-agreement

18   https://university.linkedin.com/

19   http://blog.linkedin.com/2014/02/21/high-school-students-embrace-your-skills-show-your-profession-al-side-and-create-a-linkedin-profile/?utm_source=feedburner&utm_medium=email&utm_campaign=-Feed%3A+typepad%2Flinkedinblog+%28LinkedIn+Blog%29

20   https://www.cnbc.com/2017/12/27/7-linkedin-hacks-to-boost-your-chances-of-getting-a-new-job-in-2018.html

21   http://blog.linkedin.com/

22   https://blog.linkedin.com/2014/04/09/finding-my-way-home-on-linkedin

23   http://blog.linkedin.com/2014/03/04/my-secret-career-weapon-linkedin/?utm_source=feedburn-er&utm_medium=email&utm_campaign=Feed%3A+typepad%2Flinkedinblog+%28LinkedIn+Blog%29

24   https://news.linkedin.com/about-us#Statistics

25   http://en.wikipedia.org/wiki/LinkedIn

26   https://www.omnicoreagency.com/linkedin-statistics/

27   http://www.visiospark.com/

28   https://www.linkedin.com/help/linkedin/answer/38594/changing-the-location-on-your-profile

29   https://www.linkedin.com/help/linkedin/answer/4447

30   https://www.linkedin.com/pulse/job-search-notes-relevance-searcher-determines-how-found-love-lace/

31   https://www.linkedin.com/me/profile-views/urn:li:wvmp:summary/

32   https://www.linkedin.com/feed/followers/

33   http://help.linkedin.com/app/answers/detail/a_id/6545

34   http://mashable.com/2012/08/02/higher-google-search-results/

35   https://theessayexpert.com/contact/

36   https://theessayexpert.com/linkedin-profiles/

37   https://blog.linkedin.com/2016/05/25/get-comfortable-with-being-uncomfortable-why-now-is-the-time-to

38   https://www.theladders.com/static/images/basicSite/pdfs/TheLadders-EyeTracking-StudyC2.pdf

39   https://pfpmaker.com/

40   https://blog.linkedin.com/2017/march/14/linkedin-profile-photo-tips-introducing-photo-filters-and-edit-ing

41   https://www.canva.com/

42   https://www.canva.com/templates/search/linkedin-banners/

43   http://www.fotor.com/

44   https://www.fotor.com/templates/linkedin-background

45   https://spark.adobe.com/sp/design/post/new

46   http://freelinkedinbackgrounds.com/

47   https://dashboard.visme.co/v2/create/socialmedia

48   https://visme.co/blog/canva-alternative-visme/

49   http://www.getpaint.net/

50   https://www.gimp.org/

51   http://apps.pixlr.com/editor/

52   https://unsplash.com/

53   https://pixabay.com/

54   https://www.pexels.com/search/free/

55   https://www.freepik.com/

56   https://www.linkedin.com/help/linkedin/topics/6042/6059/profile-photo

57   https://blog.linkedin.com/2017/february/17/-tips-for-building-a-great-linkedin-profile-career-expert

58   https://blog.linkedin.com/2018/august/6/make-your-experience-stand-out-with-the-new-linkedin-experience-

59   https://www.techrepublic.com/article/dont-fall-for-linkedin-phishing-how-to-watch-for-this-credential-stealing-attack/

60   https://www.egress.com/resources/cybersecurity-information/phishing/linkedin-phishing-attacks

61   https://www.linkedin.com/help/linkedin/answer/75814

62   https://www.linkedin.com/mynetwork/invitation-manager/sent/

63   https://blog.linkedin.com/2017/august/8/tuesday-tip-get-your-foot-in-the-door-with-the-alumni-tool

64   https://www.job-hunt.org/employer_alumni_networking.shtml

65   https://blog.linkedin.com/2019/september/12/tap-your-linkedin-network-to-fill-your-project-needs

66   https://www.truconversion.com/blog/social-media/how-to-create-a-perfect-linkedin-profile/

67   https://www.linkedin.com/me/search-appearances/

68   https://www.linkedin.com/help/linkedin/answer/52950/commercial-use-limit?lang=en

69   http://help.linkedin.com/app/answers/detail/a_id/1239

70   https://images.google.com/

71   https://www.linkedin.com/help/linkedin/answer/98196

72   https://www.linkedin.com/help/linkedin/answer/47081

73   Ibid.

74   http://befoundjobs.com/

75   https://www.linkedin.com/pulse/why-i-didnt-accept-your-linkedin-request-robert-p-doran

76   https://www.linkedin.com/in/brendabernstein

77   https://www.socialmediatoday.com/news/new-survey-shows-that-linkedin-users-strongly-dislike-unsolicited-dms/619180/

78   Ibid.

79   https://blog.linkedin.com/2018/july/26/voice-messaging-on-linkedin-giving-you-more-ways-to-have-conversations

80   http://theessayexpert.com/samples/linkedin-profiles/

81   http://theessayexpert.com/blog/your-linkedin-profile-summary-how-to-distinguish-yourself-from-your-company/

82   https://www.linkedin.com/in/brendabernstein/

83 http://www.slideshare.net/linkedin/representing-unique-career-paths-on-linkedin

84 https://theessayexpert.com/your-linkedin-about-section-3-reasons-not-use-resume-summary/

85 http://www.facebook.com/linkedinprofiletips

86 https://blog.linkedin.com/2016/05/25/get-comfortable-with-being-uncomfortable-why-now-is-the-time-to

87 http://theessayexpert.com/services-rates/resume-and-cover-letter-writing/

88 https://support.grammarly.com/hc/en-us

89 http://en.wikipedia.org/wiki/List_of_Unicode_characters

90 https://translate.google.com/

91 https://copychar.cc/

92 https://emojipedia.org/

93 https://getemoji.com/

94 https://fsymbols.com/generators/blackboard-bold-double-struck/

95 https://theessayexpert.com/samples/linkedin-profiles/

96 https://linkedin.github.io/future-of-skills/#explore

97 https://www.linkedin.com/help/linkedin/answer/31888/skill-endorsements-overview?lang=en

98 https://getpocket.com/

99 https://feedly.com/i/welcome

100 https://www.google.com/alerts

101 http://list.ly/

102 https://www.entrepreneur.com/article/316139

103 https://www.linkedin.com/newsletters/creator-weekly-6792913376398905344/

104 https://www.linkedin.com/help/linkedin/answer/92930

105 http://help.linkedin.com/app/answers/detail/a_id/34936

106 https://www.linkedin.com/help/linkedin/answer/78900

107 https://www.linkedin.com/help/linkedin/answer/85430

108 http://blog.linkedin.com/2014/02/19/the-definitive-professional-publishing-platform/

109 https://www.linkedin.com/legal/user-agreement

110 https://www.linkedin.com/legal/user-agreement#rights

111 https://www.businessofapps.com/data/linkedin-statistics/

112 https://okdork.com/linkedin-publishing-success/

113 https://www.linkedin.com/help/linkedin/answer/47538

114 http://www.hootsuite.com/

115 http://jetpack.me/support/publicize/linkedin/

116 http://contentmarketinginstitute.com/2016/08/linkedin-profile-tips/

117 http://www.inc.com/john-white/linkedin-changed-how-they-feature-posts-and-forgot-to-tell-anyone.html

118   https://flipweb.org/linkedin-now-factors-dwell-time-in-its-algorithm-to-improve-feed-ranking/2301

119   http://blog.linkedin.com/2015/04/13/elevate/

120   https://www.entrepreneur.com/article/316139

121   https://www.linkedin.com/help/linkedin/answer/a528144/use-hashtags-and-follow-topics-on-linkedin

122   https://www.linkedin.com/feed/following/?filterType=channel&focused=true

123   https://www.linkedin.com/help/linkedin/answer/a528144

124   https://business.linkedin.com/marketing-solutions/linkedin-live/getting-started

125   https://www.linkedin.com/help/linkedin/answer/128901

126   https://www.linkedin.com/help/linkedin/answer/a570487

127   https://www.linkedin.com/help/linkedin/answer/a569473

128   https://www.linkedin.com/help/linkedin/answer/a570528

129   https://business.linkedin.com/marketing-solutions/linkedin-live/best-practices

130   https://www.linkedin.com/help/linkedin/answer/a567498

131   https://www.linkedin.com/help/linkedin/answer/a547396

132   https://www.business.linkedin.com/content/dam/me/business/en-us/marketing-solutions/resources/
       pdfs/getting-started-checklist-for-linkedin-live-external.pdf

133   https://www.socialmediaexaminer.com/how-to-linkedin-turn-cold-prospects-warm-leads/

134   https://members.linkedin.com/creators/linkedin-podcast-network

135   https://www.linkedin.com/help/linkedin/answer/62005

136   https://influencermarketinghub.com/social-media-post-reach-engagement/

137   https://www.truconversion.com/social-media/how-to-create-a-perfect-linkedin-profile/

138   https://blog.linkedin/com/2014/02/06/welcome-bright-to-the-linkedin-family

139   http://blog.linkedin.com/2016/02/16/offering-hourly-workers-an-opportunity-to-ac-
       quire-new-skills-through-snagajob/

140   https://www.linkedin.com/learning/

141   https://news.linkedin.com/about-us#Statistics

142   https://blog.linkedin.com/2019/august/27/staying-safe-on-linkedin-during-your-job-search

143   https://www.inc.com/jt-odonnell/no-1-sign-a-job-posting-is-fake.html

144   https://www.linkedin.com/help/linkedin/answer/67405

145   Ibid.

146   https://premium.linkedin.com/

147   https://www.linkedin.com/help/linkedin/answer/75814

148   https://www.linkedin.com/pulse/new-survey-reveals-85-all-jobs-filled-via-networking-lou-adler/

149   https://www.linkedin.com/help/linkedin/answer/70033/viewing-jobs-you-ve-applied-for-on-linkedin

150   https://www.linkedin.com/help/linkedin/answer/71792

151   https://www.linkedin.com/salary

152   https://www.linkedin.com/help/linkedin/answer/68014

153   http://www.wiserutips.com/2013/09/how-and-why-to-follow-companies-on.html

154   https://blog.linkedin.com/2019/june/18/introducing-new-tools-to-help-you-prep-for-your-next-inter-view

155   https://www.linkedin.com/help/linkedin/answer/107055

156   https://business.linkedin.com/talent-solutions/company-career-pages/next-generation-career-pages

157   https://www.linkedin.com/pulse/how-contact-recruiter-linkedin-breet-chief-stripe-changer

158   https://www.glassdoor.com/blog/how-to-respond-to-a-recruiters-inmail-on-linkedin/

159   http://anymailfinder.com/

160   http://truepeoplesearch.com/

161   http://zabasearch.com/

162   http://radaris.com/

163   http://verifyemailaddress.org/

164   https://www.linkedin.com/jobs/search/?keywords=volunteer

165   https://www.linkedin.com/help/linkedin/answer/121660

166   https://www.linkedin.com/help/linkedin/answer/120698/share-that-you-re-hiring-on-linkedin

167   Ibid.

168   https://www.linkedin.com/help/linkedin/answer/71362

169   https://www.linkedin.com/help/linkedin/answer/110940

170   https://www.linkedin.com/business/sales/blog/b2b-sales/how-sales-reps-exceed-quota-make-club-and-get-promoted-faster

171   https://www.linkedin.com/help/linkedin/answer/a541653/recommendations-on-linkedin?lang=en

172   https://www.linkedin.com/help/linkedin/answer/50201

173   https://www.linkedin.com/sales/ssi

174   http://sales.linkedin.com/blog/how-sales-reps-exceed-quota-make-club-and-get-promoted-faster/

175   https://business.linkedin.com/sales-solutions/social-selling/the-social-selling-index-ssi

176   http://help.linkedin.com/app/answers/detail/a_id/50191/~/downloading-your-account-data

177   https://www.systoolsgroup.com/import/excel-spreadsheet-contacts-to-apple-address-book/

178   https://www.linkedin.com/legal/professional-community-policies

179   https://www.linkedin.com/help/linkedin/answer/62923

180   https://www.linkedin.com/help/linkedin/answer/544/turning-two-step-verification-on-and-off

181   https://www.linkedin.com/help/linkedin/answer/4788

182   https://www.link65edin.com/help/linkedin/ask/UAQ

183   https://www.entrepreneur.com/article/343987

184   https://business.linkedin.com/content/dam/me/business/en-us/sales-solutions/resources/pdfs/linke-din-cold-calling-is-dead-thanks-to-linkedin-en-us.pdf

185   https://kinsta.com/blog/linkedin-statistics/

186   https://blog.hubspot.com/marketing/linkedin-stats

187   https://www.linkedin.com/help/linkedin/answer/710

188   https://www.linkedin.com/help/linkedin/answer/44855

189   https://www.linkedin.com/products/categories/browse?trk=products_seo_home_popular_catego-ries_see_more

190   https://www.linkedin.com/help/linkedin/answer/119150

191   https://business.linkedin.com/content/dam/me/business/en-us/talent-solutions/products/pdfs/turn-ing-employees-into-brand-advocates.pdf

192   https://www.linkedin.com/help/linkedin/answer/131021

193   https://www.linkedin.com/help/linkedin/answer/132806

194   https://www.linkedin.com/help/linkedin/answer/a540854

195   https://business.linkedin.com/marketing-solutions/success/insights-and-research

196   https://business.linkedin.com/marketing-solutions/success

197   https://business.linkedin.com/marketing-solutions/blog/linkedin-b2b-marketing/2019/introducing-the-all-in-one-linkedin-insights-hub-for-marketers

198   https://www.rivaliq.com/blog/social-media-advertising-trends/

199   https://www.monsterinsights.com/conversion-rate-optimization-stats-show-what-youve-been-missing/

200   https://business.linkedin.com/marketing-solutions/linkedin-pages/best-practices

201   https://theessayexpert.com/wp-content/uploads/2022/03/LinkedIn-Profile-Completion-Check-list-2022.pdf

202   http://help.linkedin.com/app/answers/detail/a_id/190

203   https://theessayexpert.com/?s=buzzwords

204   https://business.linkedin.com/marketing-solutions/higher-education

205   https://blog.linkedin.com/2019/june/18/introducing-new-tools-to-help-you-prep-for-your-next-inter-view

206   https://university.linkedin.com/content/dam/students/global/en_US/site/img/StudentPublishMicroSite/pdfs/LNK_MM_JobSeeker_eBook_StudentEdition_Sec1_FINAL.pdf

207   https://careers.linkedin.com/students

208   https://blog.linkedin.com/topic/linkedin-for-students

209   https://www.linkedin.com/help/linkedin/answer/61169/linkedin-add-to-profile-feature-frequently-asked-questions?

210   http://blog.linkedin.com/2015/03/18/add-to-profile/

211   https://www.statista.com/statistics/264074/percentage-of-paying-linkedin-users/

212   https://www.linkedin.com/signup/cold-join

213   https://premium.linkedin.com

214   https://business.linkedin.com/marketing-solutions

215   https://business.linkedin.com/talent-solutions/recruiter-lite

216   https://business.linkedin.com/sales-solutions

217   https://business.linkedin.com/talent-solutions/recruiter-lite

218　http://www.amazon.com/gp/digital/fiona/manage

219　https://www.linkedin.com/help/linkedin/

220　https://www.lindedin.com/help/linkedin/solve/contact

221　https://www.linkedin.com/help/linkedin/forum

222　https://theessayexpert.com/how-to-write-a-winning-resume/

223　https://theessayexpert.com/write-stellar-executive-resume/

224　https://theessayexpert.com/subscribe-to-the-weekly-blog/

225　http://theessayexpert.com/job-search-success-system/

226　http://theessayexpert.com/webinars-podcasts/

227　https://theessayexpert.com/events-essay-expert/

228　https://www.amazon.com/review/create-review/?ie=UTF8&channel=reviews-product&asin=B019ELX-R8W

229　https://theessayexpert.com/linkedin-profiles/

230　https://www.amazon.com/product-reviews/162967155X

231　https://theessayexpert.com/senior-executive-resume-linkedin-profile-success-package/

232　https://theessayexpert.com/senior-executive-resume-linkedin-headline-summary-with-add-ons/

233　https://theessayexpert.com/executive-resume-linkedin-profile-success-package/

234　https://theessayexpert.com/executive-resume-linkedin-headline-summary-with-addons/

235　https://theessayexpert.com/senior-executive-linkedin-profile-complete/

236　https://theessayexpert.com/mid-level-resume-linkedin-profile-success-package/

237　https://theessayexpert.com/executive-linkedin-profile-complete/

238　https://theessayexpert.com/senior-executive-linkedin-headline-summary-special/

239　https://theessayexpert.com/product/mid-level-resume-linkedin-headline-summary-2/

240　https://theessayexpert.com/product/mid-level-linkedin-profile-complete/

241　https://theessayexpert.com/product/mid-level-linkedin-headline-summary-special/

CPSIA information can be obtained
at www.ICGtesting.com
Printed in the USA
LVHW060647030123
736289LV00001B/17

9 781629 672342